The Great Omission

Amazing Ways The Church Muddles The Message:
How To Get It Right And Tell It Right

Robert Blair

CSS Publishing Company, Inc., Lima, Ohio

THE GREAT OMISSION

Copyright © 2007 by
CSS Publishing Company, Inc.
Lima, Ohio

Scripture quotations are from the Holy Bible, New International Version. Copyright © 1973, 1978, 1984 International Bible Society. Used by permission of Zondervan Bible Publishers. All rights reserved.

Scripture quotations marked (RSV) are from the Revised Standard Version of the Bible, copyrighted 1946, 1952 ©, 1971, 1973, by the Division of Christian Education of the National Council of the Churches of Christ in the USA. Used by permission.

Scripture quotations marked (TEV) are from the Good News Bible, in Today's English Version. Copyright © American Bible Society, 1966, 1971, 1976. Used by permission.

Scripture quotations marked (TLB) are taken from The Living Bible © 1971. Used by permission of Tyndale House Publishers, Inc., Wheaton, Illinois 60189. All rights reserved.

Scripture quotations marked (KJV) are from the King James Version of the Bible, in the public domain.

Excerpts from *Faith and Public Policy*, James R. Wilburn (Lanham, Maryland: Lexington Books, 2002) used by permission.

Library of Congress Cataloging-in-Publication Data

Blair, Robert, 1936-
    The Great omission : amazing ways the church muddles the message : how to get it right and tell it right / Robert Blair.
        p. cm.
    Includes bibliographical references.
    ISBN 0-7880-2442-6 (perfect bound : alk. paper)
    1. Apologetics. 2. Evangelistic work. 3. Witness bearing (Christianity). 4. War—
Religious aspects--Christianity. 5. Christianity and politics. I. Title.

    BT1103.B53 2007
    230—dc22

                                                              2006031566

For more information about CSS Publishing Company resources, visit our website at www.csspub.com or email us at custserv@csspub.com or call (800) 241-4056.

ISBN-13: 979-0-7880-2442-9
ISBN-10: 0-7880-2442-6

PRINTED IN U.S.A.

Dedicated with praise to the Lord Jesus, who allowed a small-town Kansas kid to catch astonishing glimpses of God's incredible, eternal, active love through:

- *a spouse who continues to grow and mature in patience, understanding, and love for God;*
- *children and grandchildren, who continually make us proud;*
- *loving, supportive siblings and friends;*
- *strong, able, exemplary brothers and sisters in Christ all over the world who both challenge and encourage;*
- *the Word;*
- *God's creation; and*
- *his providential care and powerful work through his church.*

I'm very grateful to many who read parts or all of the manuscript in its various stages. They helped me improve it though none should be blamed for its deficiencies. These include my wife, Norma; my daughters, Stephanie and Janice; my brother, Don; and daughter-in-law, Pat Blair; Darcy Dreckman, Dawne Goodwin-McCullough, Doug Keen, Otto Reichardt, the late Mitzi Shows, and Suzanne Willis.

Special kudos to Judy Miller and others on the staff of the Cherokee (Iowa) Public Library who cheerfully and efficiently helped me obtain books I never thought I'd find. Thanks, also, to Janie Van Dyke and the Orange City (Iowa) Public Library.

The interest and love of people in at least seventeen different northwest Iowa churches and the Hollywood (California) Church have bolstered my faith in many ways.

It's been a pleasure and an honor to work with CSS Publishing Company, especially President Wesley Runk and Managing Editor Becky Brandt. I thank God for their confidence in the work, their competence, and their faith.

Table Of Contents

Part Two
Unadulterated Adulterators

Part Three
Fixing The Mix

Introduction

Hours before his trial and crucifixion, Jesus implored his followers for oneness. To please the Father and win the world, Jesus wanted accord. He pleaded for unity. Amity was his strategy.

How did Christians respond to Jesus' ardent appeal? With the concord of a soccer riot. Barroom brawls evidence more unity than the church. Believers argue theology, territory, and hell's torment. We dispute baptismal modes and salvation's permanence. Now another schism-carving controversy rages.

What's behind the hubbub? Let me tell you about two friends. You know a lot of believers like them. When you looked in the mirror this morning, you possibly winked at one of them.

Joe and Margot are not related. They each claim to love Jesus. Joe thinks that he's an all right disciple. Margot considers herself God's person, too. Neither cheats nor tells lies. They love their families; they contribute liberally to their churches. Each enjoys affirming friends.

Though they're both believers, ideologies divide them. When one broaches certain topics to the other, it's automatic agitation. Blood boils as though forced from cauldrons. Once they attended the same church. No longer. Margot and her family left the congregation where Joe and his family attend.

What issues divide Joe and Margot? Joe's at ease with patriotic fellow members. Although his church doesn't display American flags in worship assemblies, many congregants wear American flag pins on their lapels.

They confidently affirm that the United States distinguishes itself among all of the world's countries — indeed all history. Established on Christian principles, God chose the US for a unique leadership role.

Joe's church brothers and sisters decry current corruptive tendencies. To them the citizenry and government of the United States are fast deserting the beliefs, goals, and principles of the founding fathers.

9

Joe and his fellow believers help fund politicians who promise to reinstitute Christian values. Only those officials sharing their anti-abortion views receive their support. Joe wants the restoration of prayer and Bible-reading in public schools and the resumption of capital punishment — not in schools, of course. Joe's minister frequently preaches sermons and teaches classes on national morality or the lack thereof. Sometimes, these opinions are expressed in church announcements. Joe's church sponsors Dr. James Dobson's weekly column in a local newspaper.

Another issue divides Joe and Margot. Joe contends that the US conducts most of its wars in a just manner. Ample evidence justified the 2003 war against Iraq. The founding fathers established the United States on godly principles intending it to be Christian. Most of the attacks against the US were made by infidels, or those who have distorted Jesus' message. Therefore, it's necessary to protect not only democracy, but also this distinctive nation. Joe unabashedly shares these beliefs with coworkers.

Recent court decisions irritate and frustrate Joe and his wife. Their aggravation intensifies when ACLU attorneys win lawsuits restricting the public display of crosses, Bible texts, and Christmas decorations. The circuit court decision ordering Judge Moore to remove the Ten Commandments display from an Alabama courthouse made Joe and his wife livid. In their opinion, Judeo-Christian influence progressively suffers grievous, irretrievable losses in American courts and schools.

Though Joe doesn't agree with Pat Robertson on all religious matters, he shares most of Robertson's political stances, especially concerning prayer in public schools and the need for morality among American leaders.

Joe and his spouse fret about the future of their children. They teach them the rewards of honesty, hard work, and trustworthiness. An avid sports fan, Joe coaches little league baseball and Pop Warner football. He hopes to instill proper values in his teams. The liberal tendencies and amoral lifestyles that he sees in American society increasingly exasperate him.

Margot and her husband felt uncomfortable in a church that advocated Joe's "right wing views." Pat Robertson, James Dobson, and D. James Kennedy mortify Margot and her friends. Margot and her spouse began worshiping where many leaders openly criticized US war efforts. She actively protests armed conflict, and she generously backs antiwar movements. Margot's husband fought in Vietnam. Both deplore war in any form. They picket in front of local government buildings, and often travel to Washington DC, to protest the testing and development of nuclear weapons.

"Jesus taught love. How can we love people and then wage war against them?" say Margot and her husband. Because Jesus taught nonviolence, no individual or group of individuals should take part in aggression.

For similar reasons, Margot opposes death sentences. Margot works with other activists to remove capital punishment as an option at state and federal levels. She participates in vigils when her state imposes the death penalty.

Margot worries about the environment. Global warming disquiets her. So does big business, especially the oil industry, which she thinks severely abuses the environment. She loves to backpack in the wilderness. As they camp and hike together, Margot and her husband teach their children how to protect fragile ecosystems. They idolize those teaching and using nonviolent means. Margot wants her children to imitate people like Jesus, Gandhi, Mother Teresa, and Martin Luther King Jr.

Joe's and Margot's opposing views perplex their mutual friends. Each argues convincingly. Their associates can't make up their minds. Is Joe's Christian stance right, or is Margot's? That both are correct seems impossible.

Can it be that both Margot and Joe are misdirected? Yes. And I think that Jerry Falwell, Pat Robertson, Tim LaHaye, the Pope, Jesse Jackson, Al Sharpton, and many others are misguided, too. Many prominent religious leaders of the past like Luther, Calvin, and Zwingli erred similarly. I plan to show you how.

The Quandary For Christians

The collapse of buildings and devastation of life on September 11, 2001, fractured long-held beliefs. It created a quandary for many of Margot's pacifist friends. The militant Muslims' appalling methods created confounding questions — some that pacifists never faced in previous wars. Peace-lovers felt justified protesting the Vietnam War, the Persian Gulf War, and other recent conflicts. But the seemingly unprovoked attack that took place on American soil made this combat different. The terrorists viciously violated Bismarck's maxim, "Even in a declaration of war one observes the rules of politeness."[1]

The most notable living pacifist at the time was Pope John Paul II. The attacks apparently caused no change in his position, but the Associated Press released an article titled, "Vatican moves to dispel pope's pacifist image after terror attacks."[2] It originated from Yerevan, Armenia, where the pope visited shortly after the World Trade Center attacks. According to the report, the pope had opposed the Gulf War. He thought that dialogue could have ended the strife. The conflicts and divisions following the September 11, 2001, assaults could be resolved in the same way, he insisted.

"With all my heart, I beg God to keep the world in peace," the pope said at a mass in Kazakhstan. Shortly after the pope's remarks, many American cardinals, bishops, and church spokesmen intervened. The same AP article quoted one Vatican source, who intimated that a "just war" might "validate American military intervention."

A prominent American bishop wrote to President Bush informing him that the United States rightly claims a "grave obligation to defend the common good" against terrorists. *American Jesuit* magazine editor, Thomas Reese, said that the "People in the Vatican realize that the United States could be justified in using military force ... if conditions of a just war are met." "I don't think that the pope is a strict pacifist," Reese opined.

Later evidence suggests that the pope never gave up his rigorous antiwar position. When the United States went to war against Iraq in early 2003, the pope opposed the action. After most of the ground war ended, the pope still maintained that "the war in Iraq was neither morally nor legally justified."[3]

The pope's American representatives weren't the only prominent people scrambling for explanations immediately after

12

September 11, 2001. Another Associated Press release appeared in the *Sioux City* (Iowa) *Journal*. Headlined "Pacifist churches must cope with life in America after the attack,"[4] the article told of pacifists' inner conflicts as they dealt with the effects of the assaults on the World Trade Center and the Pentagon. To some pacifists, terrorism and war merit different responses. We "know how to behave in war," said a pacifist spokesman, "but we're still learning how to react to terrorism."[5]

One minister, noted for his attempts at brokering peace in the Middle East under previous administrations, volunteered to go to Afghanistan to help resolve the conflict. The Taliban leaders in Afghanistan invited him to help, he said. According to Taliban representatives, the clergyman did what preachers notoriously do. He invited himself. Government officials in this country told him not to go. Who can say whether the Taliban sent an invitation?

Two well-known conservative Christian leaders painstakingly nursed their wounded mouths. They jammed their feet, knees, and hips into them just after the attack. Both men alleged on national television that the 9/11 attacks evidenced God's judgment on homosexuals and other sinners in the US. The media and homosexuals launched preacher-seeking-censure-salvos at them. The pair meekly retreated from the volleys nursing their backsides, too.

I interviewed a young medical resident concerning her views of the war's rightness. She felt confused; she stated that she hadn't made up her mind. As a result, she said that she intended to leave the matter up to political leaders. She's not the only one conflicted by the recent events. A friend owns a local business and attends church nearby. Here was her take:

> *It's wrong to kill. But there are forces of good and forces of evil. God uses good people on occasions to thwart the work of evil people. That includes the use of force sometimes. There's a point when even Christians should have to stand up for what is right. I know we're supposed to be forgiving and gentle, but Satan can trick us.*

She wasn't sure at what point Christians should use force.

13

The September 11, 2001, events exacerbated the differences between Margot and Joe, but they aren't the only people at odds. Christians all over the world tried to come to terms with what happened. I'm close to people of many different churches in northwest Iowa. Their directories list lots of Joes. They record many Margots, too. In early 2003, as the likelihood of war with Iraq grew more imminent, both the Joes and Margots became vocal and anxious.

For Joe and his friends, President Bush showed ample connection between Saddam Hussein and terrorism to justify the war with Iraq. In Margot's opinion, the president didn't prove sufficient links between Hussein and the terrorists. Therefore, President Bush waged an unjust war. "It's unprecedented that the US should initiate a war," said Margot. She doubts whether any conflicts can be resolved by force.

The Bible's Mixed Signals On War

The Bible seems to give confusing signals on war's propriety. God not only approved of war in the Old Testament, he expected combativeness from the Israelites. He ordered them to annihilate certain nations. Israel's command-failures infuriated him (cf. Numbers 31:1-18; Deuteronomy 7:1-7). In contrast, Jesus emphasized loving one's enemies, and turning the other cheek (Matthew 5:38-47).

What position should Christians take on the matter of war? Is there biblical precedent for a "just war"? Why are Old and New Testament teachings at such variance? Does the Bible give us definite principles to follow?

Of the ministers that I knew in my youth, I remember only one who discussed war. During World War II, he dutifully served his country as an infantryman in the South Pacific. We sat transfixed as he told how he and his fellow troops returned fire that came at them from the surrounding hills. Whether he killed any enemy soldiers, he never knew, or wouldn't say. He said he prayed that God would keep those bullets from killing anyone or not hold him responsible if they did. He considered it a blessing that he never saw the enemy face to face.

14

I don't recall any other ministers speaking about war. Most of those preachers probably registered as conscientious objectors. Though of draft age during the World War II, they didn't talk publicly or in my presence about objections to the military. I think I know why. Many of the male church members served in the military and remained strongly patriotic. They looked with askance at COs.[6]

My Own Biases

I admit to one type of bias. When I was about eleven years old, I had a BB gun in my possession. I don't think it was mine; I couldn't afford one in those days. Near a vacant lot on our street, I saw a robin perched on a telephone wire. I aimed, shot, and killed it. As the fragile bird fell, I felt immediate remorse.

That wasn't the last time I aimed a deadly weapon at an animal. Some years later, I hunted game birds on my in-laws' farm near Needy, Oregon, blasting away with my father-in-law's shotgun. To this day, Douglas fir trees in the area probably bear my misdirected pellets. I orphaned no baby birds that day, though. The fowls flew too fast for me. The weapon's recoil left my shoulder black and blue for days. Deer hunting led to the same result. No game. Only shoulder pain.

It's probably a good thing that I didn't bring down a deer. Having to look into a dead doe's eyes would have caused more compunction than that deceased robin brought me. We live on an acreage in a rural section of Iowa. Numerous deer inhabit the area. Annually, when local hunters in their pickups chase the white-tails, my wife and I cheer for the deer.

I don't own a gun and haven't during my adult life. I can't imagine killing or even injuring another human being. On the other hand, I know that I live securely in the United States because others risk getting killed or maimed. I enjoy and appreciate the benefits of living where police officers bear weapons and imperil their lives to keep my family and me from harm.

The Army drafted my father during the World War I. I always thought he looked handsome in the pictures showing him in uniform. Dad contracted pneumonia and underwent surgery for complications of it. His recovery coincided with Armistice so he spent most of his service time in a Texas military hospital. To my knowledge, Dad never owned a gun. He so briefly served, I don't even know if he ever shot a weapon on a practice range.

My sister and three of my brothers-in-law went into the armed forces during World War II. All enlisted out of high school. I never heard any of them brag about their service. They simply felt obligated to serve their country. To my knowledge, none sustained injury or harsh psychological damage.

Some people close to me were affected. Two of my three elder sisters lost high school classmates to the war. It deeply pained them. A cousin who came back acutely troubled stayed with us for a while. My parents cautioned me about what I should say to my "shell-shocked" relative. It didn't take expert analysis to understand that my cousin suffered severe emotional harm. Even at a naive nine years of age, I sensed it.

Something else disquieted me about World War II. It distressed me more than the casualty headlines that we saw daily in the *Wichita* (Kansas) *Eagle*. Gold star pennants or flags hung in front windows of houses not only in our neighborhood, but all across the country. Stars usually illuminate, but those "haloed" heartrending gloom. They darkly signaled that a son, a husband, or a daughter would never come home.

The Korean War took place during my high school years. The conflict ended months before our graduation. My classmates and I felt relieved, but I remained subject to the draft and classified 1A. I entered college in the fall of 1954, and decided to become a minister in 1955. Though I received college deferments, I knew that any change in the international situation or in my college grades could result in my being drafted.

Some of my ministerial student contemporaries applied for conscientious objector status. I didn't. Why not apply? Whether I correctly judged my colleagues only God knows, but I felt that many of them acted cravenly. I didn't want to be considered cowardly, and I wanted to be a good citizen. If I were called, I decided, I would apply to be a medic. That way I could demonstrate my willingness to be a target. I just didn't want to shoot other people.

16

The Lord didn't test me with the tense, gut-wrenching decisions that many faced. The draft board never sent me notice. I met none of the dilemmas those passengers encountered onboard the plane that crashed in Pennsylvania that fateful September day in 2001. Some of the people on that airliner evidently showed exceptional courage. I refer to the ones who took great risk — perhaps killing or maiming one or more of the hijackers onboard in order to save innocent lives on the ground.

Our second son spent twenty years in the Air Force maintaining aircraft. He went to the Middle East during one of the tense times that occurred in the 1990s. I questioned his wisdom when he enlisted, but felt great pride when his superiors highly commended him at his crowded retirement ceremony. As you can tell, I retain mixed emotions and thoughts about military service and war.

These conflicted views possibly stem from my Church of Christ heritage. Churches of Christ boast no single founder. Instead, they evolved from the work and teaching of several nineteenth-century ministers.

As Professor Richard T. Hughes noted in his outstanding work, *Reviving the Ancient Faith*,[7] this restoration movement developed from the work of two major leaders, though the pair disagreed on some important issues. Barton Stone took a pessimistic, Calvinistic approach emphasizing the kingdom of God. He expected Jesus' speedy return to earth to establish his kingdom. Stone taught that Christians should resist participating in any organization, society, or government.

In contrast, Alexander Campbell, especially in his later life, held an optimistic, rational, and progressive view. Campbell advocated governmental support, at least in this country, because of its "Christian origins."

Much of the division between Campbell and Stone was regional. Stone heavily influenced middle Tennessee. Campbell exerted his greatest sway in Texas. Stone's effect eventually diminished to near nonexistence.

A major rift developed within the restoration movement after the turn of the twentieth century. As a result, the Disciples of Christ (the Christian church) and Churches of Christ separated. Many

Christian Churches (those affiliated with the Disciples of Christ) currently take an antiwar position.

Most Churches of Christ believe in congregational autonomy. Because they lack a headquarters and an official head, no one can officially speak for them. It's impossible to talk of a "Church of Christ position." However, my stance is, as far as I know, unlike that of most Church of Christ ministers and members.

In one important way, I differ from many in Churches of Christ. It's my attitude toward the pioneers of the restoration movement. I consider Thomas and Alexander Campbell, Barton Stone, James Kelly, and other nineteenth-century leaders of the movement as perceptive in their vision of unity. They all shared the human malady of limited wisdom, however.

Every Christian must attempt to give reasonable answers to unbelievers' questions. I've tried to disconnect myself from early influences in order to find a stance wholly from the scriptures. Still, dispassionate views come with extreme difficulty. We also face the problem that outsiders see contemporary Christianity as monolithic.

Here's an example: During the last seventeen years that we lived in Los Angeles, we enjoyed the friendship of our next-door-neighbors, Jules and Shirley Kraut. My wife and I carried on many candid religious discussions with them. For several years, the Krauts graciously invited us to share Passover with their family. They attended worship services with us numerous times at the Hollywood Church of Christ. We're still close to them even though we moved from Los Angeles to Iowa about fifteen years ago.

During the height of the Protestant versus Catholic fighting in Ireland, Jules and I conversed one afternoon in his backyard. Jules enjoyed asking hard questions. He wanted to know why Christians were killing Christians in Belfast. I don't know how my answer impressed him. Here's what I told him, though: "If they are killing and fighting, they're not following Jesus' example. I think it's a mistake to call either side Christian."

Conflict between so-called followers hasn't been restricted to Irish Catholics versus Irish Protestants. For centuries, people using Jesus' name have borne arms. During the American Civil War, Christian ministers blessed and prayed for men shooting

18

their bullets and rockets north while other fervent men of the same denomination prayed for soldiers with rifles and cannon aimed south.

The Crusaders tried to forcefully recover the Holy Land from Islam. In the First Crusade (1095-1099), Christians deliberately killed both Jews and Muslims. What was the effect of the Crusades? Don Belt, senior editor of *National Geographic* gave the following assessment:

> *Though fragmented and initially overcome, Muslims rallied to ultimately defeat the invading Christian armies, whose blood-soaked legacy — the indiscriminate killing of thousands of innocent Arabs, Muslim and Christian alike, as well as the Jews of Jerusalem — lives on in the minds of Middle Easterners to this day.*[8]

War And Turning The Other Cheek

Why did born-again people become bearers of arms? How could folks whom Jesus taught to turn the other cheek turn to killing in order to spread their faith? Furthermore, how could they justify carnage of not only unbelievers but also of one another? Why did followers of the Lamb of God begin slaying "innocent lambs"?

We'll trace the evolution of the view that Christians should defend or expand their faith by military means. The development wasn't always gradual. Some incidents brought winged development to the idea. What were those events, and how are we affected by them? I plan to show Jesus' example of dealing with war and governments.

The War Issue And Its Relationship To Other Questions

When to bear arms presents vexing complexity except for cowards and the few with a passion for butchery. It's not my intention to pass judgment on others. I desire to identify what Jesus taught and present guidance based on scripture.

In the ensuing chapters, we'll review the apparent contradictions between the Old and New Testaments concerning war. We'll also show the model Jesus taught. Although later teachers and groups failed to recognize them, Jesus left us clear examples.

19

Denominational Division And Confusion

War questions relate to a greater issue: How should Christians interact with their governments? Should we criticize political leaders? How do Christians get their governments to act responsibly and according to Christian standards? Should they even try?

How we deal with our governments on the question of war applies also to how we relate on issues like prayer in public schools, abortion, displaying Christian symbols, gay/lesbian issues, and other controversies. The contentious denominational debates over these subjects reveal gaping rifts in the Christian world that blunt Jesus' message.

Intra-denominational conflict regularly makes the news. Typical is a recent *Sioux City Journal* article written by Alicia Ebaugh. She reported that by an almost ten-to-one margin, members of Sioux City's largest Lutheran church voted to leave the Evangelical Lutheran Church of America. According to the minister, the issue was "progressive liberalism." The split centered on the denomination's alleged departure from the Word. Key matters were the ELCA's affiliation with the Episcopalian church a few years ago and the church's stand on gays, lesbians, and gay marriage. The local church also considered various theological and organizational matters.[9]

What happened within this local Lutheran church repeats itself nationwide in almost every major denomination. Representatives at the denominations' headquarters make resolutions with which the majority in local congregations disagrees. Members in local congregations become increasingly dissatisfied with hierarchal decisions.

Many denominational leaders seem either clueless as to New Testament teaching or else disregard it. One minister of a major denomination recently wrote in his church bulletin that his focus was on social justice and on his "refusal to accept any political, or *even biblical, norm that would defy the sensibilities of a loving God*" [author's emphasis] How can a "biblical norm" defy God's sensibilities? It appears that the minister uses his opinions to define righteousness, not scripture. As many ministers follow this

20

leader's pattern, there's disconnection with God's Word. Meanwhile, bearing witness to Jesus' good news tapers to nonexistence.

Why Is This Subject So Important?

Resolving how Christians should interact with their governments and the societies in which they live may be the most important issue the church now faces. The common approaches, both right and left, blunt the effectiveness of Jesus' good news.

Most Christians are sincere people, but their attitudes toward governments often destroy their witness and create unnecessary animosity toward Christ. More than that, our approach is wasteful and inefficient. Think of doctors who spend their time treating only symptoms when they have a cure available. Or a military force that bombs unnecessary targets. Or salespeople who offend most of their potential customers. Or a blacksmith who tries to shape iron without heating it.

The church may face another dark period unless we recover and reestablish Jesus' approach to governments, and emphasize anew the good news. What examples did Jesus give us? What principles did the apostles and early church leaders follow? We'll look at these questions.

------

1. W. H. Auden and Louis Kronenberger, *Viking Book of Aphorisms* (New York: Viking Press, 1966), p. 160.

2. *Sioux City Journal*, Sunday, September 30, 2001, Section B11.

3. *Ibid*, Sunday, May 4, 2003, Section A14, from Associated Press, Madrid, Spain.

4. *Ibid*, Sunday, September 30, 2001, Section A11.

5. *Ibid.*

6. Mark Elrod, Ph.D. noted in his research that in Churches of Christ, "the shift away from pacifism began either during or immediately after World War II." "Traditions of War and Peace," *New Wineskins*, Jan/Feb 2002, p. 23.

7. Richard T. Hughes, *Reviving the Ancient Faith: The Story of Churches of Christ in America* (Grand Rapids, Michigan: Wm. B. Eerdmans Publishing Company, 1996) pp. 92-167.

8. "World of Islam," *National Geographic*, January 2002, p. 85.

9. *Sioux City Journal*, Tuesday, August 6, 2005, Section A pages 1 and 6.

Part One

Unadulterated Paint

1

The Bloody Past:
The Old Testament And War

My angel will go ahead of you and bring you into the land of the Amorites, Hittites, Perizzites, Canaanites, Hivites and Jebusites, and I will wipe them out.
— Exodus 23:23

Do you like riddles? Try deciphering what the Old Testament teaches about war. The Lord sanctioned Israel's wars. He even ordered its representatives to destroy whole nations, but Isaiah prophesied poignantly of peace.

They will beat their swords into plowshares and their spears into pruning hooks. Nation will not take up sword against nation, nor will they train for war anymore.
— Isaiah 2:4

Exodus promoted aggression. Isaiah advocated war's end. What made the difference? Why did the Lord sponsor armed conflict in one era and apparently deplore it in another?

In the face of this confusing evidence, can we learn anything from the Old Testament about governmental relationships? Many reformers used the Old Testament as a basis for their intrusions into government. Were the reformers' conclusions justified? Or did they only pick and choose? Are some wars necessary or are they all evil? We need to make sense of what the Old Testament teaches.

The Genesis Wars
Genesis covers several millennia, but recounts only one battle in chapters 1 through 13. That conflict resulted in a high

25

percentage of casualties. As you know, fifty percent of the existing young people died when Cain declared war on Abel.[1]

Genesis mentions no armed combat until chapter 14. There, four kings from the lower Euphrates Valley allied themselves and traveled to the Dead Sea area where they subdued five cities and their kings. The four kings forced the subjugated people to pay tribute. After twelve full years of paying toll, the five Dead Sea area kings tired of taxation without representation. They didn't hold a tea party, but they stopped payment.

The four valley kings headed west again to recoup their lost revenue. On the way, they conquered more people west and south of them. Presumably, they exacted levies on those newly vanquished people as well. Then the valley kings turned their attention toward the five insurgent cities. Soundly defeating them in battle, they took captives, booty, and headed home.

Genesis records this incident because at the time, Abram's (God later changed his name to Abraham) foolish nephew, Lot, and his family resided in Sodom, one of the conquered cities. Lot and company became part of the battle loot and were north-eastbound, involuntarily we presume. When Abram heard about his captive relatives, "he called out the 318 trained men born in his household and went in pursuit ..." (Genesis 14:14). Some neighbors and their soldiers joined Abram's army. Abram and his allies routed the Euphrates Valley forces recovering Lot, his family, and all the spoils (Genesis 14:15-16).

When the victorious Abram returned, Melchizedek, the king of Salem (probably Jerusalem) met him and his troops. The king brought bread and wine, which he served. Genesis describes Melchizedek as:

> ... *Priest of God Most High, and he blessed Abram, saying, "Blessed be Abram by God Most High, Creator of heaven and earth. And blessed be God Most High, who delivered your enemies into your hand." Then Abram gave him a tenth of everything.*
> — Genesis 14:18b-20

According to this passage, God not only approved, he gave his blessing to Abram's war. Genesis mentions no casualties. Perhaps no one died. Abram intended to liberate his nephew. He accomplished that.

But why did Abram keep a trained army whose actions God evidently endorsed? The answer may be simple. Few central governments existed in that era. The ancient Near East was comprised mostly of individual city-states. Egypt stood as an exception. As we saw earlier, Genesis 14 relates that the kings of four Euphrates Valley city-states invaded and then exacted tribute from five city-states in the Dead Sea region.

During this period, no centralized government kept peace and protected citizens. Brigandage, robbery, pillaging, and piracy commonly took place. Skirmishes and raids settled tribal feuds. As in old western movies, if the patriarch decided to defend family honor or property by force, all of the grown sons, cousins, nephews, and hired hands readied their weapons and supported him.

The nomadic Abram grazed sizable herds and flocks moving frequently while searching fodder and water for his animals. This necessitated the retention of a substantial armed force to protect his family, his employees, and his animals. At times, Abram formed treaties with city-state leaders in order to guarantee adequate water, provisions, and feed (cf Genesis 20:2; 21:22-34). He evidently didn't conduct offensive campaigns to obtain these needs.[2]

Abram's grandson, Jacob, later settled close to the city of Shechem and purchased a nearby plot of ground. A son of Shechem's king raped Jacob's daughter, Dinah, and then wanted to marry her. Jacob's sons formed a treaty with the townspeople agreeing to intermarriage and free trade, but with one proviso. The sons insisted that all of the Shechemite men undergo circumcision. Sex and greed motivated the city-guys to submit to the rite. Three days after the surgery, those Shechemite men suffered intense pain. Jacob's sons used the opportunity to attack the city. Killing all the men, and taking the women and children captive, they completely plundered the city. (See Genesis 34.)

His offspring's rancorous behavior upset Jacob, and he decided to move before the incident became known in neighboring cities.

The Genesis account includes the episode as an aberration, not the norm. Offensive military measures weren't the patriarchal style.

There's minimal evidence that God approved killing and warfare in the patriarchal age. This seems true even though contemporary regional tribes and smaller family groups often conducted vendettas and armed clashes over food, water, and grazing rights.

The Bloodletting Beginning In Exodus

If the Genesis narrative yields little precedent for offensive armed conflict, that changed 180 degrees in Exodus. The Lord ordered his people not just into battle, but to annihilate whole cities, including women and innocent children. Why would a loving God do that? We'll examine why the Lord gave such orders and decide whether he wants Christians to use that approach.

The first several chapters of Exodus record a rare type of warfare. God's people benefited from battles they didn't fight. No Israelite lifted a sword, dagger, or even a brick against the Egyptians. The Lord carried the offense using blood, frogs, gnats, flies, animal disease, boils, hail, locusts, darkness, plagues, and his *coup de grâce*, the death of all firstborn Egyptian males. The Israelites remained passive in their flight to freedom.

When they departed Egypt, God's people weren't ready for war. As the biblical account reads:

> *When Pharaoh let the people go, God did not lead them on the road through the Philistine country, though that was shorter. For God said, "If they face war, they might change their minds and return to Egypt." So God led the people around by the desert road toward the Red Sea. The Israelites went up out of Egypt armed for battle.*
> — Exodus 13:17-18

Israel's next conflict was defensive. As they proceeded into the Sinai Peninsula, the Amalekites attacked them. Led by General Joshua, and encouraged by Moses, the Israelites successfully defended themselves (Exodus 17:8-15).

After the wilderness wanderings four decades later, the Israelites attempted to go north toward the promised land. They wanted to take the main road that led through Edom, southeast of the Dead Sea. When the Edomites refused them easement, the Israelites passively retreated and evidently headed along Edom's eastern border (Numbers 20:14-21).

As they approached their goal, Israel's passive-defensive days ended. In the southeast part of the promised land, the Canaanite king of Arad attacked the Israelites and took some of them captive. In response the Israelites totally annihilated the cities ruled by Arad's king (Numbers 21:1-3). As they traveled farther north, the Israelites came under attack from other nations located on the east side of the Jordan River. The poets of Israel remembered the conquest of that area using expressions like "consume," "destroy," "overthrow," and "demolish" (Numbers 21:27-31). Israel left no survivors.

In the promised land, the Lord wanted them to make no treaties and show no mercy. In ordering them to totally destroy the Canaanites (Deuteronomy 7:1-6; cf Exodus 34:10-16), God warned his people to bestow no compassion, and to extend no clemency. He commanded complete carnage — even the slaughter of children and babies.

Joshua led the invasion of the western bank of the Jordan. For the most part, he carried out the Lord's mandate to take no prisoners — to save no one. However, when Joshua died, the conquest remained incomplete. Most of Israel's tribes allowed former inhabitants to live among them.

The book of Judges tells the Lord's displeasure over those disobeyed orders following Joshua's death. God took umbrage with the tribes that didn't exterminate the former occupants within their borders. The Lord ordered total destruction. They didn't comply (Judges 1).

Was The Killing Justified?

What rationale justifies such calculated bloodshed including the slaughter of children and infants? How could a loving being demand pogroms? Are critics of the Old Testament God correct?[3]

Do folks rightly chafe at Old Testament scenes of killing and war? Is the God depicted in the Old Testament vengeful, bloodthirsty, and lacking in mercy? Can we explain the harsh treatment the Lord ordered the Israelites to carry out?

Answers come from various fronts. First, let's look at the connection or covenant that God formed with the sons of Jacob (Israel). The Lord's arrangement with them differed from what he required of all other nations. He specially chose Israel, but not in the way some suppose.

The Lord actively led other nations and gave them specific territories. For that reason, God told Moses not to bother the Moabites or Ammonites (Deuteronomy 2:9-23). He intended for Israel to respect their territories since Moab and Ammon received divine land-grants. Later, during the time of the prophet Amos (circa 750 B.C.), the Lord reminded Israel that in regard to receiving national soil they resembled other designated peoples.

> *"Are not you Israelites the same to me as the Cushites?"*
> *declares the Lord. "Did I not bring Israel up from Egypt,*
> *the Philistines from Caphtor (probably Crete) and the*
> *Arameans from Kir?"*   — Amos 9:7

The Lord cued Israel about feeling unique. He chose them for specific reasons, but not because they behaved better or more righteously than other nations (Deuteronomy 9:6), possessed more intelligence (Deuteronomy 8:17), or were stronger (Deuteronomy 9:1). He picked them for another reason.

Before we examine the Lord's rationale for setting apart Israel, let's note some things about the Law of Moses. The body of precepts that guided Israel differs from laws respecting life in the United States and most existing nations.

God incorporated all types of commandments into a single code for Israel. That contrasts with conditions in this country. Federal, state, county, and municipal agencies govern various areas of life. Our constitution restricts Congress from making certain types of laws. For example, local governments and agencies usually, but not always, regulate matters of hygiene and of building codes.

30

Not only that, the federal government uses numerous regulatory agencies including the FTC, the FCC, the ICC, the FDA, the FSA, the DNR, and the IRS. Look for the governmental listings in the front of your telephone directory and you will probably see agencies, bureaus, and departments you didn't know existed. Apply for certain kinds of permits in some municipalities and you may be referred from agency to agency for months. Hodgepodges of agencies and jurisdictions regulate life here.

Israel's law differed. For Israel, the Lord melded hygienic, domestic, civil, and religious law (including moral and ritual) under the Law of Moses. The Lord designed all of Israel's precepts to be interrelated and interdependent. One corpus was all-inclusive.

The US Constitution forbids the government from making laws concerning religion, but belief continued as the heart and soul of Israel's law. Though it's been traditionally called the Law of Moses, God gave Israel that law. Moses mediated it, but the Lord intended that Israel be God-ruled, a true theocracy.

The Lord informed Israel that their relationship with him was exceptional.

> *You were shown these things so that you might know that the Lord is God; besides him there is no other. From heaven he made you hear his voice to discipline you. On earth he showed you his great fire, and you heard his words from out of the fire. Because he loved your forefathers and chose their descendants after them, he brought you out of Egypt by his Presence and his great strength, to drive out before you nations greater and stronger than you and to bring you into their land to give it to you for your inheritance, as it is today. Acknowledge and take to heart this day that the Lord is God in heaven above and on the earth below. There is no other.* — Deuteronomy 4:35-39

Why God Chose Israel

Why did God give Israel special consideration? Is he biased or prejudiced toward certain people or races? Hardly. The Lord singled out Israel for two reasons. First, the Lord judged the Canaanites' behavior beyond remedy. Their wickedness multiplied to the point that the Lord deemed it necessary to destroy them (cf Genesis 15:16; Leviticus 18:24-30).

Psychiatrists, courts, and social workers today make judgments concerning the corrigibility of criminals. They attempt to determine whether murderers, rapists, kidnappers, and other violent criminals can be rehabilitated and made fit to return to society. Before their release, "experts" evaluate convicted felons and then recommend them as ready. Too often they discover that freed felons return to violence.

Authorities recently paroled a convicted rapist from a Minnesota prison. State experts judged him rehabilitated. A few days after his release, a young North Dakota woman disappeared. Police rearrested the parolee because of his presence in the area where the young lady was last seen. He's now charged with her murder. Almost nightly, we hear reports of rape — murders of young women and little children. The perpetrators frequently are previously convicted sex offenders and kidnappers.

We human beings little understand the thought processes of our fellows. Nothing illustrates that truth any better than the case of the seventeen-year-old boy named Charles Bishop, who flew a stolen light plane into the 28th floor of a Tampa, Florida, bank building.

The January 2002, incident stirred conjecture. What caused the young man to do it? The local police chief speculated that Bishop was very troubled. Authorities found nothing like drugs, mental illness, or a history of being bullied, however, that might explain the young man's motive for his aeronautical death feat. Charles' mother claimed to be close to him, yet she concluded that he hid all of his intentions from her.

Aberrant behavior repeatedly takes "experts" by surprise. In spite of psychiatric expertise, extensive testing, and wide-ranging therapies, we don't know the hearts of people. Many "mental" patients outsmart their counselors.

Years ago, I corresponded several months with a convicted bank robber while he served his second term as a federal prisoner. Professing to be reformed, he spoke of his desire to live a new life dedicated to Jesus. At least twice I visited him in prison. He told me how he wanted a respectable existence, to attend church, and to serve the Lord. I believed him. His many letters to me seemed to indicate it. He convinced experts in the system. I looked forward to working with him following his parole. I never got to see him. Only hours after his release, he robbed another bank.

Some clearly become hardened to the point of intractability. We human beings rarely discover this about our fellows until it's too late, but God knows human minds and intentions (Hebrews 4:12-13). He judged the Canaanites irredeemable.

Can a whole populace get to that point? It seems so. The Lord completely destroyed the cities of Sodom, Gomorrah, Admah, and Zeboiim (Deuteronomy 29:23; Hosea 11:8).

The Lord also promised Abraham, Isaac, and Jacob that he would accomplish something unique through them. He pledged that their descendants would own the land. He promised them more than real estate. I refer to the messianic oath to their fathers — the Christ (Messiah) would arise from the nation of Israel (Deuteronomy 9:5; cf Genesis 12:1-3). Those reasons made it necessary that the nation practice extraordinary moral standards. Israel's maintenance of those principles required three things.

First, many ancient religions practiced wanton customs. God insisted that Israel eradicate the former nations whose sexually perverted worship practices and lack of proper hygiene spread lethal diseases. The seven nations occupying the promised land evidently became infested with them. The Lord forbade Israel to intermarry or to associate with the idol-worshiping populace. In fact, he ordered Israel to totally destroy the land's previous occupants. He wanted no compromises. Yet no evidence shows that the Lord ordered the killing of people or nations that lived beyond the boundaries of the promised land.

Second, God demanded that Israel demolish all the artifacts related to idolatrous practices. Remember how quickly Israel lapsed and partied in the golden calf incident? (Exodus 32:1-6; Acts 7:37-43). Israel's later history proved their susceptibility to the practices of the people whose idols they were supposed to eradicate but didn't.[4]

33

Third, the Lord promised earlier that if the Israelites would obey his laws, they would live free from illness (Deuteronomy 7:15). Failure to keep his laws would result in "sudden terror, wasting diseases, and fever that will destroy your sight and drain away your life" (Leviticus 26:16). The Lord expected strict compliance with the laws he gave them. He permitted no exceptions.

People who violated hygiene laws, committed adultery, practiced homosexual behavior, or copulated with animals placed the whole nation in jeopardy. The Canaanites did all of the above. The swift increase of plagues and illnesses, like AIDS and syphilis in modern times, witnesses to the necessity of the hard line taken by the Lord in Mosaic times to preserve a people for the coming of the Messiah.

United States courts increasingly seem to affirm a person's right to do as he or she pleases. They tend to support freedom of expression. I'm not advocating that lobby lawmakers restore Bible morality. I'll cover my position on that issue in the closing chapters.

However, consider the consequences of practicing the types of behavior the Bible forbids. I do not consider myself homophobic. However, I consistently advocate what I think the Bible teaches — the immorality of homosexual behavior. My wife and I have had many friends who lived that way. We have lost many of them to AIDS.

Statistics unequivocally prove the so-called gay lifestyle a high-risk behavior. Through 1997, the Center for Disease Control reported 16,899 AIDS cases in males 20-24 years old in the United States. Of that total, 10,569 or 63 percent were men who had sex with men. Injection drug use accounted for another 2,101 cases (twelve percent). Men who both injected drugs and performed sex with other men accounted for another 1,767 cases (ten percent). About four percent or 706 cases came about by heterosexual contact.

The nature of the epidemic continues to evolve. Recent years show a marked increase from infected males to females. One needs only to hear current news reports from Africa to understand how AIDS tragically affects whole populations.

Strong evidence suggests that the Lord demanded stringent practices of the Israelites in order to preserve life. Strict obedience to the law would forestall an outbreak of diseases like AIDS or any sexually transmitted disease in their land. Moses' Law required quarantining people with open lesions or infectious diseases.

Thousands of innocent children now suffer and die because certain people insist on their "right" to live the way they choose. Obedience to a law similar to the Law of Moses would thwart the outbreak of diseases like AIDS, syphilis, chlamydia, gonorrhea, and other socially transmitted infections.

Strict adherence to the law's demand of the death penalty for adulterers, for those practicing sex with animals, and for those involved in homosexual behavior, would virtually eliminate suffering by innocent people. By "innocent" I refer to babies born infected with AIDS, with complications of other diseases, and having to live without one of the parents. It also includes people who in modern times become contaminated through blood transfusions.

The Canaanites practiced all kinds of forbidden conduct and apparently were so involved with it that the Lord judged them beyond cure and redemption.

> *Keep all my decrees and laws and follow them, so that the land where I am bringing you to live may not vomit you out. You must not live according to the customs of the nations I am going to drive out before you. Because they did all these things, I abhorred them. But I said to you, "You will possess their land; I will give it to you as an inheritance, a land flowing with milk and honey." I am the LORD your God, who has set you apart from the nations.* — Leviticus 20:22-24

People who follow the morals that the Bible advocates remain relatively free from many of the diseases that ravage mankind. Also, they suffer less guilt, anxiety, and fear that create depression and foster other diseases.

It's a verifiable truth that the immoral behavior we described earlier poses a lethal health threat. Real life situations repeatedly demonstrate its veracity. The mainstream press doesn't comment because of political correctness. Nonetheless, it remains true. The kind of moral behavior that the Bible advocates is healthful. It's good for the body and the psyche.

Why Were Innocent Children Slain?

The most difficult issue for me regarding the Lord's instructions to slaughter everyone centers on the slaughter of babies and children. How can a loving God allow the killing of innocent infants? Jesus mitigated the problem for me by what he taught concerning little children,

> *People were bringing little children to Jesus to have him touch them, but the disciples rebuked them. When Jesus saw this, he was indignant. He said to them, "Let the little children come to me, and do not hinder them, for the kingdom of God belongs to such as these. I tell you the truth, anyone who will not receive the kingdom of God like a little child will never enter it." And he took the children in his arms, put his hands on them and blessed them.* — Mark 10:13-16

The Lord takes care of children even if we don't. It comforts me to believe that the children who died in Canaan or anywhere else will be with God in heaven.

There's Old Testament precedent for my conclusion in 1 Kings 14. King Jeroboam's young son, Abijah, fell seriously ill. Jeroboam's wife went incognito to see the prophet Ahijah and to ask whether the boy would recover. The Lord alerted the prophet to the queen's arrival. When she got to the door, Ahijah gave her dismal news.

> *Go, tell Jeroboam that this is what the Lord, the God of Israel, says: "I raised you up from among the people and made you a leader over my people Israel. I tore the kingdom away from the house of David and gave it to you, but you have not been like my servant David, who kept my commands and followed me with all his heart, doing only what was right in my eyes. You have done*

*more evil than all who lived before you. You have made
for yourself other gods, idols made of metal; you have
provoked me to anger and thrust me behind your back.*

*"Because of this, I am going to bring disaster on
the house of Jeroboam. I will cut off from Jeroboam
every last male in Israel — slave or free. I will burn up
the house of Jeroboam as one burns dung, until it is all
gone. Dogs will eat those belonging to Jeroboam who
die in the city, and the birds of the air will feed on those
who die in the country. The Lord has spoken!*

*"As for you, go back home. When you set foot in
your city, the boy will die. All Israel will mourn for him
and bury him.* He is the only one belonging to Jeroboam
who will be buried, because he is the only one in the
house of Jeroboam in whom the LORD, the God of
Israel, has found anything good." [Author's emphasis]
— 1 Kings 14:7-13

This message about Jeroboam's son reveals God's mercy on innocent children. There's reason to conclude that no child who dies
will ever be excluded from a future home with God regardless of
the child's parents' belief or behavior.

According to Isaiah, God even allows innocent adults to die
early in order to spare them later suffering.

*The righteous perish, and no one ponders it in his heart;
devout men are taken away, and no one understands
that the righteous are taken away to be spared from
evil.*

*Those who walk uprightly enter into peace; they
find rest as they lie in death.* — Isaiah 57:1-2

What about Israel's later wars — those waged by the various
kings of Israel and Judah? In many cases, they dealt with enemies
left within their borders because they didn't obey the original orders. By that time, Israel assimilated many of those people it was
commanded earlier to destroy but did not.

The Lost Marching Orders

We need to consider something else about those wars. King David organized a military draft. He and General Joab took Israel's troops into battle. The idea that God led his troops in war had been long lost from Israel's consciousness. Kings now led the nation. Israel was a theocracy no more.[5]

Other changes took place that altered Israel's relationship with the law. First, disobedience by the people and their kings caused debilitating division. The kingdom of Israel split after Solomon's reign (circa 920 B.C.). The resultant two sectors often battled each other (1 Kings 15:6-7, 32). God also used adjoining nations to punish Israel's and Judah's disobedience (2 Kings 15:17-20, 29-30; 18:13-14; 23:26-27).

By the time of the return from the Babylonian captivity (circa 536 B.C.), Israel lacked a high priest who could read the Urim and Thummim.[6] Therefore, no priest could confirm God's will (cf Numbers 27:21; Deuteronomy 33:8-10; Ezra 2:63; Nehemiah 7:65). None could say whether God wanted Israel to go to war. After 70 A.D., there was no temple at which an Israelite could sacrifice and make atonement for sin.

Neither was there a priesthood. Apparently, all family records were lost when the temple was destroyed. That made it impossible for anyone to prove lineage connected with Aaron, the original high priest. The result of these changes: the law no longer adequately regulated life; and the marching orders that God gave Israel were forever suspended.

In summary, God doesn't want his people warring and killing. The exception was the special case of Israel — the nation the Lord chose to bring the Messiah to this planet. We've seen the rigid but restrictive instructions that the Lord gave the nation in order to preserve it for the Messiah's coming. Therefore, we cannot draw inferences from that special case to justify any current actions by nations or individuals. But, I am not hinting that Christians should try to influence governmental policy toward the implementation of any principle that we have examined so far.

Is it right for governments to wage war? The answer to that question must wait until we've explored some other issues.

38

1. The Talmud contains a thought-provoking entry concerning that battle: "Cain inflicted many wounds on Abel until he succeeded in killing him, as he did not know how death would come." Sanhedrin 37b, Quoted in *A Book of Jewish Curiosities*, David Hausdorf (New York: Crown Publishers, Inc., 1955), p. 37.

2. An entry in the Talmud demonstrates subsequent disapproval for Abram's militarism. "Compulsory military service caused Abraham to be punished in that his descendants were enslaved in Egypt for 210 years, for he gave military training to the scholars in his household taking them away from their studies." Nedarim 32a, Hausdorf, p. 242. Whether those 318 men were scholars is highly doubtful. Two generations later, Esau had an army of 400 men. (See Genesis 32:6.)

3. One of the earliest was Marcion of Pontus in the second century A.D.

4. 2 Kings 23:1-25 lists reforms instituted by King Josiah about 640 B.C., some 600-700 years after the conquest of Canaan by Israel. Israel was still tempted by many of the same gods that the Canaanites had worshiped earlier, e.g. Molech. The Lord's warning in Numbers 33:55, 56 that if Israel spared the former inhabitants that they would become barbs to them was warranted.

5. The wars against the Philistines were justified because the Philistines occupied land given to the Israelites. While king of Judah, David attacked Jebus (Jerusalem) and made it his city. The Jebusites were among the people that the Israelites were supposed to have driven from the land in Joshua's time. However, I think it worth noting that when David first became king over all twelve tribes, the Philistines mounted a campaign against David, but David did not attack them until he consulted the Lord. Even when the Philistines attacked a second time, David still did not assume that he had permission. He asked the Lord again whether he should. (See 2 Samuel 5:6-25.)

6. "Urim and Thummim" refers to a special ability given to Aaron and subsequent high priests to determine God's will. Some scholars speculate that it might have been a two-sided pendant that possibly revolved and came to rest in such a way that that the high priest could discern a yes or no answer (something similar to heads or tails). Cf Exodus 28:30, 1 Samuel 28:6, Ezra 2:63.

2

Jesus, Paul, And Their Officer Friends: *The New Testament, Military Service, And Governments*

At Caesarea there was a man named Cornelius, a centurion in what was known as the Italian Regiment. He and all his family were devout and God-fearing....
— Acts 10:1-2a

Military Service

How do current Christian beliefs about war and military service compare with what Jesus and his apostles taught? Does the New Testament warrant an antiwar and antimilitary stance? What inferences can we draw from scripture about Christians' relationships with their governments?

The Christian warfare frequently appears as a New Testament theme. Paul comfortably used militant language. He urged Timothy to fight a "good fight" (2 Timothy 4:7). Some people find New Testament military references offensive. They're too martial for them, too bellicose — out of place in a religion that preaches love. Though contradictions exist between the teachings of Jesus and the methods of war, the New Testament presents a paradox that we'll review in the coming pages.

Soldiers probably carried out Herod's heartless orders to kill all the males two years and younger in the Bethlehem area after Jesus' birth. Matthew doesn't say. The perpetrators aren't known. The New Testament, however, held Herod responsible for the horrific act.

The first military men the New Testament identifies are the soldiers who came asking John the Baptist the implications of his teaching. John's answer demonstrates that military personnel concerns haven't changed over the centuries. "Don't extort money and don't accuse people falsely — be content with your pay," John advised them (Luke 3:14). John didn't suggest or hint that soldiers should quit their military jobs.

Why is this significant? Because John the Baptist's advice to people approaching him on that occasion parallels what Jesus taught (Matthew 19:21). John instructed people with two tunics to share with those who had none. He urged those having extra food to divide it with the hungry.

After Jesus began his ministry, he met a centurion whose servant suffered a painful paralysis (Matthew 8:5-13; Luke 7:1-10). Approaching him, the military man asked Jesus to heal his employee. When Jesus offered to go to his house, the centurion humbly deferred. He considered himself unworthy of Jesus' house call. He strongly believed, though. The officer confidently affirmed that Jesus could heal his servant with a word. Jesus did precisely that commenting on the scarcity of Israelite faith. The master gave no inkling that he disapproved of the centurion's profession.

English translations tend to veil an important war analogy Jesus used in another setting. His enemies accused him of casting out demons in Beelzebub's name. Following various lines of reasoning, Jesus proved his enemies' logic erroneous. First, "Any kingdom divided against itself will be ruined" (Luke 11:17). No army intentionally kills its own troops — at least not one that expects to survive long. Not even Satan would tolerate intentional losses to friendly fire. It's too costly.[1]

Second, "If I drive out demons by Beelzebub, by whom do your followers drive them out?" (Luke 11:19). Jesus' detractors cast out demons, too. What made their attempts any different from those by Jesus? If it were logical to conclude Jesus expelled demons in Beelzebub's name, one had to deduce that the enemies' disciples did, too.

Next Jesus warned his critics using some power references.

But if I drive out demons by the finger of God, then the kingdom of God has come to you. When a strong man,

42

fully armed, guards his own house, his possessions are safe. But when someone stronger attacks and overpowers him, he takes away the armor in which the man trusted and divides up the spoils. — Luke 11:20-22

Most people concede the devil's power — he is tough. But Jesus' arrival in the flesh signaled someone more formidable than Satan. If Jesus could drive out demons by using only God's finger, the devil faces big trouble.

Satan is the fully armed strong guy. He's equipped with an arsenal like the Terminator's. The word describing his armor is the same word that Paul used in Ephesians 6, when he wrote about putting on the full armor of God. Feeling invincible, Satan assumed the security of his domain and possessions.

But the Son of God came to earth, attacked the devil, overpowered him, took away his armor, and then divided up the spoils. Jesus meant that the warfare between God and Satan resembles armed conflict. Here's the difference. God always wins.

We're still left with questions. How does a follower of Jesus engage the enemy? Does he/she fight with knives, rockets, smart bombs, and guns? Is the New Testament antimilitary? Consider more evidence.

We find sympathy for soldiers in another New Testament context. When Jesus attended the Feast of Tabernacles in Jerusalem, Jewish officials became upset when they heard what people said about him. They sent temple guards to arrest him, but the sentries returned without the much-prized prisoner. Irate over the soldiers' unsuccessful mission, the leaders wanted to know why the guards came back empty-handed. The soldiers displayed wisdom and discernment their leaders lacked, said the gospel writer. Those military guys saw something about Jesus that either their bosses didn't perceive or didn't want to admit. " 'No one ever spoke the way this man does,' the guards declared" (John 7:46; see also John 7:1-52 for full account.)

Later Jesus used a war allegory to illustrate the cost of discipleship.

43

Or suppose a king is about to go to war against an-
other king. Will he not first sit down and consider
whether he is able with ten thousand men to oppose the
one coming against him with twenty thousand? If he is
not able, he will send a delegation while the other is
still a long way off and will ask for terms of peace. In
the same way, any of you who does not give up every-
thing he has cannot be my disciple. — Luke 14:31-33

It's impossible to determine whether Jesus approved or disapproved of war from his usage of this symbolic narrative. We can
conclude only that waging war and following Jesus are both costly.
We see this in several passages.

Luke 21
Matthew 24, Mark 13, and Luke 21 present the synoptic writers' accounts of Jesus' answers to some baffling questions. Because many interpreters tend to forget the setting and the questions
in these chapters, they end up confused.
What was the setting? Jesus and the disciples were walking
through the temple area. Herod the Great built the gleaming, mag-
nificent structure that dominated Jerusalem's eastern side. The site
remains imposing. Today two Moslem mosques stand on it. During the first two-thirds of the first century, however, the temple and
its surrounding porticoes commanded attention. Though Herod
began construction in about 20 B.C., work continued through 26
A.D. (John 2:19-22). In the same way that a proud San Franciscan
might brag on the magnificence of the Golden Gate Bridge, the
disciples commented on the temple's beauty.
Jesus shocked the twelve temple-admirers. Not one stone will
be left on another. Everything will be torn down, said Jesus. The
disciple band and Jesus descended into the Kidron Valley, ascended
the Mount of Olives, and then looked back at the temple. Now
alone with him, the disciples asked Jesus, "Tell us, when will this
happen, and what will be the sign of your coming and of the end of
the age?" (Matthew 24:3).
Keep in mind the disciples' questions. The first thing they asked
was, "When will this happen?" — When will the destruction of the

temple occur? The next questions concern Jesus' second coming and the end of the age. The disciples probably never dreamed that the occurrences they asked about in questions two and three might be simultaneous.

Jesus warned about deceivers and cautioned his followers not to misinterpret events that would continually happen through the course of history, such as earthquakes, famines, wars, and rumors of wars (Matthew 24:4-8). Then he predicted persecution for present and future disciples that would cause many of them to fall away. The end would come after the gospel had been preached as a testimony to all the nations, he explained (Matthew 24:9-14).

A lot of folks misunderstand the paragraph that starts with verse 15. It's important to recognize that Jesus began there to answer the disciples' first question (such as when will the destruction of the temple happen?). Matthew's account reads, "So when you see standing in the holy place 'the abomination that causes desolation.'" At the same juncture Luke's gospel reads, "When you see Jerusalem being surrounded by armies, you will know that its desolation is near" (Luke 21:20).

The sections we're discussing, Matthew 24:15-25 and Luke 21:20-24, are best understood as referring to the destruction of the temple and Jerusalem. The razing of the city and the beloved holy place occurred in about 70 A.D. culminating a two-year siege by the Roman army. Jesus outlined the potential horrors, for example, if the fall of the city should occur in winter, or on the sabbath when Jews could flee only about one and a quarter miles (a sabbath day's journey). He rightly prophesied the misery of new mothers, some of whom out of extreme hunger would consume their own children. Expectant mothers would suffer violence from the knives and swords of soldiers. Jesus foresaw this suffering and grieved over it (cf Matthew 23:37-38).

In these gospel accounts Jesus spoke of war's wretchedness, but he made no judgments about those who commit war. He apparently wanted only to prepare the disciples for war's inevitability both in the immediate and distant future.

The Arrest And Crucifixion

The gospels tell us that the Jewish leaders sent "a large crowd armed with swords and clubs" along with Judas to arrest Jesus (Matthew 26:47-56; Mark 14:43-50; Luke 22:47-53; John 18:1-11). This group included a detachment of soldiers. Peter reacted at once by drawing his sword and attacking the high priest's servant, a man named Malchus. Whether Peter meant to detach the man's head, we don't know. If that was his intent he only slightly succeeded. He made Malchus bereft of just an ear, not his noggin. Perhaps Peter meant only to show a defensive posture. Whatever he intended, it didn't accord with Jesus' plan. Jesus rebuked him and then undid Peter's swordsmanship by reattaching the servant's ear.

Why was Peter carrying a sword? Jesus raised the subject of weapons with the disciples earlier at the Passover supper (Luke 22:24-38). Ironically, as Jesus prepared to epitomize humble service, the twelve disputed among themselves about their greatness and bravado. Peter made his audacious claim, "Lord, I am ready to go to prison with you and to death." The Lord saw through the apostle's bluster and predicted Peter's thrice denial.

Jesus also reminded the apostles of the first commission. He sent them to preach telling them to depend on their hosts for food (Matthew 10; Luke 10). He didn't want them to take money or extra supplies for future mission efforts. He asked the disciples if they experienced a scarcity of provisions when they went out depending on God ... "Did you lack anything?" "Nothing," they answered.

Then Jesus followed with a new set of orders. "But now if you have a purse, take it, and also a bag; and if you don't have a sword, sell your cloak and buy one. It is written: 'And he was numbered with the transgressors'; and I tell you that this must be fulfilled in me. Yes, what is written about me is reaching its fulfillment."

The disciples said, "See, Lord, here are two swords." "That is enough," he replied. The reason Peter wore a sword in the garden at Jesus' arrest was, Jesus ordered it.

Before we draw conclusions about this seeming contradiction, we must remember three things concerning this dialogue between

46

Jesus and the disciples. First, Jesus remained conscious of his need to fulfill everything the Old Testament prophets wrote about him (Luke 24:44-49). Jesus mentioned Isaiah's prediction: He would be "numbered with the transgressors" (Isaiah 53:12). If Jesus' cohorts brought weapons and then resisted authority at his arrest, they became transgressors.

Second, the fact that Jesus permitted only a pair of swords shows that he never plotted serious resistance. Two swords weren't adequate for rebellion, especially considering the authorities armament. Peter's awkward swipe at Malchus probably symbolized the disciples' paltry preparedness even with eleven swords. The disciples hardly possessed weapons of mass destruction.

Third, when the disciples presented their two swords to Jesus, he responded, "That is enough." The expression is similar to God's answer to Moses when the Israelite leader wanted to go into the promised land. The Lord told Moses that his time was up. Joshua would lead the people across the Jordan. But Moses pleaded to see the land of milk and honey. The Lord shushed Moses' plea with "That is enough" (Deuteronomy 3:26). The discussion was over. Moses would not make any footprints west of the Jordan River. Neither would the disciples make serious resistance to protect Jesus.

When arrested in the garden, Jesus reiterated that he wasn't leading any type of resistance movement. He emphasized that as he rebuked those who came to take him into custody.

> "Am I leading a rebellion, that you have come out with swords and clubs to capture me? Every day I sat in the temple courts teaching, and you did not arrest me. But this has all taken place that the writings of the prophets might be fulfilled." Then all the disciples deserted him and fled.　　　　　— Matthew 26:55-56

The only sword Jesus' disciples used from then on was the sword of the Spirit. No biblical precedent supports the papal claim that spiritual and temporal powers are united in the Vicar of Christ.[2]

Though Jesus forbade his disciples to bear arms, he didn't condemn those professional people who did. Soldiers oversaw the execution. Their mockery and spiteful behavior are well known. Yet their behavior hardly varied from that of other citizens. The Jewish leaders incited the crowds to call for the crucifixion. On the other hand, the presiding centurion saw Jesus' matchless behavior and commented, "Surely this man was the Son of God!" (Mark 15:39). That experienced, seasoned military man who'd probably witnessed hundreds die, recognized and declared Jesus' special nature.

Military Officers In Acts

Luke commended centurions in the Acts of the apostles. First came Cornelius, an officer of the Italian Regiment in Caesarea. The Acts historian described Cornelius and his family as "devout and God-fearing; he gave generously to those in need and prayed to God regularly" (Acts 10:2). Cornelius became the first Gentile convert to Christianity. The once-kosher Peter ate with him and stayed in his home. Not only that, Cornelius received the baptism of the Holy Spirit in the same way that the apostles had on the day of Pentecost (Acts 11:15-17).

Some of the Jewish Christians in Jerusalem criticized Peter for accepting Cornelius' hospitality. Jews didn't sup with Gentiles. But no one censured Peter because he associated with someone in the military profession. Cornelius' Gentile origins presented the problem. Neither did Peter intimate that Cornelius should forsake his soldierly duties once he became a Christian.

At Paul's and Silas's arrest in Philippi, Luke introduced another military person — a jailer. Authorities incarcerated the two missionaries in a high-security area and fastened their feet with stocks. Local officials commanded the prison officer (probably a "retired" military man) to closely guard them.

Following the miraculously timed earthquake that freed Paul, Silas, and the other prisoners, the missionary duo preached to the warden and his family. After the jailer washed the wounds of Paul and Silas, he and his family were baptized. The text gives no word condemning the man's profession. Luke did emphasize the joy the newly converted warden and his family experienced (Acts 16:16-40).

When Paul was arrested and mobbed in the temple area about 57 A.D., soldiers and their commander rescued him. Later, Paul spent considerable time with the centurion Julius, who accompanied him to Rome for trial. The book of Acts makes us wonder how many times Paul may have urged Julius to become a Christian,[3] but we see no disapproval of any centurion's profession by Paul or by Luke.

Paul And Military Service

Paul rhetorically asked the Corinthians, "Who serves as a soldier at his own expense?" (1 Corinthians 9:7). He used the imagery to support his stand that preachers and elders should be paid. Neither group should work for nothing. I think it's fair to draw the inference that Paul approved of paying soldiers. Otherwise, paid preachers stand on flimsy pulpits when they ask for pay increases.

When Timothy preached in Ephesus, he faced many challenges related to his youth. He worked in a city that enticed, baited, and lured with more temptations than Hollywood ever offered. Numerous attractions beguiled the probably shy Timothy. Ephesus boasted a long-established priesthood dedicated to Diana, the love and fertility goddess. Paul knew the social-religious conditions firsthand. He urged the youthful preacher to "Endure hardship with us like a good soldier of Christ Jesus. No one serving as a soldier gets involved in civilian affairs — he wants to please his commanding officer" (2 Timothy 2:3-4).

Paul's instructions in the epistles provide evidence that he saw several similarities between serving in the military and serving God. Both require bravery and fortitude. Each must stay focused and not be distracted by outside influences. Christians and military personnel remain true to their commanding officers.

In Ephesians 6, Paul listed the full equipment necessary for the soldier of Christ, all of it based on the stern life that Roman soldiers encountered. Peter utilized military expressions, too. He counseled his readers: "arm yourselves also with this same attitude" (1 Peter 4:1).

James

James asked his readers, "What causes fights and quarrels among you?" (James 4:1). Recall the King James wording, "Whence come wars and fights?" Jesus' half brother in the flesh used strong military language in this section, some of it not recognizable to English readers. "Fights" (wars) the first word in the phrase is the Greek word from which we derive the English word "polemic." In English, polemic usually describes controversy or disputing. The Greek word often referred to war.

James figuratively used the term referring to controversies within the church. Rhetorically asking the origin of the disputes; "Don't they come from your desires that battle within you?" "Battle" is the Greek word from which we obtain the English word strategy. Military people don't usually go to war until they have designed strategies and then deployed troops and arms.

When two countries arrange armies on a common border, there's a strong likelihood of war. And when Christians deploy anger, pride, desire, and greed, there's a good chance they will battle verbally and eventually physically with their brothers and sisters. The solution, says James: "Submit yourselves, then, to God" (James 4:7).

Paul, Peter, and James metaphorically employed war language, but the only sword God wants deployed is his Spirit. Faith is the Christian's shield. No New Testament passage suggests that we wear army garb, only an attitude of readiness for spiritual warfare and a rejection of the world's selfish, hateful, and argumentative strategies.

In summary, I find scant New Testament support for objections to Christian military service. Yet, sympathy and favorable attitudes toward officers and soldiers abound. On the basis of the New Testament it's impossible to prove whether a Christian should serve or not serve in the military.

The New Testament And Government

What does the New Testament say about Christians' relationships with their governments? Statements and actions of Jesus as well as the pens of Peter and Paul provide significant evidence. The following passages give us insight.

Mark 11:12-19

Just after Jesus' triumphal entry into Jerusalem, he went to the temple area where he forcibly removed the moneychangers and the people selling doves.[4] Was Jesus setting precedent for political activism by doing this? Consider the evidence.

We've already noted God's special relationship with Israel. It resembled no other in human history. Israel invalidated that bond, however. First century political conditions evidenced its end. Israel was no longer a sovereign nation and by no means a theocracy. Roman law superseded Jewish law in most instances.

Jesus exposed many wrongs of the Jewish religion. Clearing the temple was largely a religious act. Jesus offended the Jewish leaders in doing it, and further ignited their already smoldering anger. Yet he took no action against the Roman government and never hinted that he thought it might wrongfully be in power. We'll look more at this issue in the Romans 13 section.

Matthew 17:24-27

All Jews paid the two-drachma temple tax — an assessment used to maintain the temple and support the priests. That tax had been in effect since the Exodus (Exodus 30:13).[5] When the collectors of that levy inquired of Peter whether Jesus paid the assessment, Peter went to the Lord about it. Jesus replied that everyone pays taxes except for the kings' sons. To avoid any offense, Jesus sent Peter after a special fish with a four-drachma coin in its mouth, which the fisherman pulled from the water. The apostle used that coin to pay his and Jesus' temple tax. Jesus constantly reminded his contemporaries how they neglected, misused, and abused the law. But in this unusual way he demonstrated his submission to the acceptable laws of Israel. He paid his tax.

Next, what relationship did Jesus advocate with Caesar? Did he try to interfere with or influence the Roman government? A few New Testament examples provide insight.

Matthew 22:15-22 And Mark 12:13-17 — Taxes To Caesar

Intent on trapping Jesus in verbiage, the Pharisees sent some of their students along with the Herodians to ask him a trick question: "Is it right to pay taxes to Caesar or not?" Jesus was maneuvered into a shrinking corner, they thought. If he agreed, they'd accuse him of putting Caesar before God. If he disagreed, that would be treasonous to Caesar.

Everyone paid taxes, and the Romans heavily taxed the people of Judea. The Roman governors directly collected real estate taxes. In addition to taxes on real property, the Romans imposed taxes on personal property and head taxes. They subjected both exports and imports to custom duties. Matthew probably collected this type of duty. He and others sat at tollgates, which in some ways resembled modern truck weigh stations.

Matthew and his fellow tax collectors paid a fee to the Romans for the right to collect taxes on moveable property. Ancients called it tax farming. Those farmers usually did well. Matthew's tax collecting business was not unlike a lucrative modern franchise.

Except for the temple tax, the Jews paid their dues using Roman coinage. When Jesus requested a "coin used for paying the tax," it probably wasn't difficult to find. All Jews paid that tax using the denarius, which bore Caesar's inscription.

The Lydians invented coins in the seventh century B.C. Minted money proved to be a convenient medium of exchange. It often replaced the long-used barter system because it's easier to transport coins than goats. Leaders also discovered that coins served an added purpose. They could imprint important messages on them. To the Jews, Caesar broadcast this denarius-borne news: "I rule Israel."

By requesting his detractors to dig in their purses, Jesus forced them to admit that the money they used and probably carried in their bags bore Caesar's image and message on them. With every transaction, they affirmed Caesar's rule. They had acceded to Caesar's power and authority. Jesus then said, "Give to Caesar what is Caesar's and to God what is God's."

Most Jews regarded the Romans as idolatrous foreigners. To them, Roman forces illegitimately occupied their land (the territory God gave their forefathers). We can assume that when Jesus' Jewish contemporaries met privately, they spoke resentfully of

Rome. They probably whispered it whenever occupation troops walked by.

People gather at local convenience stores, malls, and doughnut shops today to air their gripes about taxes, the price of gasoline, and to gossip. In those days, folks used different meeting places — watering holes, town gates, and agoras — but discussed similar topics. Roman occupation and taxes were probably their biggest beef.

Whether Joseph and Mary joined in that criticism, we can only speculate, but no evidence suggests that their son ever did. I find no instances of Jesus criticizing the Roman government either in his public teaching or in conversations with his disciples.

Some might find an exception in Luke 13:31-33. There Jesus responded to the Pharisees' warning that he should leave Galilee because Herod Antipas wanted to kill him. Jesus taught in Herod's territory at the time, and the Pharisees probably hoped to frighten the Lord. Jesus gave the Pharisees a message for Herod and for them — he would continue to do his work. Describing Herod as a "fox," Jesus also informed the Pharisees and the crowds that he would die in Jerusalem, not in Galilee, that is, not in Herod's territory. God controlled the Messiah's destiny, not a fox-like subordinate of Caesar.

Jesus accurately portrayed Herod Antipas. In 39 A.D. Herod's nephew, Agrippa, denounced Antipas as a "plotter" to the Emperor Gaius. Gaius deposed Herod and the "king" spent the balance of his life in exile. Jesus wasn't deceitful. His description of Herod Antipas as a fox reminds us of what he said to the teachers of the law and the Pharisees — they were "like whitewashed tombs" (Matthew 23:27). The Master didn't need to impress anyone and didn't hanker after popularity or votes. Always candid, he spoke frankly warning all people to repent, but never to undermine existing governments.

You could accurately portray the corrupt, pagan-controlled, Roman regime as a near dictatorship by that time. Contemporary conditions inflamed numerous firebrands (cf Acts 5:33-37; 21:37-38).[6] Jesus met ample opportunities to join them. But he never advocated revolt, insurrection, or even dissatisfaction with the government.

Romans 13

Jewish Christians with latent hostility toward the Roman government were probably taken aback by Paul's instructions to the church in Rome. Two different, but related, issues ignited the interest of Roman Christians. First, the matter of freedom. Christ set his people free from the Law of Moses. Some first-century Christians possibly felt that Christ liberated them from all laws, even those of civil governments. When Christians began suffering at the hands of Roman authorities they likely assumed their new freedom released them from Roman oppression. Paul reminded them that they were to be in submission to those higher powers.

At a certain point, though, Christians should resist civil governments. The apostles established the precedent early. When Jewish authorities ordered Peter and John not to preach in Jesus' name anymore, the apostles replied that they had to obey God, rather than men (Acts 4:19-20; 5:29). The Lord wants his people to respect and obey authorities. But once a government interferes with the proclamation of Jesus and the worship of God, Christians obey the Lord.

By 90-100 A.D., when John wrote the book of Revelation, Roman authorities regularly crossed that line demanding worship of the emperor. John composed the Apocalypse to bolster the faith of Christians and encourage them to remain steadfast in their witness, even to the point of dying for their faith in the Lamb.

In all other circumstances, Christians comply with government regulations. Paul instructed: "Everyone must submit himself to the governing authorities, for there is no authority except that which God has established. The authorities that exist have been established by God" (Romans 13:1). Thinking Roman government ungodly and oppressive, some Christians may have been squirming. Paul left them little wiggle room.

"Everyone" in this verse is literally "every soul." Soul here refers to the person.

> *The Hebraism suggests prominently the idea of individuality. These rules apply to all however privileged, and the question is treated from the point of view of individual duty.*[7]

Paul listed several reasons to practice this civil obedience.

First, no authority would be in power if it were not God's will that he/she is there. Thus when we rebel against standing authority, we're actually rebelling against God.

Second, when we resist authorities, we may incur God's wrath. The Lord's anger could be expressed through the authorities themselves. Rulers carry swords for a purpose (cf Acts 12:2).[8]

Third, God places authorities in power for our good. It's important to obey them for conscience's sake. How can we live in correctness before God if we neglect the laws of the human beings that he has placed in power?

Paul concluded the section by saying, "Give everyone what you owe him: If you owe taxes, pay taxes; if revenue, then revenue; if respect, then respect; if honor, then honor" (Romans 13:7).

Titus 3:1

What Paul told the Romans, he also ordered Titus to *remind* the Cretans. His use of the word "remind" tells us that Paul, Titus, or some other teacher already taught them about submitting to governmental authority. Peter echoed almost the same instruction in his first letter (1 Peter 2:13-17). New Christians clearly received instruction concerning obedience to the state as part of their regular education.

The apostles taught humble respect, complete obedience, and submission to a government that was not Christian, not democratic, and that taxed heavily. We shall discuss why they took this position and the implications for us in the closing chapters.

Paul's Roman Citizenship

Consider one more matter here. Unlike the other apostles, Paul was a Roman citizen. At times, he used that citizenship to his advantage. The first occurrence took place in Philippi. As Paul and

Silas preached there, a woman followed them shouting, "These men are servants of the Most High God, who are telling you the way to be saved" (Acts 16:17).

Through the influence of an evil spirit, the young woman foretold the future. Enslaved, she paid her owner's bills by means of her prophetic ability. Whether they charged a flat fee per prediction or whether they took her to the hippodrome to bet on the horse and chariot races, we can only speculate.

Some might think that the recognition and free advertising the young woman gave the missionaries at the time would please Paul and Silas. Instead, it distracted from their message. When the missionaries exorcised the evil spirit from the woman they tossed her owners off "easy street."

The slave owners probably never got blisters from the handles of pickaxes or from any kind of labor. But in this case they worked hard; "They seized Paul and Silas and dragged them into the marketplace to face the authorities." The civic leaders recognized the two disciples as Jews and charged them with throwing the city into an "uproar by advocating customs unlawful for us Romans to practice" (Acts 16:19-20).

When the crowd became involved, the magistrates stripped and beat (severely flogged), Paul and Silas, then threw them into prison (Acts 16:22-24). Stocks soon confined them.

Under these circumstances, modern missionaries might urge the church folks back home to contact higher authorities, and the press, and to also hire lawyers.

Though Roman citizens, Paul and Silas didn't gripe about the illegal treatment they received (punishment prior to a trial). They waited on the Lord who freed them and gave them an opportunity to convert the jailer and his family.[9] The next day, perhaps regretting their earlier hasty judgment, the magistrates sent officers telling the jailer to release Paul and Silas. That's when Paul told the messengers:

> *They beat us publicly without a trial, even though we are Roman citizens, and threw us into prison. And now do they want to get rid of us quietly? No! Let them come themselves and escort us out.* — Acts 16:37

56

We may question Paul's decision to reveal his citizenship only after the fact. But the order of events proves the message of Jesus worth the suffering. Paul and Silas spent their night in jail without complaint. The cold, dark facility probably housed a bountiful vermin population. Chains and stocks left prisoners defenseless against such pests.

The stench of sweat, urine, and feces made acrid air. As happens in any prison, shrieks, shouts, and moans pierced the night. Paul and Silas didn't join that dismal chorus. Neither did the two missionaries intimate threat or displeasure toward those who illegally jailed them. Forming their own duet, they sang hymns, prayed, and praised God. Their behavior probably left a lasting impression not only on the jailer, but also the prisoners.

The missionaries revealed their Roman citizenship only after their night in jail, a strategy that served the church well. It's evident in their original accusations that the local people considered Jews as riffraff (Acts 16:20). By letting the authorities know about their citizenship, Paul and Silas demonstrated that followers of Jesus weren't all "lowlife" Jews. The church in Philippi evidently enjoyed peace thereafter, too. Authorities remained gun-shy about further interference with the saints in Philippi.

When he was mobbed and arrested in Jerusalem, Paul used his Roman citizenship to spare his life so that he could continue preaching (Acts 22:22-29). Had he not taken advantage of his citizenship, we'd probably be bereft of at least three New Testament books — 1 Timothy, 2 Timothy, and Titus.

In summary, what guidelines does the New Testament give us about military service and our relationships with governments?

- The New Testament sympathetically viewed most military people. When soldiers and officers became Christians, no apostle or missionary suggested they quit their occupations.
- Jesus left no example of resistance to unfair governments. Rather, the New Testament gives specific instructions regarding obedience and submission to the higher (state) powers.
- We find no support for any kind of disapproval of the state's actions, let alone any type of disobedience.

But how should Christians react when their governments do things that are clearly not Christian? We'll treat that in the closing chapters. How Christians should act when their governments directly oppose the church and its work. That's the topic of the next chapter.

---

1. The one exception might be the decimation of troops by Roman commanders in order to discipline mutinous troops. One in ten of those rebellious troops was chosen by lot and then executed.

2. Cf Rengstorf in *Theological Dictionary of the New Testament*, Vol. III, Gerhard Kittel, ed. (Grand Rapids, Michigan: Wm. B. Eerdmans Publishing Company, 1964), p. 296.

3. A soldier was assigned to guard Paul in Rome while he awaited trial there. The guard or guards must have heard the gospel countless times — cf Acts 28:16, 30-31.

4. John placed a cleansing at the beginning of Jesus' ministry (cf John 2:13-16). It's reasonable to conclude that he began and ended his ministry with this highly symbolic purging.

5. Tax = a half-shekel. In the bleaker days of the return from exile, it was a third-shekel.

6. The apostle Simon had also been a Zealot, which probably was a group that refused to offer tribute to the pagan emperor of Rome. They considered it treason to God.

7. William Sanday and Arthur C. Headlam, "Epistle to the Romans," in *The International Critical Commentary* by S. R. Driver et al Editors (Edinburgh: T. & T. Clark, Fifth Edition 1914), p. 366.

8. I think it's safe to assume that sword here is not just the modern equivalent of a gun. It probably would be likened to an electric chair or other methods of capital punishment.

9. The twin facts that the missionaries prayed and sang hymns at midnight during their painful confinement and also didn't try to escape after the earthquake had freed them must have been instrumental in changing the jailer's heart and leading him as well as his family to accept Jesus.

3

The Bloodiest Book Of All:
The Book Of Revelation And War

> *The beast and the ten horns you saw will hate the prostitute. They will bring her to ruin and leave her naked; they will eat her flesh and burn her with fire.*
> — Revelation 17:16

Revelation's Militant Language

Most New Testament books use metaphors for the spiritual warfare of Christians, but Revelation, noted for its symbolism, overflows with slaughter. Its pages sop with carnage and butchery.

In-your-face allusions start with the Son of Man vision in chapter 1, verse 16. A sharp, double-edged sword juts from the mouth of an imposing dignitary. That same weapon-in-mouth figure appears again in the letter to the Pergamum church (Revelation 2:12). Later, using Psalm 2 symbolism, the sword-in-mouth individual promises power to those who overcome so that they dominate the nations "with an iron scepter" and can "dash them to pieces like pottery" (Psalm 2:9).

Revelation reports rapid-fire explosions. Offensive, militant equestrians appear in chapter 6 — riders who satanically proclaim and ordain ruin. In chapter 9, a star from heaven unlocks the "shaft of the Abyss." Smoke-producing locusts belch from the deep. These swarming creatures torture the "unsealed" inhabitants of the earth. The only good news is that the torment doesn't last. Metamorphosing symbolism describes the locusts as looking like "horses prepared for battle." Led by King Abaddon, the destroyer, these horrific insects constitute the first woe.

More torture appears. Four angels marshal 200 million cavalry troops. Plagues of fire, smoke, and sulfur spew from the mouths of horses and riders. The hideous army inflicts a massive casualty rate. A third of the planet's population dies.

Contentious references repeat like bloodstained milestones. In certain parts they predominate. Resembling a fat man with multiple stab wounds to his abdomen, Revelation presents an especially gory midsection. Why such a warlike atmosphere in Revelation? Are these aggressive allusions meant to glorify battle and bloodshed?

In a temporary stanching of the flow, chapter 11 opens with John receiving a calibrated rod. He's ordered to measure God's temple and the number of worshipers in it. The divine voice instructs him not to gauge the temple's outer court because it temporarily belonged to the Gentiles, who would trample and defile it.

The speaker tells John about two mysterious witnesses with special power in their mouths to destroy their enemies. Halitosis isn't their strength. With abilities resembling the gifts of Moses and Elijah, these two men can cause drought and induce plagues. But foes slay the heroic duo. As a result of their deaths, their enemies exult. Rejoicing doesn't last, however, because a cloud conveys the witnesses to heaven.

The Combat Theater Expands

Combat moves even to heaven in Revelation 12. The battle commences when an enormous, powerful dragon menaces a pregnant, royal woman. The ogre intends to devour her newborn son. Readers visualize bared teeth eager to rend and consume human flesh, but the fiend goes hungry. As soon as the woman gives birth to this son, "who will rule all the nations with an iron scepter,"[1] the child is taken to heaven. The woman flees to the desert.

Conflict escalates. Michael and his angels fight against the dragon and his hosts. The dragon loses and suffers eviction from heaven. On earth the dragon intensifies his voracious campaign against the woman and the rest of her offspring.

Warfare continues in chapter 13. An evil, intimidating beast (the dragon's agent and ally) emerges from the sea. Earthly people worship both the dragon and the beast. In fact, all but God's saints (the Lamb's book of life contains their names) worship the evil

60

twosome. The vicious power and authority of the two malevolent forces seem implacable and irresistible. Then a second beast appears. He bears lamblike horns, but speaks like a dragon. This beast's power too, seems unlimited. It forces everyone to receive its mark, the mark of the beast. The mark is the dreaded, infamous number *666*.

The Tide Of War Changes

At the close of chapter 14, the devil's wins finally ebb. It's harvest time — of two different crops. The first harvest indicates the gathering of the righteous (Revelation 14:14-16). Julia Ward Howe based her popular Civil War song, "The Battle Hymn" on the second harvest. Reaping begins when an angel swings his sickle on the earth, gathers its grapes, and throws them into the great winepress of God's wrath (Revelation 14:19). God starts his judgment on iniquity.

> *They were trampled in the winepress outside the city, and blood flowed out of the press, rising as high as the horses' bridles for a distance of 1,600 stadia* [five feet high and for a distance of 200 miles].
> — Revelation 14:20

Definitive pictures of God's victory ensue. At the chapter 15 vision (based on Israel's experience at the Red Sea), God's people rejoice. They stand victorious on the far side of a "sea of glass mixed with fire," and they sing about God's conquest of the second beast (Revelation 15:1-4).

Hints of impending, punishing plagues come next. Seven terrible afflictions eventuate in chapter 16. Earthly powers conspire in an attempt to resist the divine forces. Worldly kings from the East gather at the famous battleground Armageddon. But God-ordained disaster overtakes them.

An appalling scene appears in chapter 17: a woman "dressed in purple and scarlet" and glitters "with gold, precious stones, and pearls."

61

She held a golden cup in her hand, filled with abominable things and the filth of her adulteries. This title was written on her forehead: MYSTERY, BABYLON THE GREAT, THE MOTHER OF PROSTITUTES, AND OF THE ABOMINATIONS OF THE EARTH. I saw that the woman was drunk with the blood of the saints, the blood of those who bore testimony to Jesus.

— Revelation 17:4-6a

Much like a Stephen King characterization, the woman sits on a grotesque seven-headed, ten-horned monster.

We can identity the seven-headed fiend; one of the few things in Revelation we can clearly establish. After cautioning his readers, "This calls for a mind with wisdom," John tells us that the "seven heads are seven hills on which the woman sits" (Revelation 17:9). The ancients knew Rome as the "city built on seven hills."

John left little doubt that the nasty, vicious woman represents Rome and its emperors. The seven heads, however, signify seven kings, "Five have fallen, one is, the other has not yet come, but when he does come, he must remain for a little while" (Revelation 17:10). So what's the meaning of this odd prediction?

In varying contexts, Revelation's sevens, tens, and twelves represent completeness. The fact that five kings have fallen, one is, and there's another to come informed the readers that their suffering by Roman hands would be prolonged. Though not yet over, it would end.

Developing emperor worship accompanied by the persecutions of Nero and Domitian brought severe tests for many of Jesus' followers.[2] During the latter part of the first century, Rome waged intense war against Christians in certain parts of the Empire. Virtual lakes of Christian blood flowed. God's people prayed for relief. Help wasn't immediate.

Persecuted believers should have found hope in Revelation 17. Eventually, God will judge Rome;[3] its power will falter and fail, but not soon. The prostitute will finally meet her preordained destruction. Revelation 18 and 19 portray world merchants and seamen lamenting the loss of the great commercial city. Their best customer was gone.

62

Christians could give thanks and sing hallelujahs. They had or would be delivered from the great harlot Rome (Revelation 19:1-5). God's people didn't fight any military battles, though. They won by a different approach. I plan to show what methods they used, and what the Lord wants us to employ.

In chapter 17, John gave a warning that likely caused foreboding among first-century Christians. He alerted them that,

> ... the ten horns you saw are ten kings who have not yet received a kingdom, but who for one hour will receive authority as kings along with the beast. They have one purpose and will give their power and authority to the beast. They will make war against the Lamb, but the Lamb will overcome them because he is Lord of lords and King of kings — and with him will be his called, chosen and faithful followers.
>
> — Revelation 17:12-14

This meant that other nations and kings would succeed the Roman Empire in warring against Jesus and his church. Jesus' followers would be in combat for a long time. But how should they fight? Before we answer that we need to look at the remaining battles in Revelation.

History's Quickest Victories

Chapter 19 features a man riding a white horse. The steed, the ancient equivalent of a staff car or limousine, befits a general or a king. The horseman remains unnamed. Is he Jesus? John describes him as one that judges, is Faithful, is True, is the Word of God, and wears many crowns. These crowns are diadems,[4] the symbols of royalty. "He will rule them (the nations) with a rod of iron."

The mysterious rider strikes us as a martial figure, too. His eyes blaze, and he makes war. "Out of his mouth comes a sharp sword with which to strike down the nations." With a bloodied robe, he heads the armies of heaven. John intends his readers to understand that the rider matches two Old Testament figures.

First, General Joshua met a heretofore-unidentified person the night prior to Israel's siege of Jericho (Joshua 5:13-15). Not far

63

from the city, Joshua came upon the man with a drawn sword standing in front of him. It's as if Joshua encountered a sentry, who commanded, "Halt! Who goes there?" Joshua didn't know his origin. "Are you for us or for our enemies?" he asked.

The stranger's answer probably shocked Joshua. He claimed to be for neither side, but identified himself as the "commander of the army of the Lord." Joshua knew immediately that he'd met his superior. Israel's commanding general fell down reverently and asked, "What message does my Lord have for my servant?"

The head of the Lord's army told Joshua to do exactly what the Lord instructed Joshua's predecessor, Moses, to do at the burning bush. "Take off your shoes. You stand on holy ground" (Exodus 3:1-6). There can be only one commander of the Lord's army — Jesus. He alone matches the identity of the mysterious man Joshua met.[5]

The Revelation 19 person also matches Isaiah's Messiah figure, who strode forth from Bozrah, his blood-spattered garments stained crimson, "like those of one treading the winepress." He "trampled the nations" (Isaiah 63:1-6). In the words of the Apocalypse, "He treads the winepress of the fury of the wrath of God Almighty." His robe and his thigh bore this name: "KING OF KINGS AND LORD OF LORDS" (Revelation 19:15-16).

The gory scene turns more dreadful. Vultures and other birds of prey receive a dinner invitation: "So that you may eat the flesh of kings, generals, and mighty men, of horses and their riders, and the flesh of all people, free and slave, small and great" (Revelation 19:18).

Generals and admirals pride themselves on speedy conquests. Quick victories usually come when military people obtain the fortune to fight against foes that present no match.

The beast, the world's kings, and their armies prepared to fight against the rider on the white horse (Jesus) and his army. The beast and its allies were confident in their numerical odds. They sallied forth but met sudden defeat, possibly the quickest trouncing in history.

The beast and false prophet are thrown alive into the fiery lake of burning sulfur. The rest of them were killed with the sword that came out of the mouth of the rider on the horse, and all the birds gorged themselves on their flesh. — Revelation 19:20-21

Revelation 20 gives one more look at world history. It's a grand military finale. It's told from the perspective of God's dealing with Satan himself.[6] The faithful and those martyred sit on thrones of judgment. They even come to life and reign "with Christ for a thousand years" (Revelation 20:4). After the 1,000 years end, Satan is released. The devil deceives the nations and assembles them for battle. Satan puts together an army that seems to enjoy insuperable numerical odds — "like the sand on the seashore." The massive, malevolent armed force besieges God's beloved city.

Satan's fall, however, comes as speedily as the defeat of the beast and false prophet. Fire comes down from heaven. The devil is hurled into the fiery lake to join his former allies. Their torment never ends.[7]

Why All The Gory Scenes?

Why this bloody flood in the Bible's last book? What do the gore and mayhem tell us about God's love? Do the militant scenes in the Apocalypse intimate justification for war? Can we learn anything here about how we relate to our governments?

Revelation reluctantly reveals its secrets. Few find the keys to its mysterious riddles. We can comprehend it, though, if we keep a few things in view. First, John wrote it to Christians in Asia Minor (now western Turkey) while they suffered intense maltreatment at the hands of the authorities. Christians endured persecution. Many underwent martyrdom. John sent encouragement, but warned that persecution would continue indefinitely.

Consider one particular characteristic of the martyr's suffering. Hitler largely conducted his 1930s and '40s pogroms in secret. People in other countries knew that the Jewish people lost homes and businesses, but few knew the extent of the horrors until Allied forces went into the death camps. Rumors about the "soap factories" circulated, but many in the United States and other countries refused to believe them. Later, the death camp survivor Elie Wiesel detailed the previously unimaginable Jewish torment and affliction.[8]

First-century Christians suffered intensely, but more publicly. Probably many watched their innocent brothers and sisters in Christ be tortured and die. That helps to explain the vivid, sometimes grotesque, and bloody symbols of the Apocalypse. Decades earlier Paul wrote to the beleaguered Christians in Thessalonica:

> *Therefore, among God's churches we boast about your perseverance and faith in all the persecutions and trials you are enduring. All this is evidence that God's judgment is right, and as a result you will be counted worthy of the kingdom of God, for which you are suffering. God is just: He will pay back trouble to those who trouble you and give relief to you who are troubled, and to us as well. This will happen when the Lord Jesus is revealed from heaven in blazing fire with his powerful angels.* — 2 Thessalonians 1:4-7

Early Christians suffered bloody suffering, but God would bring vengeance on the perpetrators.

But why the arcane language in Revelation? Why so much symbolism? It's this: The Lord assigned John the job of writing to seven churches located in the area that we described. He intended the book to encourage Christians to believe in God's working. The Lord wanted them to stand firm in their testimony about Jesus and to resist those trying to silence them. Revelation teaches longsuffering in the face of evil. Christians tell about Jesus, and await God's judgment on evil.

If authorities found written evidence of faithful resistance in Christian hands, it endangered the believers. The Holy Spirit helped John write in a coded language that Jesus' followers could interpret but would seem nonsense to those unfamiliar with the Old Testament and the teachings of Jesus.[9]

Following the September 11, 2001, attacks, many of the networks carried a video showing Osama bin Laden talking with some of his henchmen. United States authorities worried that those conversations contained secret messages signaling other al-Qaeda agents to attack. To those ignorant of the pre-established code, the communications would seem ordinary. But the conversations carried deadly meaning. American authorities refused to allow the broadcast of some videotaped messages.

Revelation had to be in language contemporary Christians understood, but the Roman authorities couldn't. Therefore, John used language rich in the Old Testament, rife with numerical symbols, and lively with hope. For those reasons, one should read Revelation carefully, staying mindful of its Old Testament references, expressions, and imagery as well as the numeric symbolism. The scholars, Westcott and Hort, identified 550 Old Testament references in the Revelation's 404 verses. They probably didn't find all of them.

Readers should not interpret any of Revelation's numbers literally, including the 1,000-year reign. It probably symbolizes an extended period of time that is under God's control (three symbolizes God, ten is a complete number in history; therefore 10 x 10 x 10 = 1,000).

Here's the difference between the bin Laden tapes and Revelation: Bin Laden taught his followers to take murderous vengeance. Islamic militants tutor and train hatred and retribution. Revelation gives an entirely different approach. Jesus urged love.

In what way do Jesus' followers respond to the pernicious methods of their enemies? How do they preserve the church and continue their witness? Some Christian groups teach "just war" in defense of the faith. Is there such a thing as a rightful battle? Is it appropriate to kill in certain instances?

Revelation's Main Lessons

Revelation teaches loving perseverance. God expects his people to wait for the justice that he will bring. Jesus' church in Smyrna encountered severe suffering. God's people endured slander and many died violent deaths. The Revelation letter to the church in that city warned its people that they would have to put up with severe distress. Yet neither the letter to Smyrna, nor any other letter in the Apocalypse urges anything but patience. Nothing suggests protest against the government, and there's no hint of reprisals (Revelation 2:8-11).

From what the letters of Revelation tell us we can conclude that the Lord expects the following:

- God's people glorify him and the Lamb (Revelation 4:11; 5:9-14; 7:1-17; 15:3-4).
- Christians must repent fully of their own misdeeds and their lack of faith (cf Revelation 2:4-5, 14-16, 20-24; 3:1-3, 14-20). The second and third chapters contain letters to seven individual churches. The word "repent" appears seven times in those letters. But the Lord directed those commands to repent toward wavering Christians, not unbelievers.
- The letters urged recipients to be faithful in their witness even in the face of death threats (Revelation 2:10, 13; 12:11).
- God's people are called to endure (Revelation 2:7, 11; 3:5).
- The Lord expects his people to wait for him to bring justice (Revelation 6:9-11; 19:1-2). The Apocalypse nowhere hints that we take retribution.

We need to look at one other New Testament issue. How do we apply Jesus' Sermon on the Mount teaching? Some consider it without application today. They see it as applicable only in the millennial kingdom. If it's valid today, how can we justify any type of war? If applicable to nations, can any country survive that uses its principles?

We'll examine those questions and what Jesus taught in chapter 4.

---

1. This is the same figure from Psalm 2 that we find in Revelation 2:26-27.

2. Nero reigned from 54-68 A.D. and Domitian from 81-96 A.D.

3. Alaric I and the Visigoths sacked Rome in 410 A.D. The Vandals led by Gaiseric re-sacked it in 455. Rome never regained its dominance after the invasion by those Germanic tribes.

4. Crowns given Christians are the Greek stephanoi (singular, stephanos), which were victors' crowns awarded in various contests and games. Cf 2 Timothy 4:8 (the crown of righteousness).

5. Joshua would have been even more frightened and embarrassed had he known that he bore the same name that his Lord would wear when he later appeared in the flesh Joshua = Yeshua = Jesus.

6. My interpretive view of Revelation sees the book as telling the story of history from numerous perspectives. Though written in sequence, many of the events are coincidental. An example of what I mean is the stereotypical western movie showing a bank robbery in a town. Simultaneous to the town incident, the hero or heroine is miles away involved in something else. The announcer introduces this second scene by informing us, "meanwhile, back at the ranch...." These coincidental scenes in Revelation include the standpoint that throughout history there will be wars and rumors of wars, famine, and earthquakes as Jesus predicted in Matthew 24 (Revelation 6-7). Unrepentant men will bring suffering on themselves and misery even to the created world (Revelation 8-9). Satan and his agents attack the church (Revelation 12-13). Warnings are issued to man. Men curse God, but remain unrepentant (Revelation 16). God's judgment on Rome and similar ungodly world powers (Revelation 17, 18, and first part of 19). Also we see the beginning of judgment on spiritual powers (Revelation 19:11-21). God's deals with Satan from Jesus' Incarnation, when he bound Satan, to his second coming, when he will completely vanquish him (ch. 20). Jesus "bound" him by resisting the devil's temptations (Matthew 4:1-11; Hebrews 2:14-18), by casting out his demons (Luke 11:14-22, especially v. 20), and by his resurrection (Ephesians 1:18-23; Colossians 1:9-20). Revelation brings comfort to believers because after each scene that shows world suffering and judgment, God reminds his people of his care (His people are sealed in chapter 7, reminded of their prophetic power and work in 10-11, demonstrated as God's redeemed in 14, safely sing the song of Moses and the Lamb in 15, see his judgment on the harlot and receive the wedding invitation in 19. They see visions of heaven and the garden of God in 21-22.) For a complete explanation see the video, *The Book of Revelation Made Plain*, by Robert Blair, produced by Soldiers of Light Productions.

7. It's an interesting irony that many interpreters base their understanding of the Last Days on the symbolism of chapter 20, especially verses 1-10. Instead of taking the plain language found in the gospels and the epistles and then fitting their understanding of Revelation to it, they've done the opposite. They've

interpreted the symbolic language of the first resurrection and the 1,000-year reign literally and then forced literal language to fit their theories. It's more reasonable to interpret the first resurrection as one's baptism into Christ, "being born again." Also see Colossians 3:1-4, "Since then you have been raised with Christ, set your hearts on things above, where Christ is seated at the right hand of God ... you died and your life is hidden with Christ in God. When Christ appears ... you also will appear with him in glory."

8. Elie Wiesel's chilling accounts are found in his works, titled, *Night, etc.* from *The Night Trilogy* (New York: Hill & Wang, 1987).

9. The Roman Emperor Justinian made it illegal for Jews to read, study, and teach rabbinic lore (553 A.D.). The act was meant to destroy Judaism. The rabbis resorted to a strategy of using poetic compositions (Piyut) that contained veiled allusions to "biblical, talmudic, and midrashic passages that Jewish worshipers understood but mystified the government overseers." See *Jewish Worship*, Abraham Millgram (Philadelphia: The Jewish Publication Society of America, 1971), pp. 168-177.

4

Why The Contradictions?
The Sermon On The Mount And War

> *But I tell you, Do not resist an evil person. If someone*
> *strikes you on the right cheek, turn to him the other*
> *also.* — Matthew 5:39

"Whoever eats my flesh and drinks my blood remains in me, and I in him," Jesus told his disciples (John 6:56). That's a "hard teaching. Who can accept it," some grumbled (John 6:60). The master hurled a bevy of vexing teachings. "If anyone comes to me and does not hate his father and mother." "Any of you who does not give up everything he has cannot be my disciple" (Luke 14:27, 33). Tough requirements, aren't they? But for high-impact demands, nothing equals the Sermon on the Mount.

Jesus' expectations assault every stronghold of human hubris. Like smart-bombs, they ferret into our complex, evil thought caverns. Jesus' Beatitude bunker-busters leave no safe houses for hate, revenge, adultery, greed, selfishness, or hypocrisy. Even worriers can't hide. Jesus blasted every cubicle and every millimeter of brain cells concealing human pride and mistrust of God.

Does The Sermon On The Mount Apply To The Present Age?

Questions about the sermon stack higher than Jesus' "classroom" mountain. What place should we give the sermon's teaching? Does it apply today? If it's relevant now, can nations justify going to war? Is any retaliation appropriate? If the Sermon pertains to nations, could a country survive that follows its principles?

Some consider the Sermon too demanding for people of this present age. It outlines principles for the messianic kingdom, they say. It's God's ideal for us, they contend, but not for application

71

until the millennial era arrives. Israel rejected Jesus as her king. That delayed the kingdom's advent. In the interim, the Sermon on the Mount stands as a law for a kingdom-in-waiting. Many scholars teach the above.

To conclude that God retreated to "Plan B" because of Jewish recalcitrance insults God. He formed outer and inner space. How could puny creatures force him to change plans? Generals alter strategies. Coaches revise tactics, but our Creator doesn't. He knows what he's doing from start to finish.

The sermon raises the performance bar extremely high. It's more demanding than special forces training. There's good reason for rigorous requirements. The sermon defines God's expectations for us so that we shall all reach, but never grasp.

Why should God issue rarely achieved laws? For this reason. What would we be like if we attained any of Jesus' standards? We humans clutch and carry insidious conceit. Our haughtiness and egoism inflate when we only pretend to be good. People who consider themselves accomplished in overcoming lust, anger, alcohol, or any fleshly sin exude obnoxious pride. We can't stand them. The Sermon on the Mount is exactly what human beings need now, and until Jesus returns, because pride clings closer to us than Harley riders to their "hogs."

The sermon presents this problem, however. Jesus' teachings give war no space. Nothing in the gospels intimates approval of fighting in any form. Jesus' instructions hardly allow a modicum of anger let alone armed battle. Combat methods oppose his principles. Even military people recognize the contrariety. As General Omar Bradley noted following World War II, "We have grasped the mystery of the atom and rejected the Sermon on the Mount."[1]

Have we understood Jesus correctly? Did his mountain challenge forbid war in every circumstance? Let's start by reviewing the Beatitudes and their meaning. Most of us have heard the "Blessed are" sayings almost as many times as we've heard the Ten Commandments. Not all of them apply to the war issue, but many of them do, and they involve multifaceted challenges.

72

Blessed Are The Poor In Spirit

The Beatitudes begin with "Blessed are the poor in Spirit" (Matthew 5:3).[2] Two different Greek words are translated as "poor" in the New Testament. The first of those words, *penes* (probably the root of the English word "penury"), applied to people who, if they owned land, weren't able to make a living from it. They worked to earn a wage. This included most of the freemen in first-century society. Joseph and Mary probably belonged to that class of people. *Penes* doesn't appear often in the New Testament. When it does, though, it draws attention. It was a *penes* widow who put her two mites or copper coins into the temple treasury (Luke 21:1-4).

The other word for poor, *ptochos*, appears more often than *penes*. It described beggars or those who had to depend on others for food and necessities. As Lawrence Richards noted, Jesus "went from being a member of the poor (*penes*) class ... to the state of the truly *ptochos*, being dependent on the gifts of others for his support."[3]

The word "poor" that's linked with "spirit" in Matthew's Beatitude is the Greek word *ptochos*. Adam Clarke aptly applied it to "one who is deeply sensible of his spiritual poverty."[4]

Jesus illustrated the power of *ptochos* in his story of the two men praying at the temple. The first bragged about his religious accomplishments. He wasn't like other sinners, he boasted. The other advanced timorously. "He would not even look up to heaven, but beat his breast and said, 'God, have mercy on me, a sinner' " (Luke 18:13). He understood his unworthiness.

When I candidly look at my own thoughts, motivations, and behavior, it forces me to a *ptochos* in spirit attitude. Too often that's not what others see in me. I know they spot pretense. Jesus taught that only the *ptochos* in spirit man would go home justified before God.

Being "poor in spirit" prepares us for Jesus' kingdom, but it won't help us advance or survive in any branch of the military. It's opposed to the mindset taught in martial training. A current recruiting ad runs, "Join the few, the proud, the Marines." Emphasize that you are "poor in spirit" on any job application, military or non-military, and you'll find yourself standing in an unemployment line — but it's the only mind-set that readies us for God's kingdom.

Blessed Are The Meek

Can you imagine a drill sergeant training his/her charges to proceed submissively against the enemy? From what I understand, the military severely tests timid trainees, roundly mocks them, and if they crack, sends them "home to Momma."

New Testament meekness probably refers to modesty, gentleness, and courtesy rather than our contemporary usage *submissive* or *spiritless*. Nonetheless modesty, gentleness, and courtesy succeed on the battlefield no better than passivity.

William Tecumseh Sherman led the Union Army through its devastating march through Georgia. He didn't glorify military conflict.

> *War is at best barbarism ... Its glory is all moonshine.*
> *It is only those who have neither fired a shot nor heard*
> *the shrieks and groans of the wounded who cry aloud*
> *for blood, more vengeance, more desolation. War is*
> *hell.*[5]

But Sherman wouldn't have tolerated a meek, docile, or gentle soldier under his command.

Blessed Are The Merciful

A stereotypical view of mercy pictures a soldier taking prisoners instead of killing them. It makes good movies, but it's not always practical. In some cases, it's suicidal and endangers one's fellow soldiers. Mercy can be granted only if the enemy sincerely waves the white flag.

William James noted, "The immediate aim of the soldier's life is, as Moltke said, destruction, and nothing but destruction."[6]

Mercy is sometimes granted in war, but it's the exception, not the rule. Not everyone follows the rules of polite combat. That led to many of the Vietnam atrocities. No one knew whom to trust. In the Middle East today, corpses and kids are often booby-trapped. Ambulances can convey terrorists and bombs.

Probably "pitying love" best describes the compassion that Jesus meant. His contemporaries, for their part, had no truck with the idea of pity or mercy. The Romans didn't consider it nice, either. They abhorred it.

Think about a scene in the famous Roman Colosseum. Two gladiators fight to the death (NBA, NFL, and WWF violence is like a slap on the wrist from Grandma compared to what the Romans regularly witnessed). The combatants clash in an intense, bloody battle. One finally shoves the other down, his hand gripping a sword ready to thrust through sweating flesh, rend the ribcage, and rip the heart of his fallen foe. The winner asks 30,000 rabid, screaming fans their pleasure.

They might wave their white handkerchiefs to spare the vanquished opponent. If thumbs turned down, the blade plunged on its bloody mission. Throngs sometimes decided to save fallen gladiators, but not out of pity. They spared him only because they respected his valor and wanted to see him fight again.

The Greek stoic philosophers might have agreed with rendering assistance to someone, but they doubted the benefit of showing compassion. "Doing a favor for a bad man is quite as dangerous as doing an injury to a good one," said Plautus, the Roman counterpart of Jay Leno in the third century B.C. The Manicheans, a popular religious group in the third century A.D., objected even to a god of pity and compassion.

On the other hand, the prophet Micah advised Israel, "He has showed you, O man, what is good. And what does the Lord require of you? To act justly and to love mercy and to walk humbly with your God" (Micah 6:8). And Hosea wrote, "I desire mercy and not sacrifice" (Hosea 6:6).

Jewish thinking about mercy went awry, however. Jesus' contemporaries no more willingly extended mercy than the Colosseum fans. They expected God to show compassion — but only on them. Pious Jews in Jesus' time presumed they'd receive the Creator's kosher stamp on judgment day. They looked for mercy.

One best obtained God's favor by piling up merit. How could one do that?

- Go to the synagogue regularly.
- Say daily prayers.
- Fast weekly.
- Give alms.
- Tithe and obey the law.

To them it resembled a contract. Pay your car payment every month for sixty months and the dealer sends you the pink slip.

Today we'd say, "Go to church. Pray often. Give to charity. Live right. Support your church. Performing these deeds compels God to bestow you title to a heavenly mansion someday." Jewish people perceived themselves as earning merit, deserving of acquittal, and receiving mercy on the judgment day. But as my masseuse friend, Bill, said, "Here's the rub."

The Jews wanted the Lord to show them mercy, but many of the rabbis taught that one shouldn't pity a person who lacked knowledge of the law. If you saw a man in trouble, God was punishing him for law-breaking. Leave him alone; he is a transgressor. You don't help sinners.

Many folks believed in karma then. Recall the question the disciples asked Jesus concerning the man blind from birth? "Rabbi, who sinned, this man or his parents, that he was born blind?" (John 9:1). According to first-century Jewish logic, God immediately punished evil people by afflicting them. If people suffered, they had done something wrong.

Do I consider those Jewish people hardheaded and hardhearted? Yes, but first-century Jewish hearts and heads were no more calcified than any Gentile's was or is.

Here's a crucial element about mercy or pitying love. The New Testament doesn't use "mercy" to describe an emotion or a sympathetic feeling. Jesus never stood around like politicians who look condescendingly at hurting people and say, "I feel your pain." Consider this saying of Jesus:

Sell your possessions and give to the poor. Provide purses for yourselves that will not wear out, a treasure in heaven that will not be exhausted, where no thief comes near and no moth destroys. — Luke 12:33

You may be thinking, "What's all this about giving? I thought the subject was mercy." "Give to the poor" is a verb form of the Greek word for mercy. Mercy means to give actively. It repeatedly conveys that idea in the New Testament. "He who does acts of mercy with cheerfulness," said Paul (Romans 12:8 RSV).

Matthew records the following account: "As Jesus went on from there, two blind men followed him, calling out, 'Have mercy on us, Son of David!' " (Matthew 9:27). They weren't asking Jesus just to feel sorry for them. They wanted to see. Jesus didn't say, "Boys, I feel your pain," then get on his donkey and ride to Jerusalem. In New Testament language, mercy is no emotion; it's a loving act.

It's a contradiction in terms when you harm a person to whom you extend mercy. Yet mercy isn't simply a soft heart or a nice feeling. It's pitying love translated into action. Being merciful is the opposite of doing war.

Blessed Are The Peacemakers
In verse 9 of Matthew 5, Jesus commended "peacemakers for they will be called sons of God." Are you interested in being known as God's child? Become a peacemaker. However, not everyone who speaks of peace really wants it. Cynic Ambrose Bierce defined peace this way: "Peace, (noun). In international affairs, a period of cheating between two periods of fighting."[7] Not all that go to war do so willingly. But war and peace seem eternally opposite.

Some people prefer any kind of peace to war. Benjamin Franklin seemed to believe that in 1783 when he wrote: "There never was a good war, or a bad peace." "Join the army, see the world, meet interesting people — and kill them."[8] Thus read a pacifist's badge in 1978.

Many Christian peace advocates heavily depend on this beatitude, "Blessed are the peacemakers." When Jesus made this

77

pronouncement, he seemed to align himself with Old Testament declarations of peace. The Lord said through Isaiah: "If only you had paid attention to my commands, your peace would have been like a river, your righteousness like the waves of the sea" (Isaiah 48:18).

Yet of all the beatitudes, "Blessed are the peacemakers" may least likely support the pacifists' cause. Why? Because people seem to focus on the "peace" part of the word and neglect the "maker" part.

"War-weary" describes the world of Jesus' day. Depression and frustration dominated. In the thousand years prior to Jesus' incarnation, Israel suffered from scores of civil wars and border conflicts. They fought neighbors like the Philistines, Ammonites, and Arameans. King Shishak of Egypt attacked Jerusalem only five years after Solomon's death (1 Kings 14:25-28). Beginning in the eighth century B.C., the Assyrians invaded and conquered Israel. Then came the Babylonians, the Persians, and the Greeks under Alexander, the Great.[9]

After Alexander's death (323 B.C.), two of his generals (Ptolemy in Egypt and Seleucid in Syria) and their descendants constantly fought over control of Israel. Israelite factions often sympathized with one side against the other (Ptolemies versus the Seleucids). In the midst of all that, Israel tried to regain its independence and return to sovereignty. Judas Maccabeas and his brothers led a popular, and for a while, successful revolt against the Seleucids during the second century B.C.

Though they didn't fully prevail, the Maccabeas fired Jewish nationalism. It never extinguished. The annual flames of Chanukah candles in Jewish homes and synagogues witness to Maccabean brilliance, achievement, and heroism.

Fervent nationalism ignited the hearts of Zealots in the first century. The apostle Simon had been a Zealot. A Galilean named Judas led a revolt against the Romans in 6 A.D. (Matthew 10:4). The Romans quashed it, but the spirit of rebellion against Rome never died. The Pax Romana (Roman peace) prevailed. Jewish patriots planted seeds of sedition, however, more widely and firmly in Israelite soil than winter wheat in Kansas. The blood of Jewish martyrs generated explosive germinating power.

Many Jewish young men probably muttered concerning the Roman occupation troops, "Someday the Holy One, blessed be he, will send our messiah-king, and you Gentiles and your army will get your dues." In this context, Jesus stood on the mountain and proclaimed, "Blessed are the peacemakers," or as the Today's English Version translates, "Happy are those who work for peace."

Not all first-century Jews agreed with those who resisted the Romans. Some of Jesus' contemporaries decided on another route to peace. They withdrew from the world, from commerce, and materialism teaching that one should live out in the country engaging in prayer and meditation. In that way they thought they could love every one as they should. For the Essenes, peacefulness meant passivity.

Did Jesus intend avoidance and submissiveness? I used to practice the mottoes, "He who runs away today will live to fight another day," and "Better to be a live coward than a dead hero." Do weakness and cowardice cause us to misinterpret what Jesus said about peacemaking? Ought we to conclude that Christians never fight in any situation? Is complete passive compliance the path to peace?

Jesus didn't use the word "peaceable." It's "peacemaker." Occurring only one time in the New Testament, it means "a creator of peace." It's active, not passive. Jesus commended those who attempted to reconcile feuding folks. They work to achieve goodwill in tense situations. Paul gave similar insight and instruction, "Live in peace with each other. And we urge you, brothers, warn those who are idle, encourage the timid, help the weak, be patient with everyone" (1 Thessalonians 5:13b-14). Paul didn't urge passivity. He wanted the Thessalonians to work for peace among themselves.

An elderly gentleman helped lead a church I once served. Softspoken and considered gentle, he probably never physically harmed anyone. But he also wouldn't speak up in behalf of the minorities, who wanted to worship with us at the time. He behaved passively, maybe peaceably, but not as a peacemaker. In fact, his actions (or should I say his inaction) caused pain to a lot of innocent seekers.

I can't imagine Jesus inertly watching as innocent children or the elderly suffered harm or danger due to bullying, bitterness, hypocrisy, and dishonesty by others. Can you?

Real peace includes justice. During the days of the prophet Amos, people actively participated in religious services. Peace prevailed. In fact the people felt at ease in Zion (Jerusalem) (Amos 6:1). God wasn't pleased. Those peaceful, peaceable people trampled the helpless and the needy. They cheated one another in the marketplace. And they crushed the weak. The Lord said to his people:

> *I hate, I despise your religious feasts; I cannot stand your assemblies. Even though you bring me burnt offerings and grain offerings, I will not accept them. Though you bring choice fellowship offerings, I will have no regard for them. Away with the noise of your songs! I will not listen to the music of your harps. But let justice roll on like a river, righteousness like a never-failing stream!* — Amos 5:21-24

The problem is the area of application for peacemaking. We've already noted that Israel was a theocracy; God ruled it. The instructions that the Lord gave Israel about how to correct wrongs in Old Testament times don't necessarily apply to Christians. Recall that Israel's hygienic laws, civil laws, and domestic laws were all bound together.

The New Testament gives us principles concerning church matters and personal relationships, but remains relatively silent about civil and hygienic law. Jesus gave Christians no precedent for applying civil law, criminal law, or international law. He restricted their areas of concern to the church and to personal matters.

As for dealing with church problems, the Lord wants us to play active roles. Paul made that evident in his letter to the church people in Thessalonica. He explained that in church relationships there's a place for strong rebuke. Passivity won't work in those conditions. In dealing with the world, however, we use a different procedure. We shall cover that later.

80

We've looked at the Beatitudes. Nothing in them condones war. At times in church relationships, strong rebukes become necessary. But the Beatitudes merely introduced Jesus' mountain sermon. In the main part of his discourse, he gave some radical challenges concerning war and violence.

Matthew 5:21-26 — Murder And Anger

This section assails us with demanding precepts. It starts with the great commandment, "Thou shalt not kill" (KJV). That murder is evil was a given. Everyone understood that. For most people, keeping the commandment, "Do not kill" compares to a two-inch high jump. Even Great-Grandpa can leap that high. The percentage of people who actually take the lives of other people is relatively low. But murdering another in one's thoughts presents a real problem. Just about everyone wishes on at least one occasion that a brother, a sister, a spouse, a mother, a father, or a neighbor would hastily depart this life.

The Lord radically raised the bar. Murderers aren't the only ones in jeopardy. Ire is a no-no, Jesus warned. Anger can cast you to Gehenna's torment. That's like raising the high-jump standard from two inches to thirty feet.

When Jesus condemned wrath, he implicated everyone. Not only that, Jesus wanted his hearers to work toward speedy reconciliations. As a result of Jesus' new standard, if our anger endangers us to the fires of hell, what penalties might he impose for those guilty of killing or going to war?

How should we understand Jesus' demanding requirement? Remember that the Ten Commandments only introduced the Mosaic Law. More than 600 other commandments augmented, clarified, and amplified the first ten. As we noted in chapter 1, among the other requirements laid on the Israelites was the mandate to destroy the former occupants of Canaan (Exodus 23:31-33; Numbers 31:1-2; Deuteronomy 2, 3, 4). Israel was to spare none.

Under certain circumstances, God ordered the Israelites to annihilate whole nations. It's therefore necessary to conclude that the killing referred to in the Ten Commandments meant the murder of

81

a fellow Israelite or one of the aliens that lived in the land. Otherwise, the commandment contradicts other precepts.

As we saw, Jesus based his teaching about anger on the commandment "Thou shalt not kill." He made reference to the Sanhedrin (the Jewish high court), and he used the principle in reference to brothers and neighbors. That forces the conclusion that Jesus referred to fellow Israelites in their personal relationships.

David seemed aware of this distinction when he gave instructions to Solomon concerning Joab, son of Zeruiah. During most of his reign, David retained his nephew, Joab (1 Chronicles 2:13-17), as his commanding general. Joab led the Israelites in battles that David authorized. General Joab was responsible for killing thousands of enemy troops. A brilliant strategist, Joab keenly perceived human situations that David dodged or refused to confront (2 Samuel 19:5-8).

King David held Joab responsible for two murders, however. Both victims were military men, but Joab didn't kill them in battle. He held personal animosity toward the two. Peacetime anger toward a fellow Israelite, not killing in war got Joab into trouble with his uncle. David saw that difference and wanted his son Solomon to avenge those two murders (1 Kings 2:5-6).

In Matthew 5:21-26 Jesus seemed to address the Jews' anger toward their own countrymen, their friends, family, and neighbors. Jesus probably directed his statements at those who thought that it all right to think or feel what you wanted about a neighbor as long as you didn't kill him. I question whether Jesus intended his precept for application in war. But the next two sayings that we examine can't be so easily dismissed.

Matthew 5:38-42 — An Eye For An Eye

In verse 38, Jesus referred to another Old Testament saying, "An eye for an eye, and a tooth for a tooth" (Exodus 21:24; Leviticus 24:20; Deuteronomy 19:21). The "eye for an eye" regulation, though harsh by some modern standards, was a humane advancement in its day. This Mosaic principle kept people from overreacting. It forestalled escalating retaliation and therefore seemed a good principle for its time. In many societies, no rule of law prevailed. The

82

slightest injury often provoked deadly reprisal. The Mosaic Law limited the offended person's response. For loss of a tooth, there couldn't be a smashmouth response.

Jesus raised the bar concerning this principle, too. One might hide hateful thoughts toward a brother. But Jesus' new demand meant having to turn the other cheek, give more charity than requested, and going the second mile.

We do our best to rationalize our way out of these prescripts. It's not that we consider them impossible regulations. We just don't want to follow them. Our egos loom too huge, our selfishness too entrenched, and our pride self-serving.

Jesus probably directed his "eye for an eye" principle toward those who resented the Roman occupation troops in Israel. That likely included most of his Jewish contemporaries. To get an inkling of their feeling concerning the Romans, consider how your townspeople or neighbors would feel about foreign troops on American soil. Innocent Middle-Easterners were assaulted and at least one killed by angry Americans following the WTC attacks. In this generation, many resent Middle-Easterners. But past American generations singled out Russians, Jews, Japanese, Germans, Poles, Irish, Italians, African Americans, Mexicans, Confederates, Yankees, and even the British as objects of venom.

Many scholars think Jesus formulated the second-mile principle because Roman law required that one of their occupation soldiers could force a Jew to carry his baggage for a mile. Imagine Palestinian soldiers walking the streets of your city or town and making demands of you and your family.

The temperature is 95 degrees — you are harvesting corn, playing with your children, or you're on the fourth hole at the golf course. A Palestinian occupation soldier carrying a backpack walks off the road and yells at you. He orders you to carry his eighty-pound pack for a mile. The law says that you must carry it 5,280 feet down the road. Lug it or suffer the consequences.

Here's the question. Will you gladly carry that pack or will you mutter the whole time about catching him by himself someday?

C. Roy Angell envisioned a young Jew being pressed into service by a burly Roman soldier to carry the load for a mile.[10] Instead of grousing and griping, he cheerfully picks up the pack and says to the occupation soldier, "I've always wanted to travel to Rome. Tell me what it's like there. Do you have a wife back home? Do you miss her? Do you have children? Tell me about them."

After the young man carries the soldier's pack for a mile, he says, "I've enjoyed talking with you so much that I've got my second wind. Let's go another mile. I'd like to hear more."

If one of those Palestinian soldiers got you off of the golf course or out of the cornfield and forced you to carry his luggage for a mile, would you affectionately offer to carry it two?

If that's how Jesus wants us to treat our enemies, can we even consider lifting a weapon in defense of our lives? On the other hand, if Jesus expects us to treat representatives of foreign governments in this manner, can we appropriately protest a governmental action regardless of whether the government acts favorably or unfavorably toward godly people? Jesus' second-mile requirement may preclude a tiny military step by Christians. Does it also silence Christians who protest war?

Matthew 5:43-48 — "It Was Said, 'Love Your Neighbor And Hate Your Enemy.'"

I've often said that I could probably find justification in the Bible for about any position that a person might take. Of course, I'd need to take scriptures out of context in order to make that happen. It's by that method that Jesus' contemporaries decided on the principle to "Love your neighbor and hate your enemy."

The Old Testament states that one must love his neighbor (Leviticus 19:18). But did the Old Testament say that one should hate his enemies? That isn't quite as clear. One has to play with the contexts of a few Old Testament passages to arrive at that conclusion. However, if people want they can rationalize anything. Jesus' countrymen did precisely that.

For one, they evidently based their "hate your enemies" stance on Deuteronomy 23:6. A pair of neighboring countries was the subject of that section. The Lord reminded Israel that when they earlier passed through Ammonite and Moabite territories, those two countries were hostile toward Israel. Ammon and Moab hired

84

the prophet Balaam to pronounce a curse on God's people. For those reasons the Lord forbade friendship treaties between Israel and the two nations.

But the Lord never wanted them to hate all their enemies. The next verse actually reads, "Do not abhor an Edomite, for he is your brother. *Do not abhor an Egyptian,* because you lived as an alien in his country" (Deuteronomy 23:7, author's emphasis). One has to wonder how seriously most Israelites followed those exhortations. Or how many modern Israelis or Americans comprehend them?

Psalm 139 may also have contributed some to the "hate-your-enemies" practice. There the psalmist attempted to justify himself by reminding the Lord, "Do I not hate those who hate you, O Lord, and abhor those who rise up against you? I have nothing but hatred for them; I count them my enemies" (Psalm 139:21-22). However, it's the Lord's enemies that he professes to abhor, not his own. He seems eager to justify himself by aligning himself with God.

The writer evidently recognized his pride. He concluded the psalm in humility: "Search me, O God, and know my heart; test me and know my anxious thoughts. See if there is any offensive way in me, and lead me in the way everlasting" (Psalm 139:23-24). This psalm gives little justification for hating one's enemies.

Jesus wept as he predicted Jerusalem's destruction by the Romans:

> *The days will come upon you when your enemies will build an embankment against you and encircle you and hem you in on every side. They will dash you to the ground, you and the children within your walls. They will not leave one stone on another, because you did not recognize the time of God's coming to you.*
> — Luke 19:43-44

Jesus foresaw the siege of the city by the Roman general Titus and the city's eventual demolition (70 A.D.). The fall would be bloody, humiliating, and painful for all Jews. It would occur, Jesus said, because the people failed to recognize or receive God's coming to them — that is, they rejected Jesus as the Messiah (Luke 19:45).

Not only did they rebuff him, they renounced and refused to accept Christ's precepts. Those principles included the ones we just considered: "turn the other cheek," "go the second mile," and "love your enemies." Perhaps had Jesus' contemporaries practiced those prescripts, the Romans wouldn't have been forced to quell Jewish insurrection and rebellion four decades later.

In about 30 A.D., Jesus foresaw that they would not: "If you, even you, had only known on this day what would bring you peace — but now it is hidden from your eyes" (Luke 19:41). They could have enjoyed peace by accepting him and following his advice. They didn't opt for that. We rarely do, either.

Whether a person could justify hate based on the Old Testament begged the question. By instructing us to love our enemies and to pray for those who persecute us (Matthew 5:44-45), Jesus left scarce room for animosity toward another, let alone pointing a rifle at him.

Is it wrong for governments to engage in war? Nothing in the Sermon restricts governments from warring. However, ample evidence suggests that Christian persons should not protest their governments' military actions. Is that intimated in Jesus' instruction to leave the things that are Caesar's to Caesar? Later we'll look further at that possibility.

---

1. General Omar Bradley, Address, Armistice Day, 1948.

2. There are notable differences between Matthew's and Luke's accounts of the Sermon. Instead of "Blessed are the poor in spirit," Luke's gospel reads, "Blessed are you who are poor" (Luke 6:20). Where Matthew reads, "Hunger and thirst for righteousness," Luke reads, simply "hunger now." Luke abbreviates the number of "blesseds" and adds a series of woes that Matthew doesn't include. Many scholars conclude that the two gospels give accounts of the same sermon by Jesus, but that the differences result from the varying emphases of Matthew and Luke. In other words, either Matthew added some phrases

to support his theme or Luke deleted some to support his. I find these explanations unsatisfactory. Why is it necessary to conclude that both gospel writers based their accounts on the same speech by Jesus? I think there were two different sermons. Here's why I hold that opinion. First, Matthew says that the Sermon was on the mountain and that Jesus delivered it sitting down (5:1, 2). Luke says that Jesus was standing on a level place (6:17). The phrasing and content of the two sermons are similar. But what preacher or politician doesn't give the same speech more than once if he/she has a different audience? In political campaigns, gospel meetings, and seminars, speeches are repeated all the time. Speakers typically alter and revise speeches for local audiences. I think that Matthew based his account on one occasion of Jesus' teaching and Luke on another.

3. Lawrence O. Richards, *Expository Dictionary of Bible Words*, Regency Reference Library (Grand Rapids, Michigan: Zondervan Publishing Corporation, 1985), p. 492.

4. Adam Clarke, *Clarke's Commentary*, Volume V (New York: Abingdon Press, undated), p. 65.

5. General William Tecumseh Sherman, speech, Michigan Military Academy, October 19, 1879.

6. William James, *The Varieties of Religious Experience: A Study in Human Nature* (New York: Doubleday & Company, 1902), p. 332.

7. *Devil's Dictionary* (1911), Quoted by Lance Davidson in *The Ultimate Reference Book* (New York: Avon Books, 1994), p. 287.

8. Israel's location on the eastern shores of the Mediterranean Sea directly south of where the Euphrates River could be forded, and only a few days travel northeast of Egypt made it a constant battlefield. Troops on their way from Egypt to the Fertile Crescent and from Egypt to Europe and Asia Minor, and vice versa used well-worn roadways though Israel.

9. C. Roy Angell, *Iron Shoes* (Nashville, Tennessee: Broadman Press, 1953), pp. 98-99.

5

It Began Well:
Post-Apostolic Times To Constantine

They were longing for a better country — a heavenly one. Therefore God is not ashamed to be called their God.... — Hebrews 11:16

We walked through a wind-blown cemetery near a little west Texas town. My wife hoped to find her paternal grandfather's burial place. Although we located the weathered monument, we had trouble making out the pertinent information. I felt awkward attempting to trace the decades-old inscription with pencil and paper.

Finding what Christians thought about war and military service in the second and third centuries A.D. is far more difficult to recover than ancient gravestone captions. Compare it to the lack of dependable Western intelligence reports from Iraq prior to the 2003 war.

At least two different conditions explain the lack of data. First, disciples during that era rarely found time on Saturday afternoons to curl up by the fire. Many were "fired" after being pursued, skewered to posts, and then kindled.

Survival was the contest. Staying alive was a daily challenge. Nonetheless, many believers fervently and faithfully preached Jesus' kingdom and fulfilled the Great Commission. The good news went everywhere.

There's a second reason for the scarcity of records concerning the issue of Christians and government. Today's information deluge contrasts with the slight number of surviving Christian-authored materials from this period. Mail service probably wasn't good in the caves and catacombs. Authorities likely destroyed many precious documents. Much of what remains was penned by anti-Christian authors.

New Testament teachings and examples present strong evidence for what Christians practiced. In both his Sermon on the Mount and his Sermon on the Plain, Jesus exacted demanding criteria: love adversaries, work actively as peacemakers, turn the other cheek, and bless enemies. Lovingly apply those principles, said Jesus. Evidence suggests that a preponderance of Christians did.

In that era, many Christians practiced another New Testament concept. They lived as though heaven were their home, not this planet. Not all did that of course. If they had, Peter and the writer of Hebrews wouldn't have had to challenge their contemporaries to live "as strangers and aliens."

Consider how that differs from contemporary customs. We want acceptance, rights, privileges, and recognition. Many of us consider insults and slights "sueable" offenses. Some Christians expect warm "fuzzies" in all situations. If they don't receive justice as they perceive it, countless agencies and attorneys gladly represent them so that they obtain their dues.

Currently in the US, a political-social issue rages over the rights of so-called "illegal immigrants," people who don't possess legal documentation and therefore aren't entitled to certain privileges that ordinary citizens enjoy. Some immigrants wander from place to place hoping that they will someday be considered legal and treated that way. I'm not trying to propose what's just and fair. That's not my bailiwick.

Peter and the writer of Hebrews used the terms "strangers and aliens" as analogues of our relationship to the world. Abraham and the other patriarchs wandered all over the promised land pitching their tents, but never took up permanent residence. Enjoying few rights, Abraham roamed all of his life without settling. The old patriarch gained title only to a cemetery. To the Amorites who resided in the land, Abram remained a stranger and alien.

Followers of Christ wander in the same way — we are foreigners and aliens here. As such we demand nothing. We exalt God and serve him, not protest, struggle for rights, or demand privileges. We don't strive for what the world craves because this creation passes away. Seeking permanent residence here invites disappointment.

No past person ever obtained lasting habitation on earth. Notwithstanding that, each generation keeps trying. Most folks try to settle, establish roots, and secure themselves. That neither satisfies us nor pleases God. He wants us to delight in our heavenly citizenship (Philippians 3:20).

Just after Abram defeated the kings who kidnapped his nephew Lot, Abram evidently complained to the Lord about his situation. The old patriarch recovered loads of war spoils, but at the Lord's urging, Abram gave the first tenth to the mysterious Melchizedek, King of Salem, and the balance to the patriarch's neighbor-allies, Aner, Eschol, and Mamre. Abram kept nothing for his trouble (Genesis 14).

When the Lord nudges us toward generosity, we lack confidence that he'll take care of us. "If I give so much to this cause, who will take care of me?" I often complain. In fact, I discussed that very subject with the Lord yesterday. Abram probably muttered after he gave away 100 percent of the war-spoils. That's when the Lord said to him, "Do not be afraid, Abram, I am your shield, your very great reward" (Genesis 15:1).

The Lord doesn't immediately compensate us. He wants us to accrue our savings in the bank of heaven, not in security national of Podunk. When we live this way, our neighbors consider us strange because they're in a constant funk over social acceptance and financial security.

Many kingdom-seekers of the first three centuries resembled Paul — their bodies bore the marks of their allegiance to Jesus (Galatians 6:17). They surrendered eyes, arms, legs, and skin rather than forsake their first allegiance. "They admitted that they were aliens and strangers on earth" (Hebrews 11:13d).

They longed for a "better country — a heavenly one. Therefore, God is not ashamed to be called their God, for he has prepared a city for them" (Hebrews 11:16).

We become strangers in another manner. Though we owe our first allegiance to the king of the universe, we gladly obey the laws

91

of whatever country we might reside rendering to Caesar what is
Caesar's. Paul's instruction regarding our relationships with governments paralleled what Jesus said. Paul added that God instituted the Roman government.

That probably seemed odd to most first-century folks for this
reason. The Roman government was no democracy in a republic.
Its dictators worshiped pagan gods and promoted idolatrous religious beliefs. Yet the apostles followed Jesus in teaching Christians to honor government representatives. Jesus left no examples
for resisting unfair or heathen governments.

Because Christians give tribute to whom tribute is due, they
never subvert governments or rebel against them. Disobedience is
appropriate only when governments forbid or interfere with worship of God. God's kingdom demands their first loyalty. That allegiance makes them outsiders and strangers.

The book of Revelation teaches that Jesus requires us to faithfully witness even in the face of death threats. We endure suffering. The Apocalypse never advocates taking retribution for unfair
treatment. The Lord expects his people to wait for his justice and
judgment.

What about Christians serving in the military? The New Testament yields no direct information on the issue of whether a Christian may go to war for his/her country. On the other hand, the Bible
sympathetically treats military people. We're left with inconclu-
sive evidence.

Post-Apostolic Times

Concerning the attitudes of Christians toward government during the second and third centuries, available sources yield limited
information. Most of the existing evidence came from non-Christians; we rarely read the believers' side of the issues. I don't assume that you have enemies, but if you did, would you trust them
to give a fair picture of your beliefs and behavior?

Christians encountered foes during the second and third centuries as they had in the first. One source of contention created
increasing legal problems for Christians. The Roman Empire generally tolerated religious cults. However, when officials suspected

treason, revolt, or social disorder, they reacted with force. "Christians recognized the duty of loyalty to the state, but the state demanded impossible forms for its expression."[1]

The most prominent of those "impossible forms" was veneration of the emperor. Believers offered worship only to God through Christ. That gave Rome grounds for accusing Christians of treason. Many Christians suffered martyrdom. A letter that the Roman governor of Bythinia (now north-central Turkey) wrote to the Emperor Trajan circa 112 A.D. gives us some clues as to Christians' relationships with their government, if not what they felt about war.

Governor Pliny expressed numerous concerns to his boss, the emperor. He felt at a loss as how to try believers, how to determine if they were Christians, and how to punish those "guilty" of being Jesus' disciples.

Because being a Christian was a capital offense, Pliny thoroughly queried the accused about their faith in Jesus, giving them opportunity a second and third time to renounce. Evidently a few did, demonstrating their betrayal of Jesus by supplicating the gods, placing wine and incense in front of Caesar's image, and then cursing Christ, "which I hear no true Christians will do."[2]

This early second-century letter and Trajan's response demonstrate the increased pressure Christians felt because their beliefs were at odds with those of the Roman government.

Veneration of the emperor developed throughout the first and second centuries. The Roman senate proclaimed Augustus a state god at his death. Though Tiberius didn't desire divine status unless the senate received it, too, Caligula seemed happy to claim it. Especially after Nero, Roman demands for emperor worship grew strong and at times inflexible. Christians refused to engage in emperor homage.

Though it remained a crime to be a Christian in the second-century Roman Empire, Trajan didn't want Pliny to take "witch hunts" to root them out, and he didn't wish for Pliny to pursue matters of the sort unless they came to public attention.

At times during this period, Jews brought such accusations against Christians. Earlier, the Sanhedrin pronounced the "Nazarene sect" an abomination. Because of Jewish dispersal throughout the empire, they often gained opportunity to bring charges against Christians.

Jews established themselves in such a way that the government seemed to take a hands-off policy toward them. They were a "licensed religion." Christianity was not. Jews received an additional break. The Romans usually compelled men of all conquered nations to render military service. Because the Jews stayed intractable in respect to their dietary laws and sabbath observance, the Romans exempted Jewish men from military service.

Though the government didn't actively persecute Christians at this time, some Christian behavior and beliefs brought them notoriety. Christians came to be called the "third race." Neither Jewish nor pagan, Christians took Jesus seriously when he said: "My kingdom is not of this world" (John 18:36). Paul reminded believers that their "citizenship is in heaven" (Philippians 3:20). Most Christians of that era clung firmly to that belief.

The otherworldly citizenship led Christians into conflicts with their contemporaries because heavenly hopes directed their moral standards. They always faced the question as phrased by Adolf Harnack, "In how much of this life may I take part without losing my position as a Christian?"[3]

Did Christians Serve In The Military?

During the post-apostolic period and that of the early church fathers, controversy continued over whether Christians should serve in the military. Tertullian[4] and nearly all of the Christian writers prior to the mid-fourth century condemned believers that went to war.

Tertullian based his argument on Jesus' statement to Peter at the arrest in Gethsemane. Because Jesus told the apostle to put away his sword, Tertullian assumed that the Lord forbade Christians bearing arms. Origen of Alexandria (early third century) thought that the triumph of Christianity would make war obsolete.

Most Christians apparently abstained from military service. This stand alarmed many in the empire. About 180 A.D., a pagan critic named Celsius wrote that if everyone acted like the Christians, lawless barbarians would take over. But not all Christians agreed with Tertullian, Origen, and the other church leaders of the era whose writings are preserved.

Some Christians did serve in the military. Perhaps their consciences permitted that type of service because of the prominence of New Testament centurions. One legend from the late second or early third century centers on the Roman Twelfth Legion, also known as the Thundering Legion. The Romans made an incursion into northern Moravia. A warring Germanic tribe known as the Quadi suddenly surrounded the Roman camp cutting off their water source. According to the legend, legion members knelt in prayer. The heavens soon responded with water that refreshed the parched and weary Romans.

Although the Roman historian, Dio Cassius, gave credit for this miracle to an Egyptian magician, many Christians throughout the empire credited God for the miraculous deliverance.

This Thundering Legion account gives insight into the thinking of early Christians toward the Roman army. For one, some Christians served in the military. Second, those who did unhesitatingly gave allegiance to the emperor.

How could there be such a variance between what ecclesiastical authorities taught and the behavior of individual Christians? Experiences of the twentieth and twenty-first centuries demonstrate that rank-and-file Christians often disagree with what church leaders think and practice. That applies to other issues besides war.

Unexpected Change

We need to look at an additional point about the church in the first, second, and third centuries. The number of believers increased phenomenally. Growth occurred for almost 300 years, despite the fact that most converts ran great risks to become followers of Jesus. Conversion often led to public ridicule, loss of property, torture, and death. As the early twentieth-century Catholic scholar, Guggenberger, observed:

*If we ... consider ... that an immense number of martyrs
of every age, sex and condition, have triumphantly stood
this test, it is clear that no array of merely human reasons, can explain the rapid spread of Christianity.*[5]

The word of the Lord prevailed because individuals repented, believed in Jesus, and their hearts became transformed. Converts acknowledged only one Lord and God. Allegiance to him super-ceded loyalty to the mightiest government on earth.

Though unanimity on all matters of faith didn't exist through the second and third centuries, something took place in the fourth century that affected Christians and their relations with their governments into perpetuity. It altered the original game plan and resulted in Christians forgetting it.

The most significant change occurred in 313 A.D. Prior to that time the church faced persecution from the Roman government. But that year Christianity became legal, and it received equal rights with other religions. By 380, it became the Roman Empire's official religion.

Most people know that Constantine the Great (circa 274-337) brought about different attitudes. Constantine was born in Nis (modern Serbia). As an army officer, Constantine demonstrated a military prowess that impressed his troops. In 305, his father, Constantius Chlorus, gave Constantine the status of co-emperor. Constantius died within months and Constantine's troops called him Emperor of Rome. Until 324, he encountered several rivals to the title of Emperor, but he finally prevailed in that year.

Constantine moved the seat of government from Rome to Constantinople (modern Istanbul). Like most emperors of the time, he worshiped Sol, the Roman sun god. In 310, Constantine claimed that while he was in Gaul, Sol appeared to him in a vision. One day the following year, the Emperor-to-be declared that Christ talked to him in a dream and instructed him to place the Greek letters Chi and Rho (the first two letters in Christ's name) on his men's shields. The following day Constantine reported that he saw the Latin words *in hoc signo vinces* (in this sign [such as the cross], you will conquer) along with a cross superimposed on the sun.

How much about Jesus did Constantine's army know? James Carrol explained that Constantine's army consisted of largely uneducated barbarians and peasants. Those soldiers probably wouldn't have understood the basics of Christianity.

> *Indeed, to the Teutons and Celts among them ... the cross of Christ as the standard to march behind would have evoked the ancestral totem of the sacred tree far more powerfully than it would have Saint Paul's token of deliverance.*[6]

Shortly after, at the battle of Milvian Bridge near Rome, Constantine won a victory over his rival Maxentius. He credited Christ with his conquest and *in hoc signo vinces* became Constantine's motto. At the same time, the Roman senate recognized Constantine as savior of the people.

The new period of church-state relations began. With a few exceptions, persecution ended for Christians. Constantine and his co-emperor, Licinius, jointly issued the Edict of Milan (313). The ruling mandated that Christians be tolerated throughout the Roman Empire. Favored status, legal rights, and financial donations ensued for the Christian church.

Constantine constructed church buildings in the Holy Land. His Christian mother allegedly made a profound discovery while she traveled there, claiming that she found the actual cross on which Jesus was crucified. The fellow who convinced her of its authenticity was probably in the gene pool of the first guy attempting to sell the Brooklyn Bridge. Shortly before his death, on May 22, 337, Constantine was baptized. John McManners asked:

> *Was the Constantinian alliance a betrayal of the pure essence of Christianity, with religion contributing to society and culture at the risk of its own soul, at the risk of its eternal mission?*[7]

The question is clearly rhetorical. Rarely since Constantine's time have Christians been able to plainly see how they should relate to their governments. Church and state became tightly melded, almost as inextricably bound as Siamese twins conjoined at the head. Their relationship is currently a mélange. Think of mixing a gallon of white paint with a gallon of blue, then trying to separate the colors afterward. It may be possible, but it's beyond the ability of ordinary folks.

Only by God's help can we separate governments and church. It's vital that we quickly and surely disconnect the two so we can refocus on Jesus' commission to evangelize the entire world.

In the next few chapters, we'll review how confusedly connected church and governments have become.

1. F. C. Grant, Editor, *Ancient Roman Religion* (New York: Liberal Arts Press, 1957), p. 215.

2. Quoted by Bainton, *The Horizon History of Christianity*, Marshall B. Davidson, Editor (New York: American Heritage Publishing Company, 1964), p. 67.

3. Adolf Harnack, *What Is Christianity?* (New York: Harper & Row, Publishers, 1957), p. 193.

4. Tertullian took extreme positions on numerous issues. For one, in his treatise, "De Monogamia," he condemned second marriages even for widowed men and women and also wanted married couples to abstain from sex.

5. A. Guggenberger, S. J., *A General History of the Christian Era*, Volume I — *The Papacy and the Empire* (St. Louis: B. Herder Book Company, 1931), p. 30.

6. James Carroll, *Constantine's Sword: The Church and the Jews — A History* (Boston: Houghton Mifflin, 2001), p. 183.

7. John McManners, *The Oxford Illustrated History of Christianity* (Oxford: Oxford University Press, 1990), p. 4.

Part Two

Unadulterated Adulterators

6

The First Paint Blenders:
Constantine And Other Mixers

The soldiers fight and the kings are the heroes.
— Jewish proverb[1]

Remember our blue-mixed-with-white-paint analogy? Several events and people added to the church-state blend. So far our muddle consists of one gallon each of white and blue paint. Suppose that someone else throws in some yellow, others some pink, and others some green paint. Vigorously jiggle it. With each addition and shake, recovering the original white becomes more difficult, doesn't it?

Here's our task. How do we determine the colors that polluted it so that we can restore the original? Further, how did all of those later shades get added? What forces, movements, and people caused the mixing?

Internal changes in the church created many of those hues. In this chapter, we note three people who greatly influenced the thinking of Christians toward their governments — guys who "tossed in" different colors to give us the current corrupted complexion. Two acted *within* the church. The third acted *upon* it.

Though most contemporaries recognize the "paint-mixers" names, few know how they influenced our subject. The trio varied in background. One ruled the Roman Empire. The second began life influenced by his Christian mother, believed for a while in a now-dead religion known as Manichaeism, became profligate and then turned into a Christian monk. The third was a shepherd-caravaneer who formed his own religion. Each man radically swayed church-state relationships but in a different way. The Emperor Constantine began the trio.

101

New Directions After Constantine

Constantine mingled church and state in ways that few contemporary church folks realize. For one, as the head of state, he molded church doctrine. Constantine presided at the first ecumenical council (Nicaea in 325) because he desired a unified church. Imagine General Washington setting out to establish a monolithic state church for the US colonies. Washington probably didn't have that kind of power even had he wanted it, but Constantine did. Amazingly, church leaders willingly acceded to his request.

The emperor took numerous measures not only to legalize Christianity, but also to destroy paganism and to establish Christianity as the empire's official religion. He changed laws so they would accord with Christian principles. He generously funded priests, bishops, and churches. Constantine made provisions so that worship services could be conducted in lavish splendor. By his appointments, Constantine ensured that Christians held the most powerful state offices.

The emperor's policies changed church-state relations forever. Prior to Constantine, church and state rarely mingled. Since Constantine, the two kept constant company like new lovers. But they didn't just hold hands. In some cases, they were fused. That's why most current-day Christians misunderstand proper relationships with their governments.

Christianity didn't suddenly replace paganism in the Roman Empire. The latter was too entrenched. But Constantine left Christianity in the stronger position. Christian faith spread in every direction making inroads among the Persians, Armenians, Goths, and Ethiopians.

In another historic move, Constantine initiated legislation that created a new system of church government. Even prior to Constantine, church polity (its internal system of governing and authority) underwent change. On their initial missionary journey (48, 49 A.D.), Paul and Barnabas established several churches and within a short time appointed a group of elders (Greek — *presbuteroi*) over each church (Acts 14:23).

Paul gathered on the beach with the Ephesus church presbyters-elders for a sad, final meeting with them (Acts 20). As he did so, Paul used the words elders (*presbyters*), bishops (*episkopoi* from which the Episcopal church derived its name), and a verb form of the word "pastor" interchangeably.

According to New Testament usage elders, bishops, and pastors all refer to the same office (Acts 20:28). In Titus 1:5, Paul told Titus that he had left him in Crete so Titus could "appoint elders in every town." In verse 7 of that same section, he called those elders, bishops (overseers in the NIV).

The New Testament also indicates no hierarchy in church government beyond the elders of the local churches. The apostles established church autonomy (self-government). Only the apostles or their temporary designates exercised authority over local churches.

Superior elders or bishops emerged after the New Testament period. The New Testament scholar F. F. Bruce agreed with that assessment. He saw no difference during that period between presbyters and bishops as occurred in later centuries. The Ephesus church leaders were "indiscriminately described as elders, bishops (such as superintendents) and shepherds (or pastors)."[2]

Clement of Rome has traditionally been called the third bishop of Rome. In a letter to the Corinthian church about 95 A.D., he made no reference to his being the lone bishop. Neither did he say that Rome had only one bishop at that time.

Change from the original (each church having its own local group of elders) began in the second century. Ninety years after Clement, Irenaeus claimed the Church of Rome's supremacy because, he argued, apostolic tradition could be traced to that church.[3] More alteration ensued.

By about 250 A.D., the office of presbyter (the Roman church had 46) became a distinct office from bishop (Rome had only one). It bragged about its seven deacons and many offices unknown in the first-century church: acolytes, subdeacons, readers, doorkeepers, and exorcists.

In local congregations, one elder or presbyter began exercising control over the others and became known as the *bishop*. By the time of Constantine, a bishop oversaw not just an individual church, but a *diocese* or *see* (a group of churches in a particular area).

We can trace a three-stage evolution of church government beginning from New Testament times. At first, groups of bishops (presbyters) led congregations.

Next, the monarchial episcopate increasingly predominated. A single bishop supplanted the original, apostle-instituted plurality of bishops (presbyters) in each congregation. Finally, as the church spread from urban to rural areas, "the bishop, who had formerly presided over the congregation, now comes to *preside over a larger area of the Church*."[4] That larger area became known as a diocese. A bishop then oversaw a diocese.

Constantine helped form the metropolitan system, which brought about the union of several dioceses under an archbishop or metropolitan. "In many cases the capital of the province became also the metropolitan see of the archbishop."[5] This bred the virus responsible for many current church ills and excesses. Local congregations yielded authority to leaders far removed from them. Distant bishops, archbishops, cardinals, and popes made decisions for people and received monies from folks they didn't know and to whom they didn't have to account.

By the end of the sixth century, the developing hierarchy reached a point where five major church bishops vied for authority in "Christendom." They included Jerusalem (claiming to be the mother church), Antioch (the first great Gentile church), Alexandria (the intellectual seat), Rome (which claimed connection with Peter), and Constantinople (the capital city).

This human-devised reorganization left members of local churches with little say about decisions that affected them. Faraway clergy made choices for them often collaborating with rulers and government leaders.

You're possibly asking, "What does it matter what type of government churches use?" Set aside for a moment the fact that the New Testament pattern calls for local boards of elders-bishops-pastors in every congregation. One of the greatest causes of church corruption is sole pastors, who are not accountable to anyone.

As the apostles originally organized the church, a group of mature, proven, deeply spiritual men oversaw a single congregation. The apostles gave careful instructions about their qualifications:

- married men with strong marriages, mature wives, and obedient, faithful children;
- men who conducted their lives in sexual purity;
- men of good reputation in the community and within the fellowship of believers;
- men who were gentle and not quarrelsome;
- men who were not greedy;
- men not given to drunkenness;
- men who were not novices;
- men who knew the scriptures and were able to teach them; and
- men who were proven administrators (cf 1 Timothy 3; Titus 1; 1 Peter 5).

Most church problems develop because churches don't follow these guidelines when appointing church leaders. Single ministers and priests hide lifestyles of child abuse and homosexual behavior. Alcoholism often occurs among church leaders. Ministers not held to account abscond with church funds.

Referring again to my paint analogy, the colors weren't just tossed into the same pail. The can was shaken for centuries and the concoction diluted and polluted. This mixing changed Jesus' plan for church governance and totally obscured his idea of church-state relations.

The Church's Internal Changes

As power transferred from local congregations to area bishops, it formed the climate for further transformation in the church. When direct lines of power exist, it's easier to make changes. Hierarchal authority creates rigid conformity as opposed to the spontaneity and freedom exercised by autonomous congregations.

Another type of change took place. For the first few hundred years, Christians kept busy trying to survive. After Constantine, however, relative peace prevailed. Christians had time to reflect on certain teachings and doctrines. Constantine and subsequent rulers convened church leaders in an effort to harmonize various doctrinal issues. The process began in the first quarter of the fourth century and continued through the fifth century.

One important and fundamental question related to the nature of Christ. Was he the same substance as God or only of like substance? The New Testament insists on Jesus' divinity, but doesn't make precise definitions of his relationship with the Father. In the same way that mortals lack the capacity to completely understand God's nature, neither can they fully comprehend the relationship of the Son to the Father. Nonetheless, fourth-century theologians made mighty and disastrous efforts at definitive statements.

From all over the Roman Empire, bishops traveled (300 of them) to the Council of Nicaea. Modern television cameras would have focused on men with twisted and paralyzed limbs, eyeless sockets, and horribly disfigured faces — mutilations the bishops suffered at the hands of the Emperor Diocletian's persecutions.

At the 325 A.D. council, those bishops who had endured so much were excited about resolving an issue of doctrine, but now at the behest of one of Emperor Diocletian's successors. Many of the creeds, like the Athanasian Creed and the Nicene Creed, evolved from the decisions and statements of the council. Government now influenced Christian doctrine.

Factions will always arise. They occurred in many of the churches that Paul established and addressed. The Corinthians argued social, doctrinal, and personal questions. The first-century church in Philippi suffered discord because two women, Euodia and Syntyche, quarreled sharply. Disagreements occurred in some of the seven Revelation churches. But civil authorities rarely interfered. Church and state remained separate. Since Constantine they're rarely disconnected.

Another factor led to significant change in the relationships of church and state. It developed largely in the West. I refer to what historians call the "Temporal Sovereignty of the Popes," (the involvement of religion into the secular and civil lives of all people in a region). Guggenberger described its development and argued its "necessity." He reasoned the popes didn't create the situation.

> *The temporal sovereignty of the Holy See was not founded by any particular action of the Popes. It was not snatched away from the Eastern Emperors; it was the necessary result of the position of the Popes, who were compelled by the circumstances of the time to be for the inhabitants of Italy, what the Emperors could not or would not be, the natural protectors of the people in times of extraordinary distress.*[6]

In other words, the Eastern emperors didn't send armies to protect people in the West, so the church gave citizens military protection. Peter's one sword multiplied. Plenty.

The background of this lay in the antipathy that the emperors (then in Constantinople) felt for the people out west (near Rome). Various tribes from the north attacked Rome. These included the Germanic tribes, Ostrogoths (East Goths), and Visigoths (West Goths). The Visigoths sacked Rome in 410. Also, the Vandals invaded Gaul in 406, captured Carthage in 439, and pillaged Rome in 455.

Because the Eastern emperors showed little interest in what happened in the West, the popes helped to defend Rome. As a result, popes claimed authority and possessions once the invaders departed. Guggenberger listed these entitlements as follows:

- **The Patrimony[7] Of Saint Peter**
  Wealthy Roman families often donated farms, pasture lands, even whole villages and towns to the church in Rome. The church used the revenues from these endowments to build and maintain monasteries and church buildings. It also established hospitals and hospices. Monies went to purchase the freedom of slaves and to give relief to folks who suffered because of barbarian invasions. During Gregory the Great's tenure as Pope (590-604), the patrimony consisted of villages, farms, and herds in Sicily, Africa, Gaul, and Corsica in addition to southern and northern Italy.

107

- **Imperial Grants**

  Many people came to think that popes could best take care of their worldly needs. Emperors gradually gave popes enormous temporal powers. Popes received authority to free converted slaves, administer poor laws, and supervise the business of merchants, even weights and measures. "Holy Fathers" also held authority over prisons and prisoners, and full jurisdiction over the Patrimony of Saint Peter. Popes organized armies and formed peace treaties with hostile forces. Pope Leo the Great's (440-461) armies twice saved Rome.[8]

Simon Peter's one sword proliferated exponentially. The paint was mixed, shaken, and the original white long-forgotten.

In the first century when the paint was white, the church evidently owned no property. Individuals like Barnabas in Jerusalem sold off much of their own real estate and gave the cash to the apostles. But the apostles didn't erect buildings, set up bank accounts, or establish institutions. They directly used the money to feed the poor (Acts 4:32-37). The apostles invested in no cathedrals or even chapels. In Jerusalem they met in the Jewish temple courtyards and in houses (Acts 5:42).

The only governmental influence first-century Jerusalem Christians evinced was the example of Jesus. That is, no connection. Authorities tried to silence them, and annihilate them. The apostles used no legal maneuvers or strategies to survive, however. They established no armies and utilized no police protection. They strongly and regularly exercised the two most potent influences available to every Christian — ministry of the Word and prayer (Acts 4:23-31; 6:4). Most churches now seem unaware of that apostolic example.

Augustine Of Hippo

Constantine was the first major paint-mixer, but he wasn't the only one with his hand on a pail. Fourth- and fifth-century popes and their armies swirled the mix. Augustine of Hippo mixed paint, too, in a major way. Born in 354 A.D. in Numidia (modern Algeria), Augustine spent much of his early life preoccupied with sensual pleasure. When he finally renounced the flesh and converted to Christ, he developed into a powerful church leader. Augustine colorfully described his journey from foolishness to faith in his confessions. Many people have thought, if not uttered Augustine's prayer, "Make me chaste and content, but not just yet."

Augustine later formulated several concepts for which he became well known. For example, his development of predestination brought the war issue into the fold in the following ways:

- The church is a mixture of wheat and tares (Matthew 13:24-30, Jesus' parable of the weeds [wheat and tares]), which makes it in some ways indistinguishable from the world.
- The church isn't wholly good.
- The world isn't wholly bad.

Augustine considered Rome's fall based on the above presuppositions. It involved two questions.

- Why had God allowed Rome to fall?
- Is it right for Christians to resort to war in order to repel barbarians?

Augustine dealt with these questions in his *City of God*. He concluded in the first instance that Rome's fall had nothing to do with Christian popularity and growth. Rome suffered misfortune even prior to Christianity. It fell because of its crimes. Its demise was just retribution for its wrongdoing.[9]

Augustine's Just War conclusions dealt with the second question: Was it all right to repel barbarians by force? Augustine's definition of Just War prevails in Christian thought.

Many contemporary Christians consider their beliefs under assault from two major forces. First, secular society threatens some Christians' security — a security based on the conviction that the United States was founded on Christian principles. Each time an American judge makes public school prayers illegal, refuses to allow Christians to display crosses in public places, or removes the

109

Ten Commandments from public display in a courthouse, Christians feel their faith in peril.

Contemporary Christians face another issue — the problem of Just War. When non-Christians threaten Christians' safety, do Christians have a right to defend themselves? Under what, if any, circumstances may Christians take up arms to defend their right to worship God?

Augustine thought about similar immediate challenges. He based his views on formulations that the Roman philosopher Cicero promulgated in the first century B.C.

They were in brief:

1. only the state can legitimately conduct war;
2. the restoration of peace and vindication of justice must be the objects of such a war;
3. in the conduct of war, wanton violence must be avoided;
4. the justice of the war must be determined by the rulers; and
5. a code of humanity must be observed in conducting the war (prisoners and hostages have to be treated with respect).

To these five points, Augustine added:

6. the motive for war must be love; and
7. one deals with the apparent inconsistency of a war conducted in love by remembering the New Testament principle that you can "kill the body, but you cannot kill the soul."

The major difference between Cicero's definitions and those of Augustine relates little to the points themselves. Here's the important dissimilarity: Cicero wrote as a representative of the state, Augustine wrote as a religious teacher attempting to influence state decisions. Does the Lord want Christians to influence governmental decisions in this way? That's our question.

The "Prophet" From Mecca

A third major change resulted from the church's internal reaction to external forces. The chief cause was a son born about 570 A.D. to an Arabian family[10] in Mecca. Before the birth of his child, the father died. When the boy was about six years of age, he lost his mother, too. He was reared by his Uncle Abu Talit, but soon the uncle hired out the young nephew as a shepherd's helper. Young Mohammed spent his early years tending sheep to earn his keep. "The desert was his school, and the sun by day and the stars on clear nights were his teachers."[11]

Mohammed later left sheep-handling to others and became a camel driver. He led caravans laden with products of Arabia to distant locations like Syria, Persia, and Egypt. This business led to the acquaintance of a dowager, Kadijah. A forty-year-old wealthy widow at the time with three children, her youthful beauty and appearance impressed the 25-year-old caravaneer. His broad shoulders, rhythmic almost musical speech, and his curly black hair and beard dazzled her. Mohammed managed her affairs impressing her with his honesty. Kadijah asked him to marry her. He accepted.

Mohammed and Kadijah lived happily for fifteen years. Their wealth increased, and their peers in Mecca respected them. Earlier while traveling, Mohammed met many Jews and Christians. He couldn't read, but his wife's cousin, Waraka, who had accepted the Jewish faith, read the Bible to him. When he heard the New Testament, Mohammed became convinced that his people needed an inspired prophet and leader.

In Mohammed's time, desert Arabs faced deplorable circumstances. Wilderness life wasn't favorable to serenity. Bedouins felt obligation to none but members of their own tribe. Material goods were scarce. The hot sun constantly sparked a fighting mood that led to brigandage. Males eagerly set out to prove their virility.

City life wasn't much better. Because the local politicians were at loggerheads, and there was no effective local magistrate, life in Mecca stayed chaotic. Drunken orgies bred brawls. Blood flowed without stinting. Nomads not only staked tents; they staked their wages, too. Meccan gambling could have sustained several riverboats, but tents sufficed for desert gaming. Like Las Vegas, the city never slept. "Dancing girls" drifted from tent to tent upholding the oldest profession.

The prevalent religion had slight moral effect. It was, said Huston Smith, an "animistic polytheism." According to then current lore, *jinn* (supernatural spirits as if created by a nomadic ancestor of Stephen King) inhabited the desert demonizing and frightening the desert dwellers. But they stirred neither religious enthusiasm nor moral conduct.

> *On the whole, conditions could hardly have been better calculated to produce a smoldering undercurrent which erupted in sudden affrays and blood feuds some of which stretched on for half a century. The time was ripe for a deliverer.*[12]

Conditions among the Arabs dismayed Mohammed. Influenced by what he heard from both the Old and New Testaments, he spent time in the hills surrounding Mecca contemplating how prophetic leadership could improve the sordid conditions of his fellows. Mohammed advocated improving the lot of slaves, orphans, women, and the poor.

The self-proclaimed prophet claimed that the angel Gabriel appeared to him. Kadijah believed those assertions. Mohammed imagined other appearances by Gabriel. "There is no God but Allah," he soon preached to his relatives, "and Mohammed is the prophet of Allah." The new prophet gained several followers among his relatives, but mostly encountered ridicule.

Mohammed gained confidence in his message. His wife and family believed in him, but he garnered few other disciples. His preaching about gambling, drinking, and fortune-telling created amusement. When he began attacking the rich merchants and profiteering leaders, though, the laughter ended. He received threats on his life.

Mohammed persisted in his preaching, and he found a small following. He called his new religion Islam, meaning submission. His followers were Moslems, true believers. Mohammed wanted the people to replace their tribal loyalties with Islam.

One of his followers, Abu Bekr, wrote down Mohammed's speeches. These written records became known as the *Koran*, which means "to read." When the disciples of Mohammed gathered, they read from the texts of his orations. The belief grew that God delivered them to Mohammed through the angel Gabriel. The Koran is comprised of 114 chapters of unequal length. A group of Arabic scholars prepared an authorized version of the Koran in the 650s. They tried to destroy all the other versions, but some survived.

The Meccan leaders looked on Mohammed and his followers with increasing concern. Soon they passed a law requiring that Mohammed's followers be driven from the city. Few Meccans wanted to risk losing their homes so Mohammed's teachings met increased resistance.

Kadijah died during this difficult period. But the grief-filled Mohammed kept preaching. He attempted his ministrations in Taif, seventy miles distant. Because that was a grape-and-wine region, his disapproval of drinking made him the object of fierce attacks. Mohammed returned to Mecca. Some time later, twelve pilgrims from Yathrib (270 miles from Mecca) arrived asking for an explanation of his teachings. Many Jews occupied Yathrib at the time. The twelve pilgrims had heard about the Jewish belief in one God and its hatred of idols.

Mohammed explained his succinct message:

- "Allah is the One God, and Mohammed is his prophet;
- give up idolatry;
- do not steal;
- do not lie;
- do not slander; and
- never become intoxicated.
- If you follow these teachings, then you follow Islam."

Pilgrims came to Mecca from Yathrib the next year wanting to be disciples. From this group of 75, Mohammed chose twelve men and appointed them as his apostles. He wanted them to return to Yathrib and spread Islam. When Meccan authorities got word that

Mohammed was converting the Yathrib citizenry, they plotted to kill him.

On the night of his scheduled assassination (622 A.D.), Mohammed fled on his camel to Yathrib. It's a sacred night to Moslems — his Hegira (Night of the Flight). They count time from that event. The people of Yathrib warmly welcomed him. They proclaimed Mohammed ruler of their city and changed its name to Medina (City of the Prophet).

Mohammed wanted Mecca's citizens to accept him as Allah's prophet. He had greater ambitions in Medina. He purposed to have its residents receive him as "their uncrowned ruler, maker of their laws, leader of their armies, and judge of all their affairs."[13]

Mohammed organized an army to exercise the power he desired. But Mohammed needed to fund that army. He claimed that the angel Gabriel appeared again "instructing" him to raid caravans originating in Mecca. Mohammed's previous experience as a camel driver gave him familiarity not only with cargoes, but also caravaneer's habits, and the local terrain. His men regularly plundered and pillaged Meccan caravans. Full-scale war broke out.

During one battle his men broke ranks and retreated. Left almost completely unprotected, Mohammed nearly lost his life. As a Meccan soldier swung his sword intending to behead Mohammed, a faithful follower raised his hand to defend the prophet. Mohammed retained his head; the disciple lost his hand.

The "prophet's" men ultimately subdued Mecca. According to the reports of Mohammed's followers, his success never changed him. He fed the poor, he loved children, and he always insisted on doing his share of the work. Mohammed lived humbly in a clay house and milked his own goats. He preached five important rules:

1. Believe in Allah and Mohammed, his prophet.
2. Pray five times each day.
3. Be kind to the poor and give alms.
4. Keep the fasts during the Month of Fasts.
5. And make the yearly pilgrimage to Mecca, the Holy City.

By 632 A.D. (the year of Mohammed's death), not only had Mohammed subdued and reorganized Mecca, he also controlled all of Arabia, including the armies, the police, and the civil service. Within 100 years, Islam's armies dominated Persia, Palestine, Armenia, Egypt, and Iraq. The Moslem general, Gibraltar, led his troops from North Africa and crossed the straights into southern Spain. Moslem forces then headed east across the Pyrenees into France. Many scholars think that had Charles Martel not defeated the Moslems in the 732 A.D. Battle of Tours, all of the West might now follow the way of Islam.

Those wearing the name of Jesus fought many battles with Moslems. Carl F. H. Henry edited *Christianity Today* in the 1950s. Something he wrote then seems almost prophetic when we consider the 2001 World Trade Center and Pentagon attacks. He referred to it while writing on the subject of conscience.

Henry noted that the "glory of Christian ethics is that it has provided humanity with its most highly trained conscience."[14] He meant Jesus' conscience, which the Son of God developed and demonstrated during his incarnation.

We link ourselves with this superior conscience through the influence of the Word, God's indwelling Spirit, and in association with the Christian community. Henry then correctly observed that all Christians must stay within the bounds of scripture. Also he accurately noted that

> ... only the healthy conscience, trained to react instinctively in response to the New Testament revelation of the will of God, makes for a spontaneous spiritual morality.[15]

Christians had long before lost contact with the scripture that would have helped them mold effective, lively consciences. By the time of the Crusades, most Christians surrendered their inner voices to the princes and popes of the church. As history has shown, Roman Catholic church authorities showed no qualms about drawing up infallible lists and insisting on conformance to them.

115

As the popes and princes brought knights and armor bearers with deficient consciences from the West, a different phenomenon occurred bringing warriors to the Crusades from the eastern side. Henry wrote (nearly presciently, I think) what moralists only rarely point out. Islam has "no equivalent for this term (conscience)."[16] One of the great attractions of Islam is its simplicity. Mohammed defined what one must do. The requirement was elementary, and the development of individual conscience was not on the platter.

Some explain the desperate measures taken by the extreme Moslems in this century as the poor against the rich — or disenfranchised against the franchised. Neither explanation adequately explains the situation. Many of the Moslem "martyrs" enjoyed wealth, and some apparently belonged to elite classes in their countries of origin. They exploited freedom and resources in the United States to travel, plot, and execute.

Many people in this country wondered how the suicide bombers could bring such suffering on innocent people. Their religion provided little hesitation. How did Jesus teach us to deal with religions and their representatives with deficient moral standards? That's a vital issue Christians now face. We need to find the right answers.

Jesus taught that there are two realms — Caesar's and God's. Jesus said, "My kingdom is not of this world. If it were, my servants would fight to prevent my arrest by the Jews. But now my kingdom is from another place" (John 18:36). Few Christians at this time recognize the two separate realms.

To this point, we've seen the following changes in the church's relationship with governments:

- government influenced church decisions;
- church leaders assumed many governmental responsibilities;
- churches raised armies to protect lands, possessions, and people; and
- believers in Jesus used arms to fight on several fronts and for numerous reasons.

1. Joseph Gaer and Rabbi Alfred Wolf, published in *Our Jewish Heritage* (Hollywood, California: Wilshire Book Company, 1967 edition), p. 165.

2. F. F. Bruce, *Commentary on The Book of Acts* (Grand Rapids, Michigan: Wm. B. Eerdmans Publishing Company, 1964), p. 415.

3. While it's true that both Peter and Paul visited Rome later, it appears that neither established the church there. When Paul wrote the book of Romans (circa 57-58 A.D.) the church seemed to be comprised of numerous house churches (see Romans 16). Rome was a large city and it probably was not practicable for the church to assemble at one location. If Peter founded the church at Rome as some allege, Paul grievously slighted him, by failing to mention him anywhere. Further, Paul didn't like to build on another's "foundation." The church in Rome was likely begun by Christians migrating and gravitating to the center of the Roman Empire.

4. Hans Kung, *On Being a Christian*, tr. by Edward Quinn (Garden City, New York: Doubleday & Company, Inc., 1976), p. 491.

5. A. Guggenberger, S. J., *A General History Of The Christian Era*, Volume I — *The Papacy and the Empire* (St. Louis, Missouri: B. Herder Book Company, 1931), p. 40.

6. *Ibid*, p. 121.

7. Patrimony is an estate inherited from a father or other ancestor. First, the popes claimed that they were successors to Peter's office as Bishop of Rome. Second, popes claimed that they were entitled to properties because they had defended them or rescued them from various pagan invaders. Lands and properties under the pope's control increased dramatically during this period.

8. Guggenberger, *op cit*, pp. 121, 122.

9. Some of the above is reviewed in *The Horizon History of Christianity*, pp. 132, 133.

10. Some historians say that the family was aristocratic, others that they were poor, but respected.

11. Joseph Gaer, *How the Great Religions Began* (New York: The New American Library, 1954), p. 198.

117

12. Huston Smith, *The Religions of Man* (New York: Harper & Row, 1965), p. 219.

13. Gaer, *op cit*, p. 205.

14. Carl F. H. Henry, *Christian Personal Ethics* (Grand Rapids, Michigan: Wm. B. Eerdmans Publishing Company, 1957), p. 524.

15. *Ibid*, p. 525.

16. *Ibid*, p. 524.

7

The Shameful Era:
From The Crusades To The Reformers

Let us fix our eyes on Jesus, the author and perfecter of our faith, who for the joy set before him endured the cross, scorning its shame, and sat down at the right hand of the throne of God. — Hebrews 12:2

Neither Paul nor Peter exercised political sway. They had none. Paul once held it, but renounced it when he became a Christian. It's doubtful that Peter ever wielded much worldly influence. The fisherman lacked formal education.

None of the apostles effected earthly clout. That wasn't Jesus' way. He wanted them to relinquish their place in the world. Changing society wasn't the mission. Jesus gave a singular assignment; tell the "good news." "Since, then, we know what it is to fear the Lord, we try to persuade men," said Paul (2 Corinthians 5:11).

Jesus didn't even hold the apostles accountable for whether their hearers accepted the message.[1] Resurrection testimony was the task. If people refused to hear it, the Lord held the hearers responsible for their rejection, not those who took the message.

When Paul preached before the Aereopagus in Athens, he affirmed that God "commands all people everywhere to repent" (Acts 17:30). He warned that on the last day, God will judge all people by Jesus, whom God had raised from the dead. People must choose for themselves whether to accept Jesus. None was forced, and none influenced to believe in Jesus except by preaching and teaching.

The apostles didn't permit governmental officials to mess with the message, either. When the Sanhedrin ordered Peter and John to stop teaching and speaking in the name of Jesus, the apostles answered, "Judge for yourselves whether it is right in God's sight to

119

obey you rather than God. For we cannot help speaking about what we have seen and heard" (Acts 4:19-20). In other words, you must decide whether you will listen. But we must keep talking about Jesus' death, burial, and resurrection. Later, the disciples neglected the message and the mission. We'll trace how that happened.

The Holy Roman Empire

Beginning with Constantine, political leaders shaped church policy. At the same time the church tried to mold governments. The resultant juxtaposition created unholy matrimony. The Holy Roman Empire symbolized the intertwining and mingling of church and state during the Middle Ages. Formed in 962 A.D. and lasting until 1806, the Holy Roman Empire embraced most of central Europe. It originally claimed supremacy over the church. Thus, it was called "holy." It was "Roman" because it claimed to be the successor to imperial Rome. It was never fully universal except for perhaps a brief period. The Byzantine emperors didn't recognize it. Eventually England, France, and Spain became separate nations.

The Holy Roman Empire involved mostly Germany and Italy. Emperors-elect usually went to Rome for confirmation. Only after 1562, did the emperors-elect cease acceding to Rome's demand that they be crowned by the "Holy Father."

The power of the empire ebbed and flowed. All the while popes competed with emperors for actual control. In theory, the pope held supremacy in spiritual matters and the emperors in "temporal matters." But the two rivals contended like a domineering husband and an unruly wife over the separation between physical and temporal. The matter remains unsettled between governments and many churches.

The Crusades

By the beginning of the Crusader Period (1095 A.D.), practical distinctions between church and state became vague. Churches maintained armed forces, regulated commerce, and taxed. Emperors and princes frequently influenced theology and church policy. The common person saw no clear distinctions between Caesar's realm and God's.

Four major forces then vied for control in Europe and the Middle-East. First, Islam dominated most of North Africa, the majority of Spain, and the area immediately east of the Mediterranean. As a result, three former leading Christian (Catholic) churches lost influence — Antioch, Jerusalem, and Alexandria.

Constantinople's eastern borders lay under Moslem threat, but the emperor (the second power) maintained his control there. The emperor had dominated the Eastern church for centuries. When, for example, church councils convened in the East (787 and 843) to discuss iconoclasm (whether it was right to have images), the councils met under imperial orders. Some refer to this control as *Caesaropapism.*

Various factors enabled the pope to become the third dominant power. His forces controlled most of Italy and southern Europe. Papal armies had defended Rome from the northern invaders. The popes claimed to be successors to Peter, and they increasingly gained popular support.

Fourth, like feisty harem wives, various European princes resented and contested papal domination. After Otto I revived the Holy Roman Empire in 962, popes and emperors continually struggled for supremacy. The Crusades developed amidst this power tussle.

Europe's population rapidly grew, especially in urban areas and many folks enjoyed economic resources. Merchants love it when people jingle extra spending money in their pockets. Traders saw abundant prospects in the Mediterranean region. Business aims blended well with the religious resentment toward Moslem control of the Holy Land. Christians grew infatuated with the idea that they should recoup the place where Jesus lived freeing it from Moslem infidels.

Business and religious leaders often establish joint ventures. To the delight of the tourist industry and its affiliates, ministers now sponsor guided air tours to Israel and cruises to Bible lands. What the minister usually fails to tell the people who accompany him is that the more people he enlists, the less he pays. If ministers enroll enough folks, they can cover their fares and expenses — even earn spending money.

In theory, these joint ventures bless everyone. Sometimes group travelers gain the advantage of lower fares. They also enjoy the company of other Christians and presumably benefit from the ministers' "expertise, Bible knowledge, and experience." With the Crusades, the popes hoped to profit from the whole enterprise.

The timing blossomed in the late eleventh century. People sought travel and adventure. In addition, leaders of the Holy Roman Empire, who might have opposed the Crusades, were relatively powerless. The year, 1095, found many Christians already taking pilgrimages to Jerusalem. But Moslem Seljuk Turks regularly bothered the itinerants as they traveled near the ancient city. Pope Urban II spoke in Clermont, France, in November of that year urging Christians to free Jerusalem from the hostile Moslems. Taking a crusade, promised the pope, would bring the pilgrim full penance.

Response to the pope's challenge came quickly. The next year, the First Crusade began. Few of royal or noble blood joined the venture. Lesser barons and their associates of French language and culture along with some Germans mostly comprised the group.

"It was a migration, a journey, and war,"[2] Harold Lamb aptly said. Imagine a group of society matrons, prostitutes, soccer moms, street people, CEOs, preachers, soldiers, and politicians walking or at best riding horses from New York to San Francisco to recover it from "infidels." They go without benefit of maps, cell phones, or advance accommodations.

> "A thing unheard of," said a chronicler of the day, "that such diverse people and so many distinguished princes, leaving their splendid possessions, their wives and their children, set forth with one accord and in scorn of death to seek the most unknown regions."[3]

The Crusaders were a motley crew with no leader. Numerous hostile, jealous factions vied with one another. Relationships with the church representatives who accompanied them weren't plainly defined. The pope's role in the venture remained unclear. As they journeyed, many of those "Christian" Crusaders cruelly attacked

Jewish settlements in the Rhineland.[4] And when they got to Constantinople, no one knew whether the Emperor was friend or foe. In the summer of 1099, the Crusaders finally arrived near Jerusalem and besieged the city for several weeks. During that interval, they suffered from heat, lack of water, and discouragement. But they had gone that far and nothing would deter them. Breaching Moslem defenses on July fifteenth, the Crusaders stormed Jerusalem, their long-sought goal.

On their journey, the travelers sang,

> *O Mary, Mother of God — God thy Father and Son —*
> *Our Lady, pray Thou for us, and thy Father and Glorious Son.*
> *Pray for us, who are thine.*
> *Aid thou us!*
> *Turn toward us, and behold our tears.*

But the tears of Moslem women and children garnered no pity. "Christians" ransacked houses, massacred women, and mutilated children. Mosque courtyards became battlegrounds; horsemen wielded swords and axes. Blood flowed over stone pavements. Horses' hooves stumbled over gore, offal, and body parts.

For about two centuries the Crusades continued. Moslems would regain control and another crusade would be launched to recapture the Holy City. Historians estimate that the Crusades resulted in the loss of two million lives. The Children's Crusade (1212 A.D.) epitomized folly. Thousands of young people set out. All either ended up as slaves or dead.

The Crusader Period presented a new stage in the evolution of church-state relationships. Tension between church and state wasn't the only area of conflict. Now agents of the Christian religion openly sponsored warfare against representatives of another major religion.

Attempts At Reform

In the twelfth to sixteenth centuries, several men attempted to separate church and state. They gained little attention because few of them survived. Church and governmental officials (often little distinguished the two) violently suppressed them. People known as Anabaptists carried out most of these reform endeavors. They received the name Anabaptists (literally "baptize again") because they considered infant baptism invalid. People baptized as babies must be re-baptized as adults, they taught. Only believers (adults) should be baptized.

Anabaptist groups developed diverse theology and teaching about church-state relations. At Zwickau, an industrial town in Saxony, for example, a group known as the Zwickau Prophets headed by Thomas Munzer attempted to establish a rule of the elect in a community. They went to Wittenburg in 1521 and gained the interest of Philip Melancthon, Martin Luther's associate. They didn't impress Luther. He put them down the next year. Munzer had sympathized with the Peasants' Revolt. Authorities executed him after the Battle of Frankenhausen in 1525.

Groups in Munster, Germany, also attempted to establish a kingdom of the saints. Led by a Dutchman, John of Leiden (or Jan of Leyden), they tried to set up a communistic and polygamous theocracy in Munster. Its chaotic excesses led to the leader's ouster and execution. Catholic and Protestant princes of Germany united in the destruction of the theocratic kingdom. As a result, several hundred people in Munster ended up slain along with Leiden.

Menno Simons led a group of Swiss Anabaptists. At first called Swiss Brethren, they later took the name Mennonites. In Zurich the group seceded from the state church (1523-1525). Practicing non-resistance and pacifism, Mennonites rejected participation in government and also refused to take oaths. In 1683, many of them settled in Germantown, Pennsylvania.

Another group known as the Swiss Brethren arose in Zurich about 1525. They also practiced non-resistance and rejected Christian participation in civil government. Modern-day Mennonites, Swiss Brethren, and affiliated groups widely influence peace movements in the United States. We shall more fully discuss these sects later.

One Anabaptist deserves special attention. He advocated the need to use scriptural authority for positions on church-state relations. In taking that position, he differed from many of his peers.

124

Balthasar Hubmaier

Balthasar Hubmaier was born about 1481 in Freiburg. Scholars know little of his parentage; they were likely peasants. Hubmaier received religious training probably because the church customarily financed the education of promising youths. He began his matriculation at the University of Freiburg in 1503 and received his master's degree in 1511. At Hubmaier's graduation the distinguished Dr. Johann Eck gave an oration commenting on the industry and diligence of his student.

Hubmaier apparently received an appointment to teach at the university but left with Eck and went to Ingolstadt. Eck evidently quarreled with his superiors over his salary. Hubmaier was ordained as a priest and preached in the Church of the Virgin. Because of his popularity, he received a calling from Regensburg to minister in its cathedral.

Hubmaier's reputation there continued to escalate, but he became involved in an anti-Jewish movement and left in 1520. There's no evidence that the transfer was in any way related to his theological beliefs. Hubmaier next labored in the small city of Waldshut. Evidently, in this more leisurely atmosphere, change came to his life. He zealously promoted Catholic doctrine, but he became absorbed in a study of the scriptures, especially the writings of Paul.

This learning led him to conclude that salvation was in Christ, not in the church and its sacraments. In 1522, Hubmaier visited Switzerland to confer with other religious leaders. One of those was Erasmus of whom Hubmaier said, he "speaks freely but writes cautiously."

Hubmaier returned for a brief time to Regensburg but in 1523 went back to Waldshut. Upon his arrival, his theological position became clearer. He communicated openly with Ulrich Zwingli and discussed with the Zurich reformer such subjects as infant baptism.

Hubmaier and Zwingli didn't stay bedfellows long. At an October 1523, council in Zurich, the two leaders compared their teachings. They discussed the mass, the use of images, and the authority of scripture. On these points they agreed in principle, but Zwingli and Hubmaier differed over methods. Zwingli was too much the pragmatist for radical action; Hubmaier too much of biblicist to resist carrying out his beliefs.

Zwingli agreed with most of Hubmaier's objectives but like a politician, wanted to study whether the people would accept his ideas before he publicly pursued them. Hubmaier returned from the conference determined to activate his beliefs. He drew up a series of theses. The townspeople of Waldshut were receptive to Hubmaier's views. For political reasons, Hubmaier fled Waldshut, but he returned in 1525.

In the meantime, Zwingli faced difficulty in Zurich. Some of that city's reformers insisted that Zwingli carry out his publicly advocated intention of following the scripture. These "more radical reformers" adamantly claimed that the only church in the New Testament was a congregation of "true believers in Christ." The church should be reorganized on that basis. The "radicals" also contended that the only baptisms in the New Testament were of believers who had confessed a personal faith in Christ. Thus the true church could be composed only of persons who had been born again by the Spirit as adults according to the commandments of God.

Hubmaier gave aid and comfort to these "radicals." It forever severed relations between him and Zwingli. Hubmaier gained a following in Waldshut. William Roublin baptized Hubmaier along with sixty other people, who had been driven out of Zurich. Hubmaier himself, on Easter Sunday of the same year, baptized 300 men with a milk pail full of water. Some think that he also practiced foot-washing. It's difficult to say how many milk pails that took.

Not long after Anabaptist Conrad Grebel visited him, Anabaptists recognized Hubmaier as a leader. Hubmaier fled Waldshut again and went to the unlikely place of Zurich. He eventually escaped to Moravia. The Austrians extradited him in 1528, however, and executed him.

Hubmaier's great strength lay in his acquaintance with the Bible. He resolutely clung to the authority of the scriptures and a rejection of all other influences. In this area he evidently saw few peers.

Hubmaier became known for this rule of interpretation: one must take a "plain text in its plain meaning, applying to its" interpretation and explanation "the principles of grammar and ordinary common sense." Never interpret difficult passages in a way that contradicts plainer passages. Also, don't accept God's Word secondhand. All should study for themselves.

Hubmaier possessed admirable gravity, distinct lack of vitriol, and an unwillingness to go beyond the authority of the scriptures. He never disputed with civil authorities. To him they were according to the "order of Christ." How he harmonized that view with his involvement with the Peasant's War,[5] is problematic.

The Anabaptists profoundly affected modern views of church-state relations. Many contemporary anti-war movements have grown from Anabaptist roots. Anabaptist emphasis on using scripture as authority left a rich legacy.

Major sixteenth-century reformers ostensibly based their views on scripture, but took divergent positions concerning church-state connections. In later chapters, we'll discuss the reasons for this.

The Major Reformers — Martin Luther

The scriptures strongly affected Martin Luther, too. Most people know the details of his life and experiences better than they do those of other reformers so we won't spend time reviewing them. Luther became incensed over the sale of indulgences, the condition of the sacramental system, and the preeminence of works over faith in the church's teaching. On these and other points he remained admirably intractable.

Luther's appearance before the Diet of Worms illustrates the interlocking of church and state in his day. Church officials and state representatives joined forces to silence him and to force his recantation. The pope's men assembled with the Holy Roman Emperor, Charles V, and various German princes to intimidate Luther at Worms. When the pope excommunicated him, Luther burned the paper on which they wrote the order. He refused to change his mind and spent a year in hiding.

In the interim, the reform movement gained momentum. Lutheranism developed into a new religion supported by most of the peasants and merchants, the lower clergy, and the princes of Northern Germany. The pope, his higher church officials, and the Emperor stood opposed. In the subsequent struggles, church and state officials on both sides met to work out compromises.

The Peace of Augsburg illustrated contemporary church-government involvement. Although the pope's full authority officially ended in Germany, church-state blending didn't. At that time, Germany's princes numbered about 300. Each of them could decide whether to become Catholic or Protestant. Though the princes could freely choose their religion, they didn't grant their subjects that liberty. The treaty permitted princes to force their chosen faith on their subjects. As a result, Germany became half-Catholic and half-Lutheran.

Luther inconsistently viewed church-state relationships. As the biographer, Bainton, noted, "The charge has been leveled against Luther that he relegated the Christian ethic to private life and turned over the state to the Devil."[6] Luther saw that the Sermon on the Mount was meant for personal relationships and that the civil government has been charged with the regulation of society as outlined in Romans 13.

> When a magistrate condemns to death a man who has done him no harm, he is not the enemy. He does this at God's behest. There should be no anger or bitterness in the man's heart, but only the wrath and sword of God. Also in war, where in defense, one has to hew, stab, and burn there is shear wrath and vengeance, but it does not come from the heart of man but from the judgment and command of God.[7]

To Luther, the church and state represented opposites in God's nature — mercy and wrath. He viewed the church as God's agent of the former and the state of the latter. In Luther's mind, God gave a calling to both magistrate and minister. Yet Luther felt it the minister's duty to remonstrate the magistrate when he practiced injustice.

We should wash the fur of the magistrate and clean out his mouth whenever he laughs or rages. Christ has instructed us preachers not to withhold the truth from the lords but to exhort and chide them in their injustice. Christ did not say to Pilate, "You have no power over me." He said that Pilate did have power, but he said, "You do not have this power from your self. It is given you from God." Therefore he upbraided Pilate. We do the same. We recognize the authority, but we must rebuke our Pilates in their crime and self-confidence. Then they say to us, "You are reviling the majesty of God," to which we answer, "We will suffer what you do to us, but to keep still and let it appear that you do right when you do wrong, that we cannot and will not do." We must confess the truth and rebuke the evil. There is a big difference between suffering injustice and keeping still. We should suffer. We should not keep still.[8]

Luther's use of the Word to support his rebuke of civil authorities seems to some scripturally sound and logical. Here's the problem with that view. The Son of God can make judgments and assessments that we mortals can't. Jesus upbraided Pilate, but the Lord never gave us that kind of authority.

Jude recognized this distinction, "But even the archangel Michael, when he was disputing with the devil about the body of Moses, did not dare to bring a slanderous accusation against him, but said, 'The Lord rebuke you!' " (Jude 9). Paul also recognized the need to leave judgments to God (1 Corinthians 5:12-13).

Because of liturgical and doctrinal inconsistencies in Germany, Luther took a curious stand. The reformer placed the burden of determining the proper religious course upon the state. Governments should deal with heretics and put a stop to all false teaching as well as carrying out their state responsibilities. Ironically, Luther felt, with sufficient justification, that the civil authorities were more to be trusted than the various and sundry church leaders.

The Major Reformers — Ulrich Zwingli
Zurich is located about fifty kilometers south of Switzerland's most northern border with Germany. Travel fifty kilometers west

129

and there's an area called Sankt Gallen, Zwingli's birthplace. Born on the first day of January, 1484, Ulrich received his education at the universities of Vienna and Basel. At age 22, he was already an ordained parish priest in Glarus about sixty kilometers southeast of Zurich.

Swiss farmers in the area gained fame as mercenaries. They fought well and enjoyed the ample extra pay. Glarus was the local army recruiting center. Zwingli served two different terms as a chaplain. After seeing gruesome fighting, he publicly denounced the mercenary system. That was like protesting tobacco in Raleigh, North Carolina, or beer in Golden, Colorado. Zwingli retreated to Einsiedeln and began his ministry there.

The Rotterdam-based textual scholar, Erasmus, had recently published a Latin translation of the New Testament. Zwingli not only read it, and copied it into notebooks, he memorized those notes. Zwingli's reading of the New Testament led him to the conclusion that the church had departed greatly from the New Testament origins. He found no justification for indulgences, the adoration of relics and saints, or for the miraculous cures churchmen kept promising. His forthright, biblical preaching gained him wide popularity.

On New Year's Day, 1519, Zwingli was appointed as a priest at the Great Cathedral in Zurich. Several forces and thoughts swirled around the city. Zwingli gained an interest in humanism.[9] Zurich had long attracted people who shared that belief. After his move to the city, Zwingli began studying the Bible in its original languages and started to preach textual sermons using his knowledge of Hebrew and Greek. This contrasted with typical Catholic teaching, which depended on the Vulgate and the church fathers' teaching.

One of his disciples gave Zwingli access to a printing press; his teachings gained wide circulation. In 1519, Zwingli found encouragement from his recent exposure to Martin Luther's writings. His Bible studies led him to make a bold move. The next year, Zwingli influenced the Zurich city council to forbid all teaching that lacked scriptural authority.

Pope Adrian VI banished Zwingli from the pulpit. The supreme prelate wanted the city council to disclaim the reformer. When

Zwingli went before the council, he insisted on the Bible's precedence over church teaching and dogma. He explained that the sacramental view of the Eucharist[10] lacked scriptural basis. Zwingli also condemned enforced celibacy and the worship of relics, images, and saints because they were deficient in biblical foundation. As a result of his influence, Zwingli's disciples destroyed not only images and pictures, but crucifixes throughout Zurich.

The council supported Zwingli by withdrawing the canton of Zurich from the local bishop's jurisdiction. "Extreme austerity succeeded the profusion of ornaments. The bareness of protestant worship banished the ceremonies and display of catholicism."[11] Zurich adopted the Reformation. Zwingli established a theocracy there overseen by him and a Christian magistrate. The pair instituted numerous reforms including removal of religious images, elimination of confession and the Mass, and conversion of convents and monasteries into hospitals. As had Luther, Zwingli also married a widow, Anna Reinhard.

A group of radical Anabaptists opposed Zwingli's Zurich authority in 1525. They failed to usurp him; he banished their leaders. The issue was infant baptism. Zwingli compared it to Old Testament circumcision, a rite performed on males the eighth day after their birth. But the Anabaptists saw baptism as an adult decision.

Zurich resolved most conflicts by meetings of the town council. Members listened to the evidence and then deliberated their decisions. Zurich leaders wanted to maintain religious unity in their reform movement.

The Anabaptists threatened that unity by baptizing adults and separately celebrating communion. Confining the offenders in a Dominican monastery, the council also fined them. The Zurich leaders still hoped to preserve unity by a series of meetings throughout 1525. Zwingli argued leniency for the offenders who promoted adult baptism. Still, the Anabaptists persisted. They were rearrested, detained, given a diet of bread and water, and warned not to teach the offensive doctrine again.

Numerous vocal Anabaptists including Conrad Grebel, Felix Manz, and George Blaurock, suffered for refusing to renounce their doctrine. Zurich authorities bound Manz hand and foot and flung him into the Lake of Zurich. Zwingli explained, "By water he had sinned, by water he must perish." Zwingli ordered Blaurock whipped, expelled, and sent to Austria. Catholic authorities there burned him as a heretic. Conrad Grebel died of the plague, but his father was beheaded along with Hans Bulmann.

Zwingli biographer, Jean Rilliet, asked, "Once the legitimacy of the use of force in vindication of the honor of God and the gospel is admitted, where is one to stop?"[12] Zwingli seemingly disregarded the halt signs. Rilliet sympathized with Zwingli and Calvin because less blood flowed in Zurich and Geneva than in Germany, Austria, or France. Whether the Lord considers violence toward a few people less reprehensible than violence toward a multitude, only he can judge.

Zwingli seemed strongly affected by the Old Testament, particularly the Law of Moses. He spent much of his ministry studying and expounding the Old Testament. Mosaic Law appears the basis for many of the changes instituted in Zurich. Zwingli's reforms went far beyond what the Mosaic Law outlined, however.

In 1525, Zwingli urged the formation of an ad hoc committee comprised of six judges, including two pastors, to meet every Monday and Thursday to deal with marriage issues. A few samples of their decisions suffice. The committee solved matrimonial disputes and set the legal age of marriage. A couple planning to marry had to pre-announce it from the pulpit. In 1525, an adulteress had to wait at least five years before she could remarry. Yet in 1531, one former transgressor waited only a year and another only three months.

By 1526, a tribunal wholly supervised the city's moral life. The panel held property owners responsible for their tenants, and they often questioned innkeepers. Heini Genner operated a brothel, but his operation couldn't admit married men. The city became a hotbed of informers. If neighbors witnessed unusual visitors, heard cries, or questionable talk, they were obligated to report it to the authorities.

In Galatians, Paul used the analogy of the Law of Moses as a schoolmaster that leads us to Christ. Zwingli viewed the civil government as a schoolmaster necessary to stabilize society from anarchy that human passions create. Zwingli thought that God would raise avengers to deal with civil tyrants. He distended the teachings in Romans 13:1-7 respecting governmental taxation. Zwingli's position on church-state relationships underwent change from 1526-1528. It became difficult for him to separate the two realms. City decisions grew to be church decisions. Using the biblical example of sabbath enforcement in Jesus' time, Zwingli thought it all right for the state to compel obedience to certain religious rules. He failed to make any distinction between ordinances of the church applicable to believers and laws for all city residents whether believers or not.

In 1527, both magistrates and clerics formed a commission of superintendence in Zurich. They intended to administer the church and to oversee the conduct and work of ministers. By 1528, this body became an official synod that controlled spiritual life in the city. Zwingli himself instigated most of the synod's decisions.

Zurich at that time had two councils, the Little and the Great. The synod, at Zwingli's behest, forbade membership in either body to anyone who refused to partake of the evangelical Lord's Supper. Next, no one could solicit votes for public office who would not declare publicly that he was a Lord's table communicant.

The following year Zwingli's teaching regarding church and state evolved further. He obliged all citizens to attend worship services. Later it became a punishable offense for Catholics who attended mass in neighboring cantons to worship in Zurich. Zwingli's practices seemed to set a precedent for John Calvin, who instituted similar church-state measures in Geneva decades later.

Zwingli met with Martin Luther in 1528 in an attempt to resolve some of their differences. That conference known as the Marburg Colloquy accomplished little. Zwingli's wing of the Reformation met with continued success in Switzerland. Six of the eleven cantons adopted the reform movement. Those that didn't became known as the Forest Cantons and stayed faithful to the pope.

Later in 1528, civil war broke out between the Catholic and Protestant factions. Zwingli acted as chaplain and standard bearer for the Protestants. He was wounded on October 10, 1531, at Cappel.[13] Catholic forces later executed him. The Catholics have since prevailed in the mountainous regions and Protestants in the cities and valley areas of Switzerland.

When people die in middle-age, it presents questions about what they might have done in their mature years. Had he reached a more contemplative stage in life, might Zwingli have resolved the church-state conflict in a different way? Given the forceful flux of sixteenth-century society in which Zwingli made his decisions, only God knows.

Our next reformer had the advantage of building somewhat on knowledge gained in Zurich. We'll see how he dealt with the conflicts.

The Major Reformers — John Calvin

John Calvin also based his views on scripture, and yet he differed with both Luther and Zwingli. Luther vacillated some in his attitude toward church-state relations, Zwingli's views evolved, but Calvin seemed fully committed to the preeminence of church over state.

After Calvin studied theology at the University of Paris, he began to doubt his vocation, and he turned to a law emphasis at Orleans in 1528. Strongly influenced by the Protestant Melchior Wolmar, Calvin (1533) came to the conclusion that God had called him on a mission to restore the New Testament church. That led to a complete break with the Catholic church.

Calvin spent some time in prison for his beliefs. After his release he fled to Basle in order to escape further persecution. He wrote his *Institutes of the Christian Religion* in 1536. In that same year, when Calvin visited Geneva, Guillaume Farel persuaded him to help reform that city. Also in 1536, Calvin published his *Articuli de Regimine Ecclesiou*. This work contained stern regulations about how to administer the Lord's Supper. Calvin insisted that all citizens should have to take a profession of faith. Failure to do so would result in exile. Two years later, the town fathers requested Farel and Calvin to leave.

Calvin spent the next few years in Strasbourg where he met and married a widow, Idelette de Bure (someone needs to study why the reformers went for widows). Calvin also developed a friendship with Martin Bucer, who had corresponded with Luther beginning in 1518. Bucer's influence led to a 1539 revision of the *Institutes*. In addition, Calvin befriended Luther's associate Philip Melancthon.

The Genevans changed their minds in 1541 and asked Calvin to return and lead them in church reform. He held no public office and didn't become a citizen until 1555. The city paid Calvin, though, and provided him a house. For fourteen years he worked on reforming Geneva and setting up a theocracy modeled after Old Testament examples. Even household conduct was held up to rigid inspection. A consistory of laypeople and pastors compelled citizens to act according to Calvin's standards. They forbade card-playing, dancing, playing dice, and other popular forms of recreation.

A party known as the Libertines opposed Calvin, but he suppressed them. He executed numerous adversaries including Jacque Gruet, Raoul Monet, and Michael Servetus, whom he burned at the stake in 1553. By 1555, no resisters remained. Calvin ruled Geneva from 1555 to 1564 enforcing his strict morality on the city. He also gave assistance to other cities interested in reform.

To Calvin's credit, he founded the Academy of Geneva and strongly fostered education by his development of a municipal school system, but he never compromised his conviction that the state is subject to the church. Calvin believed that the government should protect the church, enforce sound doctrine, and create civil righteousness.

Somehow Calvin — as had Zwingli — failed to distinguish between the theocracy God established for Israel in the Law of Moses and the separate realms of Caesar and God that Jesus explained and that Paul advocated in Romans 13.

One of Calvin's disciples, John Knox, convinced the Scottish parliament to adopt Calvinism. In 1560, they embraced a book of discipline and confession of faith similar to the ones used in Geneva. Thus Parliament created the Scottish Presbyterian Church with its polity.

Other Reforms And Reformers

England's reform movement originated differently than the ones we've examined so far. It didn't share the grassroots beginnings that formed in France, Germany, and Switzerland. Katherine of Aragon's "failure" to bear a son frustrated King Henry VIII (we now know it was his fault). The monarch wanted an annulment. The pope refused to grant it. A question arose about the validity of Henry's first marriage; the pope had given him a special dispensation so he could marry Katherine. The Holy Father refused Henry's wish to divorce her. After all, she was a good Catholic.

Henry decided to get a second opinion — and a third and a fourth. He consulted well-known reformers and the faculties of Europe's great universities. Eight university faculties supported him. So did Ulrich Zwingli and the theologian Johannes Oecolampadius. Luther and Melancthon opposed. In 1533, Henry married Anne Boleyn. The Archbishop of Canterbury made the king's divorce from Catherine official.

Events soon turned and twisted like a drunken snake. The pope excommunicated Henry. The king responded in 1534 by getting Parliament to appoint him and his successors head of the English church. Parliament and the king quickly ended the sending of monies to Rome and terminated the pope's religious and political authority in England. Turmoil simmered and broiled until 1563 because some of Henry's successors were Catholic. For example, Mary I attempted to restore Catholicism and ordered many Protestants burned at the stake.

Neither Henry nor subsequent English rulers for generations cared a whit for Christian liberty. Henry attempted to suppress Lutheranism by urging Parliament to enact the Act of Six Articles. Even though Henry denied papal power in England, he still wanted the theological tenets of medieval Catholicism taught in the English cathedrals. Later, Edward VI encouraged Protestant preachers. In both cases, the state controlled church decisions. After 1563, when Elizabeth finally restored Protestantism, Catholics often suffered persecution.

What changes took place in the English church? As the British playwright, Sir Richard Steele (1672-1729) commented, "There is a difference between the Church of Rome and the Church of England: the one professes to be infallible — the other to be never wrong." A host of dissenting and nonconforming groups became active, however including Brownists, Presbyterians, Puritans, Quakers, and Separatists. These groups advocated a host of positions on the church-state issue.

Though the reformers generally taught respect for the scriptures, most lacked completely biblical views of church-state relations. But the severity of our judgment needs tempering because the reformers were for the most part men of their time. Tradition and violent waves of social force shaped their theology. Long-established emphasis on the Church Fathers' teachings halted and obscured the study of scripture. Using the Bible as a guide was a relatively new experience.

The reformers helped in some cases to clarify matters of faith, grace, and individual responsibility before God. They did little, however, to filter or purify the muddied, multicolored paint that obfuscated church-state relations. Rather they poured the sullied paint into a hundred other containers of unequal sizes and then mixed it with scores more new shades and hues.

The Thirty Years' War (1618-1648) added gory mixing and spilling. Though fought mostly on German soil, the war involved Bohemia, Denmark, England, France, Sweden, and what we now know as Switzerland and the Netherlands. Much of the war's origin lay in roots of dissatisfaction with the ineffective Peace of Augsburg. In 1555, that treaty ended Protestant-Catholic fighting in Germany. Dynastic rivalries continued, however, in Germany. Tension between the Holy Roman Emperor and the Protestant princes remained high.

During the Thirty Years' War neither side seemed reluctant to kill. Numerous bloody battles took place throughout Germany and spilled into neighboring countries. On May 23, 1618, Protestants in Prague threw two of the king's ministers out of a window. As the war continued, the Protestants couldn't even agree. Divisions between Calvinists and Lutherans resulted in heavy Protestant losses. Some estimate that the war cost about twenty percent of the German population with some cities suffering as much as a fifty percent loss of their inhabitants.

Exploration and settlement in the New World, attempts to reform the Reform movement itself, nationalistic feelings, the rising middle class, and the pursuit of political liberty added further paint pails and pots, all with their own tinges and tones. We'll look at some of those new hues and those who mixed them in the next chapter.

---

1. When Paul told the Ephesian elders that he was "innocent of the blood of all men" (Acts 20:26, 27), he used the prophetic principle given to Ezekiel (Ezekiel 3:16-21; 33:1-9). Preachers (prophets) are like watchmen who are assigned the task of cautioning people about imminent danger. If the prophet warns and people do not heed, the prophet has fulfilled his duty. He can only tell the message. He cannot and should not force his hearers to heed it.

2. Harold Lamb, *The Crusades* (New York: Bantam Books, 1962), p. 5.

3. *Ibid.*

4. James Carroll, *Constantine's Sword: The Church and The Jews — A History* (Boston: Houghton Mifflin, 2001), see pp. 276-277 regarding attacks against the Jews during and after the Crusades.

5. The Peasant's War (1524-1526) occurred in Germany when urban lower-class people and peasants revolted against the oppression of their feudal overlords. They demanded the abolition of serfdom; they wanted the right to kill wild game and to fish. They also wanted to choose their own ministers. The Anabaptist leader Thomas Munzer led a successful revolt in Thüringen, but it was later suppressed, and he was executed. Altogether about 500,000 peasants gave armed resistance. About 100,000 of them died in conflict. Though much of the revolt was fomented by the freedom people felt because of the preaching of Martin Luther, he was shocked by their violence, and opposed them.

6. Roland H. Bainton, *Here I Stand: A Life of Martin Luther* (New York: Mentor Books, 1963), p. 186.

7. *Ibid*, p. 187.

8. *Ibid*, pp. 189-190.

9. The perspective of the humanist begins with man and not God. Humanists want to develop all the potentialities of human reason, skills, and abilities. In the Renaissance, they emphasized classical (especially Greek and Roman) literature, the arts, and music.

10. What Zwingli objected to was Transubstantiation, the idea that the Lord's table bread and wine literally become the body and blood of Jesus, not symbols, but actually flesh and blood in every way but appearance.

11. Jean Rilliet, *Zwingli, Third Man of the Reformation*, translated by Harold Knight, (Philadelphia: The Westminster Press, 1959), p. 86.

12. *Ibid*, p. 146.

13. May also be spelled Kappel.

8

It Really Got Mixed:
Eighteenth- To Twentieth-Century Teachers And Movements

*By this gospel you are saved, if you hold firmly to the
word I preached to you. Otherwise, you have believed
in vain.*
— 1 Corinthians 15:2

The Protestant Reformation blended with and was inflamed by intense longings for individual liberty. Other dynamic factors affecting the mix included the invention of the printing press and latent nationalistic feelings — indeed all aspects of the Renaissance.[1] These causes and others whipped, blended, and bloodied our paint.

Some imagine the Reformation as unified and uniform. Coherent, it wasn't. Each major wing of the Reformation spawned its own dissenters, reformers, and restorers. National parties arose. That intermingling of forces created escalating and accelerating religious diversity. The Reformation splashed, spattered, and flung paint colors.

Most major reform parties approved the use of force to protect or to build their religious societies. That wasn't new. But something unseen for centuries came to the fore. Many Anabaptists now taught pacifism. Several modern groups evolved from those Anabaptists. We shall examine them more fully in the next chapter. First we'll explore how other major influences affected the course of church-state relations.

The Puritans
The European reform movements resulted in the formation of state or nationalistic churches in many countries. In some nations,

141

efforts to restructure those new churches created significant outcomes. One of the most powerful influences stemmed from a descendant of Anne Boleyn and Henry VIII's marriage.

Recall that Henry divorced Katharine of Aragon because Katharine couldn't produce a son for him. She delivered a daughter, Mary. Because Henry annulled his marriage to Katharine, that left Mary in "illegitimacy." Gory and unpredictable battles between Anglicans and Catholics for supremacy in England raged at the time. In order to survive, Mary, though a Catholic, pretended to be Protestant.

Meanwhile, poor Anne succeeded no better with Henry's chromosomes than her predecessor Katharine. She produced a daughter, Elizabeth. Anne never gained the people's support. Her bad renown coupled with Henry's no-son displeasure resulted in Anne's execution. It's also possible that Anne's eyes, shape, voice, and pheromones no longer attracted Henry. Whatever the real reasons, Anne was no more. Now Anne's daughter, Elizabeth, pretended to be something she wasn't. Though a Protestant she claimed to be Catholic. Some considered Elizabeth illegitimate after Anne's death, but in 1544, Parliament gave her right of succession to the throne after Mary.

Mary became Queen of England in 1553. The pope forgave her for renouncing the church under Protestant pressure and declared her legitimate. Bloody Mary, as she became known, persecuted Protestants and married Philip II of Spain. Mary ascended to a shaky throne.

Pollsters would have given her low numbers. Her English subjects counted three strikes against Mary. They disapproved of her new alliance with Spain. Her pro-Catholic position brought disdain, and it upset the populace when Mary lost Calais back to France in a war Mary and Philip waged. Mary died in 1558.

It would have been a mistake in those days for English churches to order many copies of letterhead stationery. At Mary's death, Elizabeth became queen. Once she established her power, she sided with the Anglicans and took harsh measures against Catholics.

The Elizabethan Era (1558-1603) is known as one of the greatest in English history. Under Elizabeth, England developed into a great sea power. Commerce and industry prospered and colonization rapidly advanced. How much Elizabeth's policies deserve credit or other factors already in motion caused the success, only God and possibly some historians know.[2]

During Elizabeth's reign, several leaders thought it necessary to reform the state church. They objected to the hierarchical organization and also wanted to be rid of the ritual and vestments. By 1567, a group from London that worshiped after Calvin's pattern established itself in Geneva. Other congregations soon joined the movement. They aimed to purify the English church. Many of them became separatists. The group included Presbyterians and Independents (later known as Congregationalists).[3] Calvinism with its strict ideas of morality based on Old Testament law predominated among the followers.

The Puritans (as the group became known) largely succeeded in their mission, but then started quarreling among themselves. During the Puritan Revolution (first half of the 1600s), England's kings and Parliament vied for authority. They disputed nearly everything. Among the chief areas of contention: the divine right of the king and church governance.

Many Puritans migrated to New England. The movement lost its identity to its various factions, but its ideas strongly influenced the region into the eighteenth century and later. Some party leaders held passionate attitudes toward church-state relations. This led to a variety of beliefs. We'll consider some of them.

Puritanism In The New World

Here's what we've seen about the Reformation so far. Church-state boundaries were barely discernible. How to align and harmonize the two while maintaining separation provides the basis for this nation's current angst and conflict. In 1776, more than 95 percent of the population claimed a Protestant background. Some estimate that in the Revolution only about 25,000 Catholics lived in the colonies.

Many of the people lived on the frontier where kings and rulers possessed few enforcement powers. Historian Sidney Ahlstrom noted that French and Spanish pressure on Queen Elizabeth I forced

143

the "English 'empire' to intensify ... its Protestantism."[4] When it crossed the Atlantic, that profound English Puritanism shaped the moral and religious landscape of colonial America. Awareness of these influences creates better understanding of the religious trends and forces still at work in this country.

From its inception Puritanism embodied pluralism. One group wanted to retain the episcopal (single bishop overseeing a congregation) form of government and seemed satisfied with having a national church. They chiefly aimed to clear or purify the church of any Roman church vestiges. Calvinistic in their theology, they promoted an austere lifestyle.

The Presbyterians practiced strictness, too. They also wanted a national church, but as disciples of John Knox they wished to follow a Scottish example. Congregationalists thought the local churches should be self-sufficient, but they suffered divisions as well. Many of them didn't object to a national connection. But another party, the Separatists, felt obligated to leave the national church. They were unwilling to wait for the king, Parliament, or the bishops to make up their minds on Reformation issues.

Most Congregational groups practiced infant baptism. But another wing, the Baptists, performed believer's baptism. In addition, they contended that the church could consist of only regenerate "visible saints." That necessitated separation from the state.

Following the lead of George Fox, the Quakers originated from English Puritanism. Born in 1624 to an English Puritan family, Fox claimed at age nineteen that he received revelations. In these mystical experiences, God "told" him that he should follow only Christ. Soon he began to assert that every person should seek guidance through this type of "inner light." Fox insisted that he received these revelations during a calm frame of mind. Paroxysms or quaking (thus Quakers) usually preceded those placid states.

Fox actively preached against Presbyterianism and other formalized religions. He objected to authority, both religious and political. Fox also denounced slavery and war. Human activity should be directed both by God-inspired inner contemplation and by social conscience, Fox taught. His teaching gained wide acceptance in England.

Fox's objection to authority lacked consistency. During the last part of his life, while he helped establish Quaker schools and communities in England, Fox lobbied Parliament for it to pass the Act of Toleration. As a result, in 1689 his group received acceptance. But Fox sought no such privileges for Roman Catholics and Unitarians.

William Penn became one of Fox's most famous followers. He helped create the colony of Pennsylvania noted for its acceptance of various religions. Many religious groups that suffered persecution in Europe found haven in Penn's colony. They included Amish, Dunkards, Mennonites, and Moravians.

The Effects Of Philosophers On Church-State Relations

Other forces influenced and still impinge on the relationships of church and state. The teachings of certain philosophers shaped what modern church people and non-church people think. For example, the English-born (1588) Thomas Hobbes developed the idea of a secular justification for the political state. The philosopher-theorist opined that the Reformation caused too much decentralization. He feared anarchy would result. Hobbes correctly predicted religious disunity. But his concerns about political disorder seem unjustified, at least in this country.

John Locke (born 1632 in England) developed an opposing view. Locke contended that the people were sovereign, not the state. The state could be supreme only if bound by what he termed "natural law." The writers of the United States Constitution derived the basis of it from Locke's thought. He expounded the idea that it is government's duty to protect individual rights. Citizens possess natural rights and property rights. Locke also taught the rule of the majority, but he showed no tolerance for atheists. According to him they threatened society.

Locke promoted the idea of checks and balances in government. He wanted a separate church and state. Locke's thought strongly affected the American Revolution. Prior to the Revolution, many American preachers promoted his ideas. Most current Americans agree with his principles. It's the practical application

145

of them that becomes difficult as we're witnessing in the twenty-first century.

Church and state were not separate at first in this country. In the early years, most of the states had established religions. Virginia became a Royal Province in 1624. Only church members could vote. There was Congregationalist establishment in Connecticut and Massachusetts. The Catholic church was established in Maryland. But the Baptists and Presbyterians opposed any form of establishment. The move toward disestablishment came gradually state by state.

Theologian-Philosophers

Numerous theologian-philosophers also helped shape church-state relations. It's impossible to relate all of the contributors, but some had lasting impact. During the nineteenth century, philosophers, thinkers, scientists, and religious teachers advocated an abundance of social theories. They dealt with issues not publicly discussed for centuries, and in some cases never anticipated by previous thinkers. I refer to conditions caused by the rising middle class, exposure to new scientific knowledge, and varying directions taken by rapidly multiplying denominations. All of these influences forced new assessments of long-held beliefs.

The German preacher, Friedrich Schleiermacher (1768-1834), sought to reconcile evangelical religious beliefs and current social theories. Perhaps foremost of the era's liberal theologians, Schleiermacher wanted to shift the focus from God to humanity. The heart of the believer is the most important thing. Each one's personal experience creates its own realm, has its own proof, and validity.

Schleiermacher taught that religion is a universal and deep-rooted experience of all human beings. He thought it impossible to separate knowledge of the human soul from one's knowledge of God.

Though I'm not aware of significant direct pronouncements Schleiermacher made about Christians and governments, he sowed the seeds of the "I think" mentality current in our society that fosters so many opinions independent of scripture. Richard Neibuhr wrote of Schleiermacher, "His greatest achievement is his articulation of the self-consciousness and the God-consciousness that relate to feeling."[5] We can probably blame Schleiermacher more than anyone else for the fact that not only has the church-state paint been poured into many buckets, all now own their own little pots of multi-colored paint.

In his truncated life, Sören Kierkegaard (1813-1855) possibly influenced the thoughts of twentieth- and twenty-first-century theology and philosophy as much as anyone other than Jesus. Existentialism, the idea that you can't speak about generalities, but must begin with each individual in his/her own real situation is the basis. Kierkegaard's influence remains strong among both Christians and unbelievers.

Kierkegaard felt that abstract thought, though necessary in science and mathematics, can't be wholly applicable in religion. We need to live truth, not just know it, he said. Effective religion leads a person to consider, "What must I do?"

Kierkegaard protested the idea that either God or man can be an object that a scientist or a mathematician might study. A number is a lifeless symbol with no feeling. So are numerous facts in nature. But, neither God nor any individual should be considered as an object.

Kierkegaard seemed strongly affected by the citizenry of his home country, Denmark. That nation maintained a state church. Though most Danes considered themselves Christians, Kierkegaard regarded them as nominal believers. One doesn't become a Christian simply from knowing a set of facts or belonging to an organization. One must be transformed by divine grace. One strives to become perfect but never fully reaches that goal.

Becoming a Christian also requires a leap of faith. For Kierkegaard, one never fully knows God. God transcends us. We can't use the methods of science to prove God's existence or to demonstrate his essence. Most God-seekers find only images of themselves.

God offers salvation to people, but most of them seek only a good life. In fact, as folks pursue their dreams they never come to terms with their underlying insecurity and anxiety. "Faith means the betting of one's life upon the God in Jesus Christ."[6] This life might be lonely and include suffering. The Christian life can't be done without God's help.

Horace Bushnell (1802-1876) was a Puritan preacher of New England background. He spent most of his life in local ministry, but he became an activist in social causes. In Bushnell's notion, the New England area enjoyed health, wealth, and societal excellence. He credited Puritanism and the genius of Anglo-Saxons for those successes.

Bushnell figured that the ideal New England society suffered from the immigration of Irish and Catholics into the factory towns and cities. In order to resist the effects of the Catholic migrants, Bushnell actively helped form the Protestant League and Christian Alliance. He showed little interest in the creeds of the alliance. Rather, he wanted to promote a unity among Protestants against Catholics.

On other fronts, he opposed slavery, but he didn't call for abolition. Bushnell reckoned that slavery would eventually expire on its own. He regarded the Republicans snooty, but liked Lincoln. According to Bushnell, both sides were culpable in the Civil War, and God chastised each side.

It's evident from Bushnell's public statements and writings that preachers commonly spoke out on societal and church-state issues during the nineteenth century. Bushnell typified the period's liberal theology.

Notwithstanding Bushnell's railings against Catholic immigration, he and fellow liberal theologians held optimistic views of man's destiny. They adopted some of Darwinism's tenets. That is, they concluded that the course of human history evolves upwardly. By means of their reformation, therefore, the kingdom of God could be realized by human effort.

If those thinkers had worn religious emphasis as clothes, they'd have been barely clad. Some used no Christian basis for their efforts. They emphasized societal improvement. Most important: man's relationship with his neighbors. In dealing with these challenges, some in the movement accented subjective things like intuition and feeling. Scriptural examples or authority meant little to them.

Many scholars of that era created doubt about the Bible's reliability. "The church was understood less as a supernatural agency, less as 'the Body of Christ,' and more as an agency for the propagation of an ethical message and the advancement of the kingdom."[7]

Liberals of that era wanted religious freedom. They advocated social, ecclesiastical, and doctrinal free expression. There was some validity for their quest. But as with most protest movements, they crossed far over the centerline. Here's how H. Richard Niebuhr described their message: "A God without wrath brought men without sin into a kingdom without judgment through the ministrations of a Christ without a cross."[8] The liberals mixed countless pastels into the church-state issue. The muddle wasn't finished.

The Social Gospel

Burgeoning industrialism and ever-increasing migration to large cities intensified urban problems in the late nineteenth century. Walter Rauschenbusch, a Baptist, and Washington Gladden, a Congregationalist, voiced two major concerns. First, they wished to give dignity to working class people. Second, they wanted the proletariat to learn religion. Among their interests; child labor, the right of all workers to have a living wage, and improved conditions for women in the workplace. Rauschenbusch and Gladden advocated, too, that all workers receive a day off per week. Along with other social gospel advocates, the pair felt that too many leading clergymen "shared beds" with prominent, wealthy capitalists.

The year 1893 brought severe economic depression to the United States. As a Baptist minister in New York, Rauschenbusch saw firsthand the squalor and other devastating effects the downturn produced. Through a periodical that he published, he encouraged the formation of a Christian socialist movement. In 1908, Rauschenbusch and Gladden persuaded the Federal Council of the Churches of Christ in America to draw up a "social creed of the churches."

The influence of Gladden, Rauschenbusch, and like-minded ministers of their day strongly affected the perspective many denominations now take. Advocates of the social gospel felt that simply preaching the biblical gospel never suffices. They saw the

149

gospel as only hellfire insurance where policies are sold individually. "There is no use saving individuals one by one when a corrupt social system is damning them by the thousands."[9]

According to social gospel promoters, if we live in a corrupt society, it will corrupt us, because society molds us. Only making society perfect corrects the problems. In their search for relevancy, ministers voiced wide-ranging concerns. These included the issues of slavery, labor's right to organize, religious intolerance, and agricultural dislocation. Two matters dominated: race relations and peace. Most felt that the kingdom of God could not appear until war had been abolished.

Did social gospel advocates succeed? Without question they helped ameliorate many effects of injustice. Was there a better way to accomplish what they did? We'll assess that in the closing chapters.

The social gospel philosophy remains lively in twenty-first-century religion. It's seen in ministers who feel compelled to speak out on social and political issues. Some religious leaders spend nearly all of their time dealing with present conditions, and almost no time on the gospel.[10] "The social gospel could be regarded as, in a sense, reform with a Protestant gloss, the gloss interesting but inessential. Reform first, religion second."[11]

Social gospel advocates face many obstacles. For one, hardly anyone agrees on what constitutes a perfect society. Indeed the perfect culture that nineteenth-century leaders preached, expected, and endeavored to bring about never arrived. Twentieth-century events caused many to question what man "had wrought."

Human-organized-kingdom advocates boldly prophesied. But, if humankind was evolving upwardly, why the 1929 stock market debacle, the ensuing depression, two world wars, Hitler's ovens, and Stalin's pogroms? Later in the century, the Cold War not only killed earlier optimism by its chill, it iced the kingdom's cadaver.

Neo-Orthodoxy

The term "neo-orthodoxy" seems oxymoronic — a contradiction. Orthodoxy usually means conformance to something established or traditional. Neo intimates something new. How can you

150

have something new that's established? Nonetheless, the term was struck, and it stuck.

Neo-orthodoxy showed few traditional features. On the contrary, the twentieth-century second-trimester movement became notable for increasing varieties of religious thought. It displayed more forms than a tide-washed oil slick. Too diverse to be really orthodox the word amorphous may best describe it. Many regarded neo-orthodoxy as nothing new at all, only an updated social gospel.

Facing dismay over Western society's failure to achieve earlier goals and the bad news from numerous fronts, theologians attempted to form new concepts and theories. Religious thinkers promoted fresh premises taking contemporary conditions into account.

Some of the controversy centered on the authority and reliability of the scriptures. Theologians and ministers also argued over domestic social problems, foreign policy, and church authority. We shall limit our discussion to issues of church and state. Some of neo-orthodoxy's prominent leaders and their positions on the subject follow.

Reinhold Niebuhr (1892-1971)

A Wright City, Missouri, native, Niebuhr received his education at Elmhurst (Illinois) College, Eden (Missouri) Seminary, and Yale Divinity School. After serving as a minister in Detroit, Niebuhr joined the faculty of Union Theological Seminary in New York City. He taught and lectured there for more than thirty years. Niebuhr became the foremost and widely read American-born theologian of the twentieth century. "His books are read carefully by many who would not normally be 'caught dead' reading theology," wrote William Hordern.[12]

The years Niebuhr spent in Detroit changed his liberal ideas of the church's mission. He found little application for what he learned in seminary. Detroit, the motor city, ranked among the most industrialized American metropolises. Niebuhr witnessed firsthand industrialism's effects on men and was dismayed that the church failed to minister to them.

Niebuhr actively involved himself in the affairs of trade unions and politics. In the 1930s, he joined the Socialist Party. About ten years later, Niebuhr helped to form New York State's Liberal Party. Despite his own participation in it, he understood the inconsistencies of Christian social involvement.

Pride lies at the heart of human difficulty, said Niebuhr. He defined three pernicious pride areas. First pride in power leads to false security. Man's lust for power corrupts his dealings with his fellows resulting in racial discrimination, totalitarianism, and imperialism.

Knowledge pride causes people to claim they possess the unadulterated truth and nothing but that. No one ever knows all the truth. Man's pride keeps him from admitting his limited understanding. His fanatic efforts to cover his limitations separate him from his fellows.

Moral arrogance is a third type of pride. Jesus told the story of the two men who went to the temple to pray. The Pharisee thanked God that he wasn't like other sinners, especially the publican standing not far from him. How the Pharisee saw the publican through his praying eyelids Jesus left to our imagination. Religious people often make judgments of this type and find their security in the supposed knowledge, power, or presumed moral goodness of their own groups.

Niebuhr recognized the inherent flaw in the liberal quest for the perfect society. The liberals thought that civilization's defects could be corrected through education and by changing society. Here's the rub. Sin causes society's evils, it doesn't result from them.[13] That creates a dilemma.

Regardless of the origin of the insights we possess concerning the political order, it's important to keep in view the high potential for justice in all situations. Yet we must recognize "that the twin perils of tyranny and anarchy can never be completely overcome in any political achievement."[14]

Niebuhr saw no way to completely make history safe. One works in behalf of justice, understanding that perfect justice is unachievable. But one can't escape the quest for it simply because perfection can't be attained.

Niebuhr overcame that inconsistency by taking an apocalyptic view of world history. He saw history moving toward a fulfillment. Popular predictive elements didn't interest him. Niebuhr felt that those who continually forecast the end of the world pervert Jesus' second coming and apocalyptic teaching. On the other hand, Niebuhr thought that Christians must take a view of history that goes "beyond history."

Considering the fact that history will be fulfilled, Christians may thus choose from various professions. One option: become a prophet in the way Niebuhr did. Condemn society when it doesn't conform to the absolute demands of Christ. Prophets must quicken the consciences of men, he said. While Neibuhr insisted that Christians can't form God's kingdom in history, they still must participate in God's action within history. Christians must be actively involved in social causes.

Niebuhr thought that others could choose to be compromising statesmen. They might become politicians or military personnel. Sometimes, a Christian simply must choose the lesser of two evils, Niebuhr contended. In accepting that compromise, however, one can never be proud. Rather he/she proceeds with sorrow and repentance. Niebuhr achieved a singular accomplishment in his proactive thorough devotion to the job of outlining his idea that man should mediate between society and God. How to intercede is the painful question.

In his treatise "The Christian Attitude to Government," Niebuhr observed flaws in both the Lutheran Reformation and the radical sects. He considered the Lutherans too pessimistic, and they uncritically sanctified government. He thought the radical sects too optimistic; they completely rejected government. Moderate Anglicans and later Calvinists came closest to his ideal because they understood government as both vice and necessity. Though there must be free interplay of social forces, this freedom contains peril.[15]

Niebuhr took exception to Paul's advice in Romans 13. To him, it became a "vehicle for a too uncritical devotion to government." This he regarded as a peril of biblicism. Later, Christian rulers assumed it gave them divine right. In my view, we can't blame the Bible or Paul's teaching. Followers of Jesus knowing they are answerable to God and who do not submit in true humility must bear the guilt.[16]

Though Niebuhr didn't mention the United Nations by name, he either foresaw its formation or referred to it in his treatise entitled "Justice and World Community."[17] He felt that the developing interdependence of nations gave opportunity to bring justice and order to the world stage. In his opinion, dominance of the stronger powers was inevitable, and yet he recognized that this arrangement would bring new perils of imperialism. Only a world constitution giving protection to weaker powers could deal with the problem.

Niebuhr considered the approaches of the pessimists, cynics, and idealists as flawed. He saw the new world order being built by staunch men who "when hope is dead, will hope by faith." Niebuhr's outlook reflected uncertainty in men's ability to accomplish what he saw as necessary. His "ace-in-the-hole" so to speak was God's judgment on history.

Helmut Richard Niebuhr (1894-1962)

Though H. Richard Niebuhr received similar early education as his elder brother, Reinhold, he spent his teaching career at a different institution. He ended up at Yale as a professor of Christian ethics. H. Richard brought a new approach to church-world relations in the form of a question. In a book titled *The Church Against the World*, he asked, "What must we the church do to be saved?" Niebuhr based the question on the Pentecost query, "What must we do to be saved?"

Niebuhr saw the church infected by the world within it as well as affected by the world outside. Compromise with the world puts the church into a retreat stance. Hosts of church people heard commands to halt, were reminded of their mission, and then instructed to wait for new orders, felt Niebuhr. Thus the question, "What must the church do to be saved?"

The church intimately involved itself with capitalism, with individualism, and imperialism, Niebuhr lamented. He recognized that the church could prepare for its work only by turning away from worldly involvement and re-engaging in "eternal relations."

That requires penitence and silence. Niebuhr pleaded for a return to the scriptures because he felt that the church would find in them the commands and promises that first impelled it.

In regard to capitalism's connection to the Protestant church, Niebuhr wryly noted that Protestantism and capitalism had formed such a close bond "genealogists have suspected kinship."[18] Niebuhr wasn't sure which gave birth to the other, but the linkage troubled him. Those connections included churches' great economic interest through debt structure, their endowments derived from capitalistic dividends, and their dependence on gifts from the privileged, wealthy classes of society.

Niebuhr noted further evidence of the capitalist-Protestant marriage in the fact that many church people confuse building God's kingdom with the enlargement of church ownership, and generally with society's economic advancement. For many, the church's mission became saving capitalistic civilization.

Niebuhr saw an even more insidious relationship than the one with capitalism. He thought the church was in bondage to nationalism. He didn't regard either private ownership or nationalism in themselves as wrong — only when worship of nations and intense desire for power and glory develop. Niebuhr saw the evil in nations that attempt to make the glory and might of the nation as their chief aim.

While insisting that "Internal life does not exist without external embodiment,"[19] Niebuhr urged the church to seek its independence. He wisely warned against allying the church with other agencies and associates. He feared the inherent evils when churches try to deliver mankind by playing messiah.

Niebuhr properly assessed that the church must depend on God. Glory and power belong to God alone. Decades after Niebuhr wrote his evaluation, many American Christians fail to note the distinctions between what is truly of Christ and what is related to national pride, worldly influence, and capitalistic fervor. I plan to show some biblical distinctions in the closing chapters. Niebuhr correctly understood this, however: we must start with repentance and faith.

155

Karl Barth

Barth received a good start in life because he chose the right parents. His father, Fritz, was a New Testament scholar and a Swiss Reformed minister. Though born in Basel, Switzerland (1886), Barth was reared in Bern. He received his higher education at four different universities; Berlin, Bern, Marburg, and Tubingen. Barth served professorships in Gottingen and Munster and then went to the University of Bonn (Germany) as a professor of systematic theology.

Adolf Hitler and his National Socialism rose to power in the early 1930s. Many churches sponsored opposition to the National Socialists by means of a six-article work known as the Barmen Declaration. Barth authored most of it. The Nazis expelled Barth from Bonn in 1934 and then later deported him to Switzerland because of his refusal to take a loyalty oath to Hitler's regime.

Barth wrote prolifically. His commentary on the book of Romans in 1919 broadsided liberal theology. In that and other works, Barth insisted that we can know God only through divine revelation. He regarded humanism and feeling as worthless. His study of Romans led Barth to conclude that the living God delivered perplexed, self-contradictory people like him from their sins through Jesus Christ's power.

Barth emphasized some important matters for our study. First, in reaction to increasing belief in the immanence of God (that God is very close to or in every human being); Barth believed in God's transcendence — "Wholly Other."[20] God has always existed apart from his creation. Immanence was the basis of the worldview used by many of his liberal contemporaries. That belief started from man and built upward using the building blocks of mystical experience, natural theology, and reason.

What man discovered by that method was only a pale reflection of himself. As a result, when ministers preached about God, "they sounded as though they were doing little more than speaking about man in a loud voice."[21] Barth also objected to the liberal optimism. He rightly argued that man is in crisis. We are "dying men speaking to dying men."

Barth emphasized the Word of God. He took exception to the fundamentalist view that identifies the words of the Bible with the Word of God. Barth regarded the words of Jesus and scripture as "tokens." The expression "token" may be unfortunate. Before we harshly judge Barth for his terminology, it helps to recall what Jesus said to his contemporaries:

> *You diligently study the Scriptures because you think that by them you possess eternal life. These are the Scriptures that testify about me, yet you refuse to come to me to have life.* — John 5:39-40

Possession of accurately translated scripture and the ability to read doesn't guarantee that the Word will be heard or understood. I think what Barth recognized was that simply reading or hearing the Word does no good unless it speaks to and affects the heart of the person. Until people read scripture allowing God to speak forcibly and unequivocally to their own hearts, they had just as well read Shakespeare, Milton, or Langston Hughes.

Barth effectively brought much of the religious world back to the Word. Unless the Word becomes the authority, we are lost in shifting tides of opinion.

In addition, Barth emphasized the New Testament view that the church is, by nature, a pilgrim church. It should not try to settle down anywhere as an earthly institution. For the church to do so brings the threat of being conformed to the world. This aligns with what Paul wrote in 1 Corinthians 10 and is a vital part of the theme of Hebrews. Here is an example:

> *And so Jesus also suffered outside the city gate to make the people holy through his own blood. Let us, then, go to him outside the camp, bearing the disgrace he bore. For here we do not have an enduring city, but we are looking for the city that is to come.* — Hebrews 13:12-14

Although the word pilgrim isn't used in the above passage, the text emphasizes that the Lord wants us to be on the move. That

157

may be part of the basis for Barth's insistence that the church lives between the time of Jesus' reconciliation and his final redemption. In Barth's opinion, churches don't believe enough in God. That explains their ineffectiveness. That evaluation might be one of Barth's most important contributions.

Barth cautioned against identifying the church with any political movement. To do so would be an attempt to establish the kingdom of God within time. The kingdom can come only at the conclusion of history, at the end of time, and the beginning of eternity. In the interim, the rule of the state will be at times unjust, but it is still necessary to prevent chaos and strife.

Reinhold Niebuhr disparaged Barth's view of government. Niebuhr thought Barth indifferent to the problems of social injustice, until the crisis of Nazi tyranny brought a strong response. According to Niebuhr, Barth backtracked from that point taking a different position. The change included criticism of the Reformation, because it saw government as an ordinance of divine providence, but did not set government under God's judgment.

Martin Niemöller and Dietrich Bonhoeffer

We need to mention two more exceptional theologians before we close this chapter; Martin Niemöller and Dietrich Bonhoeffer. Each opposed Hitler. The Nazis incarcerated both. Similar to the fate of Zebedee's sons, one suffered execution at a relatively young age and the other lived a full life.

Niemöller (1892-1984) commanded a U-boat in World War I. After the war he studied theology at Munster. When Hitler's National Socialism Party was formed, as a minister at Berlin-Dahlem, Niemöller welcomed it. His approval soon soured because the Nazis advocated various pagan and anti-Semitic policies.

Niemöller joined other German Protestant Christians in forming the Confessing Church and became one of its leaders. The group firmly opposed the National Socialists. The Gestapo arrested Niemöller placing him first at Sachsenhausen concentration camp and Dachau later. He was freed near the end of World War II and went on to lead the restructuring of the Protestant church in Germany. Niemöller served as president of the World Council of

Churches and actively opposed both atomic weapons and the rearmament of Germany.

Dietrich Bonhoeffer (born February 4, 1906) received his education at Tübingen and Berlin universities, and Union Theological Seminary in New York. In 1931, he lectured on theology at Berlin. Bonhoeffer joined Niemöller as part of the Confessing Church. He left Berlin in protest of Hitler's anti-Semitism. After spending two years in London where he served German-speaking congregations, Bonhoeffer was asked to lead a Confessing Church seminary in Pomerania. The Gestapo closed it.

In the early '30s Bonhoeffer preached pacifism. He said that God ordered the world's preservation in our time through international peace. On the other hand, he regarded that order as provisional, and relative if truth and justice should ever be endangered. He saw Hitler's regime as a threat to that order.

After World War II began, Bonhoeffer became active in political resistance to Hitler. Bonhoeffer did more than criticize the fuhrer. He secured credentials so he could travel to Sigtuna, Sweden, for a meeting with the Bishop of Chichester, England. In May of 1942, at the meeting, he gave the bishop documents meant for the British government. The information contained plans for the overthrow of the Nazis.

Hitler's agents arrested Bonhoeffer in 1943, imprisoning him near Berlin. On July 20, 1944, there was an attempt to assassinate Hitler. The Germans discovered Bonhoeffer's connection to the group responsible for the failed attempt. They transferred him to a maximum security prison and then hanged him April 9, 1945.

Niemöller and Bonhoeffer demonstrated extraordinary courage. I reluctantly judge their actions, especially knowing that I've never faced the threats they encountered. Notwithstanding their valor and faith, we still must ask, "Did they follow either apostolic example or Jesus' example in their approaches to the religion-government issues they faced?"

In the next chapter, we need to treat movements and teachers of the late twentieth century up to the present.

1. Interest in this world and faith in man were chief features of the Renaissance. Reason was important; faith in God of questionable meaning. Immanuel Kant taught that religion should be kept within the bounds of reason.

2. There's considerable question about the historians.

3. The chief difference between Congregationalists and Presbyterians was the formation of church government. Congregationalists, as their name indicates, believed in congregational rule of churches. The Presbyterians had elders (*presbyters* in Greek). They had few theological differences. In fact, in the early days in this country, Congregationalist and Presbyterian ministers could often fill one another's pulpits.

4. Sydney E. Ahlstrom, *Theology in America: The Major Protestant Voices from Puritanism to Neo-Orthodoxy* (Indianapolis-New York: The Bobbs-Merrill Company, Inc., 1967), p. 24.

5. Richard R. Neibuhr, "Friedrich Schleiermacher," *A Handbook of Christian Theologians* (Cleveland, Ohio: The World Publishing Company, 1967), p. 33.

6. William Hordern, *A Layman's Guide to Protestant Theology* (New York: The Macmillan Company, 1962), p. 126.

7. *Op cit,* Ahlstrom, p. 70.

8. *Ibid,* p. 71. Quoted from H. Richard Niebuhr, *The Kingdom of God in America* (1937). Reprinted in paperback (New York: Harper & Brothers Publishers, Torchbook, 1959), p. 193.

9. *Op cit,* Hordern, p. 94.

10. There are numerous areas of society that religious people want to fix. Some focus almost exclusively on the war issue, others race relations, others abortion, and other issues.

11. Donald Meyer, *The Protestant Search for Political Realism, 1919-1941,* Second Edition (Middletown, Connecticut: Wesleyan University Press, 1960, 1988), p. 2.

12. *Op cit,* Hordern, p. 147.

13. Actually, sin causes the imperfections and more sin results from imperfections. It's a double-edged sword.

14. Reinhold Niebuhr, *The Nature and Destiny of Man*, Part II, Man's Destiny (New York, Charles Scribner's Sons, 1949), p. 284.

15. This treatise is found in *The Nature and Destiny of Man*, Part II, Human Destiny, pp. 269-284. See also his criticism of Karl Barth's eschatology on p. 309, footnote 12.

16. In Ephesians 6:9, Paul reminded Christian slaveholders that they were answerable to God. I have a feeling the Roman Governor Felix heard an even stronger Apostolic warning that he was answerable to God in the Judgment. See Acts 24:25.

17. *Op cit*, Niebuhr, pp. 284-286.

18. *Op cit*, Ahlstrom, p. 603.

19. Clyde A. Holbrook, *A Handbook of Christian Theologians* (New York: Meridian Books, World Publishing, 1967), p. 389.

20. Immanence refers to the nearness of God and often includes the idea and feeling that God is within you. Transcendence is the opposite. God is distant, far-off, and unknowable unless he chooses to reveal himself. Barth taught that God revealed himself through Christ.

21. Quoted by Daniel Jenkins, "Karl Barth," *A Handbook of Christian Theologians* (New York: Meridian Books, World Publishing, 1967), p. 398.

9

The Presumers:
Mid- And Late-Twentieth-Century Influences

Through him (Jesus) you believe in God, who raised him from the dead and glorified him, and so your faith and hope are in God. — 1 Peter 1:21

Many forces create weather systems, meteorologists tell us. Ocean temperature, barometric pressure, wind direction, the jet stream, and factors no one yet understands all contribute. Predicting weather beyond five days ahead enjoys a success rate slightly better than crystal ball gazing. Bookies do a better job betting on horses. In the same way, we don't know all the things that create weather systems, we can't explain the copious color in all of those church-state paint pots.

There's space only to consider some major paint mixers and splashers. In this chapter, we'll look at a few mid- and late-twentieth-century dye slingers. Though differing in backgrounds and working dissimilarly, they shared assumptions concerning societal improvement. I omitted some influential people. The ones I've included give an adequate cross-section.

After we review the teachings of these noted spokesmen, I plan to show the flaws in their thinking. Areas of concern include the Christian's task, the place of Christian witness, and our relationship with the kingdom of God.

The first "mixer" strongly swayed Christians during the post World War II period. Popular, much-read, and of Quaker background, he authored fifteen books. Elton Trueblood profoundly affected his generation, yet contemporary historians tend to neglect and/or forget him. Trueblood's *Foundations for Reconstruction*

163

typifies the belief that use of biblical principles, especially Old Testament ones, will change society.

In his opening chapter titled "The Ten Commandments in Contemporary Life," Trueblood insisted that his book wasn't about the Ten Commandments but was focused on a "philosophy of civilization."

> *It seeks to discover the necessary planks for a platform on which civilization must be rebuilt if it is to be rebuilt in enduring fashion."* [1]

Trueblood saw society's greatest challenge as a moral one. He reviewed Moses' commandments presenting them as building blocks for an anticipated changed social order. Trueblood stated that Western society resembles that of Rome in its declining years. That theme, prominent in the mid-twentieth century, resounds still from American pulpits.

Present humanity may be in the midst of a Roman-like decay, but it's impossible to know all the parameters for quantifying something like morality. How can anyone gauge another person's heart?

Trueblood erred in one assessment, I think. As he saw the "decline" in Western morals, he expected a concomitant failure of science and technology. God will judge whether morality is failing, but current science and technology show few signs of foundering except in the ethics of some scientists and technicians.

Noah gave his world a limited time to repent, but he directly received his message from God. Unfortunately — I should say fortunately — modern prophets lack the express-connection the Old Testament prophets enjoyed with our Creator. Today's "Noahs" forecast, but the tsunamis they predict rarely result. Sometimes hardly a ripple occurs. I doubt that Trueblood and other Christian spokespeople of that time expected American society to remain intact into the twenty-first century. Here we are, and Christian ministers continue to "forecast" God's plans.

Let's return to Trueblood's stated purpose. He hoped to establish a "sound ethical creed" for society, one that could serve as a standard or a moral reference point. Trueblood rightly saw the dangers of ethical subjectivism as expressed in the saying, "There's nothing either good or bad, but thinking makes it so."

The teachings of the famous Greek triad, Plato, Socrates, and Aristotle complemented the Hebrew Decalogue, thought Trueblood. He set great store in the Greek trio's conclusion that there is real right, and there is real wrong. The Ten Commandments, wrote Trueblood, effectively identify good and bad.

Failure to define rightness lies behind the moral morass Western society faces. Controversy currently rages over gay marriage. Talk show hosts and various social experts keep trying to outline individual rights and marriage. No one agrees because no standard exists.

At one time, Mosaic Law served as the basis for much of this country's civil law. Recent court actions tend to sever existing ties to that base. Our society will become increasingly dismembered as lack of accord progresses. For the near future, courts will define morality, and they will decide on the basis of the judges' political and social leanings. I am, at this point, merely assessing current conditions in American society. What Christians should do about it, I'll treat later.

Trueblood advocated the Christian faith because it respects reason, which produces science. It also honors the sacredness of individual personality. That leads to "true charity." Trueblood saw this as the only hope for the world. It could, he said, "do for our time what it did for the decaying culture of classical Greece and Rome."[2] In order to accomplish this, we must stop saying that one religion equals another or that a person's faith is his own business.

Tolerance of all types of behavior, as political correctness demands in contemporary culture, must be replaced with a "burning faith." Also a true missionary spirit must be evident that speaks of God, the Lord of life, not a god that we've created or invented.

Only Hebrew synagogues and Christian churches aim to preserve the moral and spiritual principles necessary for a decent world. The church's chief task, Trueblood taught, is to help bring about a proper life for civilization at this dreadful time — so that people can enjoy a decent existence on earth. The society that Trueblood most eagerly defended is democracy.

Martin Luther King Jr.

The major events in Martin Luther King Jr.'s life are as well known as any twentieth-century American's. For that reason, we'll relate only pertinent information about Dr. King.

The racial climate of the 1950s differed radically from today's, especially in the South. Blacks rode only in the backs of public buses. Authorities often obliged them to yield those seats when public transportation became crowded. Blacks drank from separate public water fountains. They suffered other abuse and humiliation.

In Montgomery, Alabama, blacks discussed how to improve their circumstances. They wanted greater dignity and respect as they rode public transit. Ending segregation seemed a hopeless goal.

Enter Rosa Parks, a prominent member of the National Association for the Advancement of Colored People in Montgomery. On December 1, 1955, a bus driver ordered Ms. Parks to yield her backseat to a white passenger. She refused. Authorities arrested her and took her to jail. Because many knew and respected Ms. Parks, local NAACP leaders saw this as an opportunity to rally Montgomery blacks for a protest. They formed the Montgomery Improvement Association in order to formulate a bus boycott.

In their search for a leader who could unite them, Martin Luther King Jr. answered their need. He had recently located in Montgomery to preach at the Dexter Avenue Baptist Church. Because he was new to the area, he had no local adversaries. That meant that he wouldn't ignite automatic resistance to a boycott led by him.

King's sober appeals to American idealism and Christian brotherhood impressed many northern whites. He effectively drew awareness of the cause. Some black protestors became victims of violence. That bolstered media attention. Segregationists reacted by bombing King's home. The MIA brought a lawsuit seeking an injunction against seating practices on the local bus lines. A federal court ruled in MIA's favor. In November 1956, the Supreme Court upheld the ruling. As a result, King became a national figure.

In 1957, a group of black ministers and churches formed the Southern Christian Leadership Conference. They recognized King as the dominant intellect, personality, and fundraiser. The organization intended to protest discrimination by using nonviolent methods. Using marches, boycotts, and demonstrations, they, at times, provoked violent responses from whites. The federal government intervened.

King allied himself with influential northern whites, including numerous Caucasian ministers, and some Jewish radical activists. The latter proved to be good sources of money and advice. King relied heavily on an influential Jew named Stanley Levison, a sometime member of the American Communist Party.

The year 1959 was pivotal for King. He went to India so he could learn Mohandas K. (Mahatma) Gandhi's methods of nonviolent persuasion. King also moved from Montgomery to Atlanta to co-pastor the Ebenezer Baptist Church with his father.

King gained national attention in 1961, when his SCLC joined forces with local blacks in Albany, Georgia. They demonstrated against segregation in hotels, housing, restaurants, and public transportation. Their plan: overwhelm local authorities with the size and scope of their protests so police would counter with violence. The police failed to respond the way protest planners expected. The SCLC ran out of steam and funds.

In neighboring Alabama, the Birmingham police "accommodated" them. SCLC leaders encouraged black school children and teens to protest segregation by marching. Eugene "Bull" Connor, the police commissioner, reacted in the way the SCLC hoped. He used police officers braced with attack dogs and firefighters equipped with high-pressure hoses against the black youths. Pictures of Connor's aggressive tactics dominated front pages around the world. Strong sympathy for blacks ensued in many quarters.

King was arrested and jailed. Local ministers criticized King's methods. Contending his moral rightness and responsibility in disobeying unjust laws, King wrote a work while confined titled "Letter from Birmingham Jail." Many lauded the writing. It effected a gain in standing for King as a moral leader, an increase in support for black civil rights, a negotiated end to much of Birmingham's segregation, and national legislation in opposition to color or racial separation.

In 1963, King and other leaders enlarged the scope of their mission by organizing massive marches on Washington DC, on behalf of civil rights and jobs. At a meeting on August 28 before more than 200,000 civil rights supporters, King delivered his famous "I Have a Dream" speech. The influence of that oration coupled with the high-impact demonstrations in Birmingham led to the Civil Rights Act of 1964.

The next year, the SCLC promoted a protest march routed from Selma, Alabama, to Montgomery. The objective: end voting rights discrimination against blacks. Just outside Selma, police beat marchers and used tear gas on them. Violent scenes filled television screens across the country. That day became known as "Bloody Sunday."

The SCLC obtained a court order that barred police from interfering with any subsequent march. A fortnight later, about 3,000 participated in a new march from Selma to Montgomery. On their arrival, King addressed more than 20,000 people gathered in front of the Capitol Building.

For several reasons, King's successes began to wane following the Selma-Montgomery march. First, many American whites felt the civil rights mission accomplished. Two, King began actively and publicly protesting the Vietnam War. His opposition upset President Lyndon Johnson and angered many white Americans. Conversely, King gained the support of other white Americans who opposed the war.

A challenge to King's popularity grew in the mid-1960s from another front. Stokely Carmichael's Student Nonviolent Coordinating Committee became popular with young blacks. Carmichael and others considered King's protest strategies and moral idealism passé. Some objected to ministerial involvement. Jealousy also factored into this. SNCC leaders felt like they did all the hard work and King would show up in time to receive media attention.

In the face of these conflicts, King embarked on a new mission. A Chicago apartment became King's new headquarters for his goal of protesting housing and economic discrimination in the Windy City. Again, King met resistance. Many local black ministers publicly disagreed with King's tactics. His efforts gained little there. In addition the Ku Klux Klan and the neo-Nazis violently opposed the SCLC.

King spent increasingly more time on the theme of economic issues. He argued for a redistribution of wealth to blacks in order to compensate for centuries of injustice.[3] King began drawing new plans. He wanted the United States Congress to rectify racial economic disparities. King traveled to Memphis, Tennessee, in the spring of 1968 to support striking black garbage workers. On April 4, 1968, he was assassinated.

Many blacks and whites idolize King for his courage and moral leadership in overcoming racial divisions and inequities. Largely forgotten are his harsh criticism of US foreign policy, his upstaging of brothers in the cause, and his own questionable lifestyle.

King's methods differed from Elton Trueblood's, but the two shared similar goals. Both tried to improve society. That King helped bring about positive advances by blacks is indisputable. But a more important question must take priority: "Did Martin Luther King follow biblical precedent and use Jesus' model in pursuing his dreams?" He learned the nonviolent methods of Mahatma Gandhi, but did Dr. King advance the cause of Christ? Did the kingdom progress as a result of King's ministry?

Numerous churches today take positions on economic causes and social issues. They show genuine concern for crucial needs in present society. But did Jesus assign his disciples the task of correcting social ills? Is that what Jesus meant us to accomplish or did he send the church on another mission?

Francis Schaeffer

Francis Schaeffer was a widely respected American-born theologian-philosopher, who relocated to Switzerland. He and his wife, Edith, founded L'Abri Fellowship there in 1955 (L'Abri is French for shelter). The organization still operates with European, Asian, and American branches emphasizing international study and discipleship. The group also promotes the arts and accentuates the totality of life.

Schaeffer died in 1984, but authored more than twenty books. *Whatever Happened to the Human Race*, he cowrote with

C. Everett Koop, M.D., former United States Surgeon General. The subjects of this latter book include abortion and euthanasia. The copy I read came from a Catholic school library in Sioux City, Iowa. Tire marks blackened several of the pages. I wondered whether the copy inadvertently fell into the street from someone's backpack or suffered intentional defacing by a pro-abortionist. I knew that a euthanasia victim hadn't disfigured it.

Of Schaeffer's many works, the most pertinent is *A Christian Manifesto*, first published by Crossway Books in 1980. The work dealt with a Christian's relationship to civil disobedience, law, and government. In respect to those areas, Schaeffer deemed the following as the major difficulty for most twentieth-century Christians: they saw "bits and pieces," not the total situation. Thus, Schaeffer regarded abortion, pornography, permissiveness, and family breakdowns as symptoms of a greater problem — of worldview.

The present societal lapses arise, he said, from "the idea that the final reality is impersonal matter or energy shaped into its present form by chance."[4] This contrasts with the belief that God designed and built the universe. The two positions stand in antithesis.

Schaeffer noted that many "Christians" are merely humanists. He defined humanism as the belief that man should be at the center of all things and that everything should be measured by man.

The authority problem troubled Schaeffer. Everyday authority comes from the state, from the church, and for some people, from scripture. He thought the Reformation was beneficial because it emphasized the authority of scripture. That restoration helped clarify doctrine and also gave a basis for law.

In Schaeffer's view, neither church nor state should be above that law. By *law* he meant the Law of Moses. Schaeffer reasoned that the freedom and democracy, which provided this country's success can't work in nations that lack the Law of Moses' basis for it. Humanism without that necessary foundation or law leads to chaos, he said.

In a chapter titled "Foundations for Faith and Freedom," Schaeffer pointed to the understanding between government and one's worldview that the US founding fathers apparently possessed. He noted the important contribution made by John Witherspoon, the only minister to sign the Declaration of Independence. Witherspoon served as the president of the College of New Jersey (now Princeton). Witherspoon, in turn, fostered ideas promoted by the seventeenth-century Scotsman, Samuel Rutherford.

Rutherford gained fame for writing *Lex rex* (law is king). Nearly all kings assumed their "divine right" on the basis of *rex lex* (the king is law). The new definition meant that kings can't be a law to themselves. They and their governments must be subject to law. Later in the seventeenth century, John Locke formulated a secularized *lex rex*. Thomas Jefferson, a deist, stood in the *lex rex* tradition.

Schaeffer noted that Jefferson and his peers "understood the basis of the government, which they were founding."[5] They established the country on the Judeo-Christian concept. In regard to the famous phrase "certain inalienable rights" one can assume that government or the state doesn't give those rights, God does. It was possible to make law the king, because God, the lawgiver granted those inalienable rights. William Penn tersely verbalized it, "If we are not governed by God, then we will be ruled by tyrants."

The First Amendment was accepted, said Schaeffer, for two purposes; first to prevent there ever being an established national church (they didn't want a Church of the United States as there was a Church of England). Two, the First Amendment was passed to keep government from impeding or interfering with the free observance or performance of religion. Humanists now work effectively to reverse the intent of this last purpose. The rash of recent court decisions that prohibit public religious expressions witnesses their success.

Immigration to the US of those with a non-Christian (also non-Protestant) background results in a pluralism laden with beliefs and ideas that no longer flow from the Reformation. Schaeffer said that Christians must demonstrate Christianity's truth in freedom's marketplace.

Nonetheless, pluralism leads to the idea that one choice is as good as another. It becomes a matter of personal preference for each individual. No option is inherently better than another. The late astronomer, Carl Sagan, stated the crux of this view: "The cosmos is all that is or ever was or ever will be."

Schaeffer deplored the fact that courts in this country now foist the humanistic idea on all citizens of this country. He laid much of the blame for the present state of things on Christians, especially Christian lawyers and ministers, who did little or nothing to forestall the prevalent humanist-based situational ethics. Legalized abortion results from this humanistic "material-energy, chance concept of the final basic reality."[6]

Schaeffer rightly saw that the communications media now act as a fourth branch of government in this country. Public television, for example, refused to consider the airing of Schaeffer's video, *Whatever Happened to the Human Race?* because of the film's anti-abortion stance.

A battle plan exists, said Schaeffer, for countering this false doctrine. That includes using the freedom currently available to Christians. He faulted Christians for forsaking their task of being agents of change. Christians need to be culture's salt and light.

The Wesley and Whitefield revivals, wrote Schaeffer, exemplified the way Christians can approach the problems of secularism. Wesley and Whitefield called people to personal salvation and thousands responded. But, Schaeffer noted, their revivals also created social improvement. He pointed also to the preaching of William Wilberforce, who perhaps more than anyone else, motivated England to turn away from slavery before the United States did.

Christians face challenges due to court decisions not favorable to Christianity or to advocating Christ or his ethics in public places. In a chapter titled "The Limits of Civil Disobedience," Schaeffer asked about the believer's relationship to the state. At issue was Jesus' well-known dictum, "Give to Caesar what is Caesar's and to God what is God's." Schaeffer observed that Jesus didn't intend us to understand from this that God and Caesar were equals. From this, Schaeffer concluded that civil government must always stand under God's Law.[7]

Schaeffer then deduced that when the state or any office abolishes God's authority or law, it must be disobeyed. The state is a delegated authority; it has no autonomy. The state should be an agent of justice. It also, by punishing wrongdoers, restrains evil. But the state loses its authority, when it doesn't do justly and when it protects wrongdoers. Then it's tyrannical and lawless. Who should make the call about whether the state does justly Schaeffer didn't explain.

Schaeffer discussed what one should do when the state breeches its rightful function. Early Christians were thrown to lions, he noted, because they refused obedience to the state in civil matters — the chief matter being that those believers refused to worship Caesar. According to the Romans, that was a political crime. From this example, Schaefer drew a "bottom line." At certain points, he concluded, Christians have not just a right, they have a duty to become disobedient to the state.

From this one example of early Christians, Schaeffer journeyed far. He started with the model of William Tyndale (1490-1536), who disobeyed the state and the church when he promoted his new English translation of the Bible. Then Schaeffer used numerous examples of the Protestant Reformation in Sweden, the Netherlands, Denmark, Germany, and Switzerland. Reformers in those countries used armies to fight against the established Catholic church and various state authorities.

The reformer, John Knox, seemed a favorite of Schaeffer. Knox departed from Martin Luther and John Calvin[8] in respect to his thoughts about the right of rebellion. The latter two reformers maintained the principle that only civil authorities hold rights to rebel. John Knox insisted that common people may civilly disobey when state officials make rulings that conflict with biblical teaching. If they don't rebel against civil authorities in those circumstances, it would be tantamount to rebelling against God.

Schaeffer drew his principles from certain religious philosophers; one of them the seventeenth-century Scotsman, Samuel Rutherford, whom we mentioned earlier. Schaeffer presented Rutherford's arguments for resisting unlawful governments. First, Christians honor God when they resist tyranny because of tyranny's satanic nature. Second, since rulers have conditional power, subjects may, if the conditions aren't fulfilled properly, abandon their sanction of those rulers.

Schaeffer thought that circumstances present in the latter part of the twentieth century gave license to civil disobedience. The reason: humanism's effects debased long-established structures of society founded on the Law of Moses.

In his chapter, "The Use of Civil Disobedience," Schaeffer listed Rutherford's "appropriate" responses when the state interferes with the citizen's liberty. The levels of resistance are these:

1. The private citizen should take advantage of legal action by protesting.
2. Providing protest becomes ineffective, the citizen may flee.
3. If necessary, a Christian may use force to protect himself. However, one shouldn't use force if he can flee. Rutherford offered the example of David fleeing from Saul rather than employing force against him.[9]

Both Rutherford and Schaeffer acknowledged that in the case of individual or corporate use of force, one must carefully differentiate between lawful resistance and lawless uprising.

Schaeffer wanted to preserve or restore the ideal United States of America as originally established. He saw the rise of humanism as a chief cause of this country's loss of state's rights. Humanists, he wrote, don't have a god so they put the state at the center.

In a chapter titled "The Use of Force," Schaeffer advocated that Christians actively picket, protest, and take political action necessary against clinics and hospitals that perform abortions. He also reaffirmed the principle that under certain conditions Christians must disobey the state.

Schaeffer interestingly acknowledged the difference between the Old Testament theocracy that God formed in Israel and the relationship of the New Testament church to the state. He warned against confusing the kingdom of God with the United States. But then he reasserted his frequent theme: this country was founded upon a Christian consensus. Therefore, it's necessary to operate this country by Judeo-Christian law and principles.

Schaeffer worried that the state would become too powerful and that God's primacy would be usurped. Government might supplant God, he fretted. As to Christianity's potential influence, Schaeffer pointed to the effects of early Christian revivals on the formation of this country — to a great extent revivalists sowed the seeds of the American Revolution.

Living by the scripture, Schaeffer taught, requires practicing alternatives that the scriptures command. At times, however, he made no distinction between Old Testament commands to Israel and New Testament principles of Jesus. Schaeffer quoted Romans 13 and 1 Peter 2:13-17, but his writings seemed void of any New Testament examples of church-state practice.[10]

His desire to minister to the whole person, I think, skewed his perspective of the Christian life. Ideally, all people should enjoy the arts. But Jesus emphasized seeking his kingdom first. Paul certainly observed and possibly admired the art on display in Athens when he visited there. But Paul had a singular purpose — preaching about Jesus (Acts 17:16-34). Later I'll cover how we are to deal with the secular society and the loss of certain freedoms.

Richard J. Foster

Richard J. Foster gained renown as a Quaker author and the founder of Renovaré "an infra-church movement dedicated to the renewal of the church in all her multifaceted expressions." Possibly you ask, "Why another Quaker?" Foster represents a later generation, and he deals specifically with individuals in this current age. Foster writes insightfully and humbly.

I've read two of his books: *Celebration of Discipline* and *Money, Sex & Power*, and often recommend both works to folks I counsel. "Christians need a fresh articulation of what it means to live faithfully in these areas," he wrote at the beginning of *Money, Sex & Power*.[11]

A few pages later, Foster noted the social implications of these subjects on business, government, and marriage. He reasoned that each of those three institutions inheres destructive forces that must be transformed by God's power for the benefit of human society. Foster praised the Puritans' efforts to use the state's authority to bring moral fiber to public life. But he noted, too, that some Puritan efforts went awry as in the Salem, Massachusetts, witch trials. He referred to that as "Church-power gone sour."[12]

In the section titled "Power," Foster advised his readers on practical matters of control, influence, and clout. For one, he encouraged Christians to face up to our heart-gripping prestige and pride. However, he seemed to shift from confronting the evil powers and temptations that we find in our own hearts to confronting evil in the hearts of school board members that make decisions detrimental to children. In the same fashion, one must, he said, also confront those responsible for unjust laws and corrupt corporate structure.

Foster admitted the difficulty of proper discernment. He cited how Hitler first proposed a platform that would improve education, enhance health standards, and encourage faith in "positive Christianity." Some ministers like Martin Niemöller recognized the Nazi perversion, others didn't.

When Foster wrote of militarism, it's almost as if he borrowed the language of his Quaker peers without circumspection. The insightfulness he brought to other subjects seemed absent when he assayed that the divine plan for "military power is to restrain chaos."[13] Now, he thinks military power primarily tries to destabilize the world. "Terrorism and spy networks are the order of the day."[14]

Foster apparently forgot the tactics of the twelve spies that Moses ordered into Canaan, the spies Joshua sent to Jericho, or how the left-handed Ehud secreted a long knife into King Eglon's palace in Moab and stabbed the overweight monarch. Ehud sank his knife to the hilt — in fact, so far that he had to leave it in the dying king's obese belly. Did Foster forget the tactics used by the Jewish Zealots and other opponents of Rome in Jesus' day and the decades prior to the destruction of Jerusalem?

After Paul's third missionary journey, the Roman commander who arrested him speculated about Paul's identity. He asked the apostle, "Aren't you the Egyptian who started a revolt and led four thousand terrorists out into the desert some time ago?" (Acts 21:38). Some translations render terrorists as "assassins" in Acts 21:17. Of the Greek word *sikarioi*, F. F. Bruce wrote that it's a loan-word from Latin.

The sicarii ... "dagger-men" (from Latin sica, *"dagger"), made their appearance (circa 55 A.D.) ... as bitter enemies of the Romans and pro-Roman Jews. They mingled with crowds ... with daggers hidden beneath their cloaks, and stabbed their opponents by stealth.*[15]

Spy networks, brutal war, and terrorism are as old as nations. Foster contended that it's the responsibility of Christians, especially those who live in democracies, to hold states accountable for justice. He recommended praising the state when it does a good job in that area and confronting it when it doesn't. He quoted an old Quaker adage, "speak truth to the power."

Commendation and strong support should be given governments when they provide true justice, he suggested. When the state fails, however, Foster thought it incumbent on Christians to bring prayer, fasting, lamentation, and mourning to the table. That's not all. He also advocated nonviolent confrontation, vigorous protest, and even civil disobedience. Foster insisted, though, that one must do these things with perfect love. The objective, he said, "is to make the evil visible and to prick the social conscience of the people."[16]

Foster thinks it possible to positively affect the state this way. First, Christians become employees of the state. Second, those believers exert influence. He warned, however, about the inherent dangers of this approach.

The idea of complimenting the state when it does a good job sounds noble. But here's the problem: Christians can't always effectively evaluate the state's performance. The worth or value of programs may not be known for decades. And I've not yet found a person who loves perfectly. Measuring the heart and motivations of a politician, a preacher, or anyone, for that matter, involves more risk than predicting the behavior of a rabid skunk.

Many people commended Lyndon Johnson's efforts to build the Great Society. Grant that he and Congress acted with good intentions (that's a huge allowance), the money and energy hardly produced the advertised result. One doesn't necessarily help another person by giving him/her things. In many cases, it produces

177

laziness and an expectation for more. Human beings can't accurately judge the hearts of their fellows. What seems right at one moment in history often proves a bane in the next.

Here's the important question: Did Jesus commission his followers to change society? Or did he assign them another task? This question eluded Francis Schaeffer. Richard Foster never answered it. Neither did Martin Luther King nor his followers. Elton Trueblood seemed not to consider the question.

Billy Graham

Billy Graham stood unrivaled as the preeminent religious force in the United States during the latter half of the twentieth century. He likely preached to more people in his lifetime than populated the planet contemporary to Jesus' incarnation. Graham led thousands of people to belief in Jesus. He befriended numerous US presidents, advised them, and prayed with them.

Graham emphasized personal faith in Jesus. He encouraged believers to help the poor and to be concerned about the state of the planet. He lived an exemplary life free from the scandals that ruined the ministries of numerous gifted evangelists. Graham relied on the Bible as the central authority for faith and practice for Christians.

I wasn't sure of Graham's Christian-government position. It wasn't evident to me in other works that I read about him or works by him. However, in his book, *Approaching Hoofbeats*, he outlined his suggestions for world leaders in respect to weapons of mass destruction including nuclear arms. His stated aim was to save the "sacred gift of life from nuclear catastrophe."[17]

Graham's recommendations included calling world leaders to repentance, asking them to commit to peace and justice, taking specific action toward peace, calling all people to prayer, and rededication to being peacemakers. He also advocated the destruction of all nuclear weapons.

Approaching Hoofbeats contains Graham's interpretation of the so-called "four horsemen of the Apocalypse" found in Revelation 6. In referring to the black horse, that most commentators agree signifies famine, Graham understood the Bible to warn that there will be increasing suffering and inequities. In Graham's words, "The Scriptures teach that famine and pestilence will continue and intensify until Christ comes back...."[18]

In support of his thesis that certain types of suffering indicate or precede the end-time, Graham along with many teachers linked Revelation 6 with Jesus' words.

> *You will hear of wars and rumors of wars, but see to it that you are not alarmed. Such things must happen, but the end is still to come. Nation will rise against nation, and kingdom against kingdom. There will be famines and earthquakes in various places. All these are the beginning of birth pains.* — Matthew 24:6-8

Graham and his fellows seemed to bypass what Jesus said in verse 6, "See to it that you are not alarmed. Such things must happen, but the end is still to come."

For many years, I taught a bimonthly Bible class at St. Anne's Home in Los Angeles. St. Anne's provided superb care for young unwed mothers. At the time, the home could accommodate about seventy girls. During the fifteen or so years that I taught there, I talked with hundreds of young women. At almost every session, one or more young ladies would say that they'd had labor pains, been taken to the hospital, and then were sent back to the home after being informed by the doctors that they still had several days, if not weeks, to go. The "beginning of birth pains" doesn't always mean that giving birth is imminent.

In the same way, history is replete with wars, famines, and earthquakes. No generation has completely avoided all three. But in every age, as soon as the frequency of war, earthquakes, and famines appear to increase, so does the number of gloom-predictors. Christian "prophets" always stand ready to predict that "it's time for the hospital."

What Jesus taught in Matthew 24, and what Revelation teaches, is that Christians of every age will face trials. We need to be prepared for them and at the same time remain faithful to Jesus and not be alarmed. Earthquakes, famines, and war occur aplenty in every era.

179

Graham told of making a motion picture with Sargent Shriver, who, during John Kennedy's administration, headed the United States poverty program. Addressing nearly 200 members of congress, Graham shared various scriptures with them. Among these were selections from Proverbs 14:21, "Blessed is he who is kind to the needy." Also Proverbs 29:7, "The righteous care about justice for the poor, but the wicked have no such concern." As far as I know Graham spoke boldly, forthrightly, and without political bias. Few ministers receive the honor of speaking to members of the United States Congress.

During the Eisenhower administration, Graham visited with John Foster Dulles at the former Secretary of State's home. Graham wished to describe to Dulles the poverty that he witnessed on a tour of developing countries. He strongly urged Dulles to influence the US to give surplus wheat to poor countries. In his book Graham noted the powerful teachings on the need to share with the deprived that James and John emphasized in their epistles.

Would it be a good thing if rich nations shared with the poorer ones? Yes, for the most part. Should the wealthy be urged toward generosity? This certainly seems to accord with what Paul instructed Timothy:

> *Command those who are rich in this present world not to be arrogant nor to put their hope in wealth, which is so uncertain, but to put their hope in God, who richly provides us with everything for our enjoyment. Command them to do good, to be rich in good deeds, and to be generous and willing to share. In this way they will lay up treasure for themselves as a firm foundation for the coming age, so that they may take hold of the life that is truly life.* — 1 Timothy 6:17-19

One problem with commanding the rich to contribute is that few persons are in a position to do that. Billy Graham could urge Secretary of State Dulles to use his governmental influence to create economic sharing. But Graham was in no position to "command" and probably wouldn't have if he could have.

The only reason that Paul expected that of Timothy is that Timothy was a young evangelist, a protégé of Paul whom the apostle had sent to Ephesus. Ephesus was a prominent city in what is now Turkey. The rich folks that Paul referred to were almost certainly Christians. According to the apostle, Timothy might command people, but his purview was restricted to his brothers and sisters in the Lord.

Most commentators agree that it is wealthy Christians Paul had in mind. Paul himself disapproved of passing judgment on non-Christians so it's hard to imagine him instructing Timothy to do that. We try to bring non-Christians to faith in Jesus by telling them his good news, but we have no authority over them. Later we'll discuss this in more detail.

In a chapter titled "The Black Horse," Mr. Graham insisted that all Christians are obligated to do everything possible to "feed, medicate, house and clothe the poor of the world."[19] Graham used Jesus' compassion for the poor as an example. He called on Christians of all occupations to do this. He then expressed the aspiration that the black horse's advent can be slowed by the generosity of Christians. A few paragraphs later, he voiced the same hope.[20] He believed the judgment of God can be delayed for a period of time.[21] In this interim (of withheld judgment) Graham urged Christians to work as "allies in the salvation of the lost and in social justice."[22]

The question remains: "How involved should Christians become in the battle for social justice?" Scores of social issues exist. Which ones does a conscientious Christian choose? During my four plus decades of ministry, I've watched helplessly as dozens of widows, widowers, and elderly couples have wasted monies on social cause scams and charlatan-operated charities.

It's also evident that Jesus helped the poor, the disenfranchised, and the needy. But he never swerved from his oft-stated main task — preaching the kingdom. He addressed problems as they came to him, yet created no specific social reform programs. The Jerusalem church cared for needy church widows and orphans (Acts 6, 7). But Paul later counseled against putting young widows on the roll because they tended to become lazy gossips. He advised them to marry. If widows had adult Christian children, those children were to care for their mothers.[23]

One also has to be careful with whom he allies himself. I spent many years working with a church in Hollywood, California. Outside promoters and sponsors asked us to be involved in many social causes. In one instance, churches of several denominations planned a joint effort to help the community's poor. The Hollywood-based Church of Scientology was asked to participate. They are not Christian. In fact, they are an anti-Christian cult with a power-and-control agenda. According to the guidelines set up for the cause, the Scientologists had to be included. We chose not to cooperate with that venture.

In 2 Corinthians 6:14-18, Paul warned about being "yoked together with unbelievers." Many commentators have seen this as a caution concerning marriage of believers and unbelievers, but Paul seemed to include relationships of any kind that compromise Christians. At the close of this book I plan to describe a sound biblical method for dealing with the poor and addressing other social causes.

1. Elton Trueblood, *Foundations for Reconstruction*, Revised Edition (New York: Harper and Row, 1946), p. 8.

2. *Ibid*, p. 30.

3. This theme has been carried on by Jesse Jackson, Al Sharpton, and other black leaders into the twenty-first century.

4. Francis A. Schaeffer, *A Christian Manifesto* (Westchester, Illinois: Crossway Books, 1981), p. 18.

5. *Ibid*, p. 32.

6. *Ibid*, p. 48.

7. There's no question that government is subject to God's Law. Here's the issue: "Whose job is it to hold the government responsible?" I think that the Lord will eventually take care of the matter.

8. John Calvin may have taught this, but in his Geneva experiment, he combined church and state. He was the civil authority.

9. I regard this as a flimsy and inappropriate example. The only reason David didn't use force against Saul was that he regarded Saul as the duly anointed king of Israel. He refused to do harm to the Lord's anointed. See 1 Samuel 24:5-7. David had no qualms about killing Nabal, who had offended him (cf 1 Samuel 25).

10. Most notable is Acts 4:1-31. The apostles were commanded to desist their preaching about Jesus. They didn't protest or begin legal action against the state. They simply kept preaching.

11. Richard J. Foster, *Money, Sex, and Power* (San Francisco: Harper & Row Publishers, 1985), p. 2.

12. *Ibid*, see footnote on p. 11.

13. *Ibid*, p. 188.

14. *Ibid*, p. 188.

15. F. F. Bruce, editor, "Commentary on the Book of Acts," *The New International Commentary on the New Testament* (Grand Rapids, Michigan: Wm. B Eerdmans Publishing Company, 1964), p. 437, footnotes.

16. *Op cit*, Foster, p. 226.

17. Billy Graham, *Approaching Hoofbeats* (Waco: Word Books, 1983), p. 142.

18. *Ibid*, p. 153.

19. *Ibid*, p. 177.

20. *Ibid*, p. 178.

21. *Ibid*, p. 216. It's at this point that Graham's interpretive view of the end-time comes into place. For one, Graham referred to the conversation between the Lord and Abraham concerning the fate of Sodom (Genesis 18). Sodom was corrupt and the Lord intended to destroy it. Abraham, knowing that his nephew lived there, hoped to save the city from destruction. He began bargaining with the Lord, "What if there are fifty righteous people in the city? Will you really sweep it away and not spare the place for the sake of the fifty righteous

people in it?" The Lord told Abraham that if he could find fifty righteous people there he would save it.

Then Abraham began reducing the numbers, as any good haggler might, from fifty to ten. The Lord promised that he would spare the city if ten righteous people were presently in residence. Graham neglects an incontrovertible fact. The Lord knew from the beginning of the bargaining session that there weren't ten people there. If there were, he wouldn't have planned to destroy Sodom. The process demonstrated God's righteous judgment and sovereign will to Abraham. It said nothing of God's willingness to defer judgment. He did defer Nineveh's judgment, but that's because he sent Jonah there to give them a chance to repent and the Ninevites heeded the warning.

I think that Graham and many other interpreters fail to interpret Matthew 24 correctly. They err in not seeing that Jesus answered at least two and possibly three different questions that the disciples asked about Jesus' comments concerning the destruction of temple in Jerusalem. Jesus told the apostles that not one stone would be left on top of another. The apostles then asked the following questions: 1) When will this (that is the destruction of Jerusalem) happen? 2) What will be the sign of your coming? and 3) What will be the sign of the end of the age?

It's important in Jesus' discourse to separate those events that refer to Jerusalem's destruction (that occurred in 70 A.D.) from the end-of-the-age questions. If we see that verses 15-25 refer to the Jerusalem's destruction in 70 A.D., it helps avoid many of the interpretive problems that ensue as a result of thinking that all the circumstances Jesus described refer to the end-time. As an example, Graham sees vv. 21, 22 referring to events preceding Armageddon where he says history will "bottom out." He does not see them as applying to Jerusalem's 70 A.D. destruction.

22. *Ibid*, p. 216.

23. See 1 Timothy 5 for these and other instructions concerning widows and their care.

10

Will We Ever Get It Right?
Where We Are
In The Twenty-First Century

You have been chosen by God Himself, you are priests
of the King, you are holy and pure, you are God's very
own — and this that you may show to others how God
called you out of darkness into His wonderful light.
— 1 Peter 2:9 (TLB)

As I write this, we stand at an early point in the twenty-first century. Not only are there countless pots of theological paint, colors are splashed, flung, and slopped everywhere. Each generation variegates the patterns more. The spectrum shows more shades than a mutant kaleidoscope.

Several religious groups actively advocate their church-state beliefs. Mennonites, Amish, Quakers, Church of the Brethren, and Roman Catholics publicly promote their positions. So do the boards of many mainline protestant denominations. Views abound; we'll summarize them. Though most represent themselves as teaching according to Jesus, many lose sight of what Jesus and his disciples practiced.

Two outspoken, media-oriented religious teachers grab headlines and microphones in this first decade — Tim LaHaye and Pat Robertson. Most know LaHaye as a cowriter of a series on the rapture. He has written or coauthored about thirty books that have sold millions of copies. LaHaye serves as president of Family Life Ministries and his wife, Beverly, founded Concerned Women for America.

LaHaye currently specializes in writing about Armageddon and the end-times. At one time, he wrote prolifically about how Christians should try to effect change in American culture. He dedicated a 1986 book, *The Race for the 21st Century* to Francis Schaeffer.

In that work, LaHaye referred to the old axiom, "Politics is a dirty business." Many ministers and church leaders used to excuse themselves from political involvement, he said, because politics isn't clean.

LaHaye regarded that as a false teaching. He condemned church leaders who choose to spend their lives trying to advance God's kingdom and who leave politics to "nice, civic minded people."[1] While decrying those who take that approach, he stated that as a result (in 1986) the people in government aren't nice and aren't civic (he didn't name any names). Our once Judeo-Christian nation with the motto, "one nation under God" is now, LaHaye observed, a libertine, "secular nation."

I wonder when "nice" and "civic" people ever dominated government. Politics is "the conduct of affairs for private advantage."[2] The well-known cynic, Ambrose Bierce, wrote that about ninety years ago. Mark Twain showed politicians even less charity: "Public servants: Persons chosen by the people to distribute the graft."[3]

Anyone concluding that the American government should maintain neutrality toward religion, LaHaye assumed, is deceived by secular humanists, namely the American Civil Liberties Union. LaHaye faulted former president, Jimmy Carter, for much of the current American moral malaise. In his opinion, Carter deceived Christian leaders. "He (Carter) campaigned as a Christian conservative, but ran his administration as a Christian liberal."[4] Carter taught Sunday school and met with conservative religious leaders, but he often nominated liberals to the court. The then president wouldn't halt anti-abortion legislation, LaHaye lamented, or abortions that were government-funded. Carter disliked the School Prayer Amendment.

LaHaye described a White House meeting that he and other conservative leaders attended. Carter invited them so they could ask about administration policies that troubled them. The president insisted that written (nothing impromptu) questions be submitted in advance. Dr. Jerry Falwell queried Carter about the abortion amendment; why did the president oppose it? D. James Kennedy asked Carter to explain why, in view of the Communists' build-up of their military, he wasn't strong on national defense.

186

Considering the Equal Rights Amendment's potential bad effects on families, LaHaye wanted to know the reason Carter favored it. Carter gave inadequate answers and seemed not to enjoy the meeting, reported LaHaye. A minister from Dallas asked the president why his cabinet lacked any known Christians. Reportedly clearing his throat in discomfort, Carter responded by declaring the appraisal unfair. Vice-president Walter Mondale's father was a minister, and he attested that the vice-president was very religious. Carter also mentioned his public relations person, Ann Wexler, and his wife, Rosalind.

The answer further dismayed the conservative group. LaHaye described Mondale as a humanist. Wexler was purportedly Jewish. As he waited for the car that transported the ministers home, LaHaye said that he prayed that God would remove Carter from office in the next election. LaHaye remembered that the meeting depressed him and left the other ministers melancholy. LaHaye told of preaching the message about Carter's politics in three separate churches and distributing copies of those tapes to numerous ministers. LaHaye and his fellows felt that they reawakened the Christian church as to how important politics are to restoring traditional values.

In a 1987 work titled *Faith of Our Founding Fathers*, LaHaye remained gloomy over the state of this country. He related results of a research project conducted by a New York University psychology professor. The educator examined sixty popular textbooks used in this country's elementary schools. The professor reportedly found the Christian religion virtually absent from them. Though the books included references to Amish, Catholics, Jews, and Mormons, they contained almost nothing about evangelical Protestants and the contributions they made to building America.

LaHaye related the case of an Ohio public school teacher, who for fifteen years practiced giving a Bible to every student in her class. She evidently got permission of the parents, went to the students' homes on Saturdays and Sundays, and offered the Bibles with no conditions. No parent registered a complaint. Nonetheless, the school superintendent urged the school board to stop the teacher because the practice violated principles of church-state relations.

187

The above examples typify how LaHaye bolstered his contentions: Christians receive unfair treatment, and humanists are taking over American society. He urged Christians to do something about waning religious freedoms, because Christians might lose them. After all, the United States Constitution guarantees religious freedom.

Court decisions unfavorable to Christianity, LaHaye noted, happen at a time when humanism's anti-moral philosophy deleteriously affects children in this country. The result: rampant sexual permissiveness, venereal disease, unwanted pregnancies among teens, and high youth suicide rates.

"Whom do you blame?"[5] asked LaHaye. He wrote that you can't hold churches accountable for the problem; they adequately warn kids concerning the consequences. Don't blame parents either, insisted LaHaye. Permissiveness, venereal disease, and unwanted pregnancies result from humanism's increasing control of our educational system over the past several decades.

Let me share some details of a chat that I heard recently. I went to visit a neighbor in the hospital. A mutual friend was there when I walked into the room. The conversation led to their boyhood days. They attended the same rural school in northwest Iowa and graduated two years apart in the mid-1930s. They spoke of the class between theirs. To the best of my recollection, it was the 1935 graduates.

That group of students gained notoriety, my friends said, after several girls in that small class got pregnant prior to graduation. They lived in a devoutly religious community where few people ever heard about humanism. I wonder whom LaHaye would have blamed for that local outbreak of rural, mid-continent, 1930s depravity.

King David of Israel got Bathsheba pregnant and ordered her husband killed to cover up the infidelity. David knew nothing of humanism or situational ethics. He saw a desirable woman and let his sensuous nature take control. He didn't think about his obligation to her, her husband, or his country, let alone God.

Are churches partly responsible for the current problem? Yes. The emphases some church leaders place on certain issues leave openings for temptation. When I was younger some of my contemporaries told me that they preferred to date girls who went to certain conservative, Bible-believing churches. My friends knew that the girls in those denominations received considerable parental and church instruction about not using makeup and lipstick, but no one cautioned those girls about keeping their clothes on in the backseats of young men's cars.

It's evident to me that many Christian parents share the blame. Some parents give their kids too many opportunities; the parents don't stay home enough to see what their children are doing. Other parents avoid talking about moral responsibility with their children. In numerous cases, the children get excessive allowances and too many liberties.

Am I refuting the fact that humanistic ideas infiltrate our educational system? Hardly. But to blame the humanists for it all is not realistic. I have counseled hundreds of people who faced conflict with others. In those disputes, only rarely was one party free from guilt. In the same way, it's also unfair and unrealistic to fault the humanists for all of society's ills.

In a chapter called "Who Fathered America?" LaHaye made no claim that America was founded as a Christian nation though some of the original colonies had established churches. He used an expression employed by Francis Schaeffer — America began with a "Christian consensus." That part can be verified according to LaHaye. In 1770, the great British leader and orator, Edmund Burke, spoke the following to Parliament about the American colonists:

> *The people are Protestants; and of that kind which is the most adverse to all implicit submission of mind and opinion ... This is a persuasion not only favorable to Liberty, but built upon it ... All Protestantism, even the most cold and passive, is a sort of dissent. But the religion most prevalent in our northern colonies is a refinement on the principle of resistance; it is the dissidence of dissent, and the protestantism of the Protestant religion.*[6]

Considerable evidence supports the theory that the founders of this country didn't intend to form a Christian nation, contended LaHaye. Still, Christianity dominated the culture, he said. The schools welcomed Christianity, and education centered on a godly base. Morality was established on Judeo-Christian ethics.

In his 1987 book, LaHaye urged Christians to:

- pray for social, moral, and spiritual revival, and pray that the country will in future elections elect God-fearing presidents;
- vote and to remind fellow Christians to vote also; and
- be politically active.

He saw the near future as decisive for the twenty-first century. According to LaHaye, the founding fathers did a good job. It is up to contemporary Christians to retain what the fathers built.

LaHaye implored Christians to be politically active. In answer to the question, "Is it scriptural?"[7] he quoted a well known, but unnamed Christian leader who expressed disapproval of politically active ministers. That leader referred to Jesus' example — Jesus never taught his disciples to resist or to overthrow the Roman government. LaHaye gave what he termed "an extended answer." First he noted that in Matthew 5, Jesus taught his followers to be "the salt of the earth" and "the light of the world." He opined that Christians were good lights, but poor salt.

LaHaye then drew conclusions based on a Gallup poll showing the threefold increase in Christian population during the prior fifty years (presumably from 1936-1986). But LaHaye contended the American culture was morally worse than when it had fewer Christians. He reasoned that it's because Christians withdrew from government, an institution that God established. Secularists took over from the Christians and now control it.

According to the poll LaHaye quoted, only ten to fifteen percent of elected officials were committed Christians, but Christians comprised four out of ten persons in this country. From that, LaHaye reckoned Christians under-represented. LaHaye then made a long leap, "Yet three times in Romans 13:1-6," he wrote, "God calls government authorities 'ministers of God ... for good' " (KJV).

Resembling an ice dancer bounding from one chunk of thin ice to another, Tim LaHaye jumped from one deduction to another. Here's what I mean. He conveniently based his argument on the term "minister" that the King James translators used in Romans 13:6. But minister simply means servant. It's translated "servant" in the NIV and the New American Standard Version. In other words, Paul simply meant that rulers are servants of God.

In the paragraph following his quotation from Romans 13:6, LaHaye leapt to the question of whether it's biblical for "pastors" (ministers) to challenge their parishioners to "fulfill God's description of our leaders." He thought so.

Then LaHaye turned for "support" to the Old Testament. He contended that the Old Testament called numerous governmental leaders "ministers of God." His list included Moses, Samuel, Solomon, Daniel, and Isaiah (Did the prophet Isaiah ever hold a governmental position?).[8]

My investigation of the word "minister" in the KJV showed Samuel ministering in the temple as a youth (1 Samuel 3:10), but none of the other Old Testament persons LaHaye listed was called a "minister." The Old Testament word consistently means to serve. It applied mostly to the priests who worked in the tabernacle and temple.

David's officials selected the young lady Abishag to sleep with the aged king. They appointed her not for sex, but to serve as a heating blanket. The KJV reads that she "ministered" to him (1 Kings 1:1-4). I failed to find the term "minister" applied to Moses, David, Solomon, or Daniel. That makes LaHaye's evidence shakier than cold, old King David. Nonetheless, LaHaye asserted that it's unscriptural for folks to say that Christians shouldn't be involved in government.

LaHaye also thinks that pastors should identify and flag political leaders who don't adequately carry out their responsibility as "ministers of God for good." Christians should call to account judges who rule in favor of abortion, he said, and who are soft on pornographers and criminals. He used Ephesians 5:10-14 as a basis for this action. This passage teaches us, according to him, that God wants us to "expose the unfruitful workers of darkness."

191

LaHaye made a curious switch in his quotation. I consulted the King James Version, the New King James Version, the New Revised Standard Version, the New International Version, and the original. None reads the "unfruitful 'workers' of darkness." Most refer to " 'works' of darkness"; the NIV reads "fruitless deeds of darkness."

Here's how this passage reads in the New Revised Standard Version:

> *Try to find out what is pleasing to the Lord. Take no part in the unfruitful works of darkness, but instead expose them. For it is shameful even to mention what such people do secretly; but everything exposed by the light becomes visible, for everything that becomes visible is light. Therefore it says, "Sleeper, awake! Rise from the dead, and Christ will shine on you."*
> — Ephesians 5:10-14

I can find no serious commentator who thinks that this passage relates to anything except what goes on among Christians and within the church. In fact, Paul wrote in 1 Corinthians 5:12 that it is not our business to "judge those outside the church." In verse 13, Paul wrote that "God will judge those outside."

Still, LaHaye concluded the better we apply salt to our society (he meant involvement in politics), the more effectively we become shining lights for the good of our country's lost souls. I find the opposite to be true and will discuss this at more length, later.

If LaHaye serves as a conservative Christian spokesperson in the print media, his friend, Pat Robertson, leads in the television medium. His daily program airs weekday mornings on the local NBC affiliate opposite popular shows on the other networks. Robertson also authored several books. In the Prologue to his recently published *The Ten Offenses*, he wrote, "those who founded the United States consciously intended America to be a Christian nation, guided ... by truths of the Bible."[9]

This nation's formers operated on principles found in the Ten Commandments and Jesus' Sermon on the Mount, Robertson continued. Revisionist historians try to obscure the truths about history, he wrote, but there's too much documentation to suppress it. Adequate evidence exists, he said. Starting in 1607 when English-speaking settlers planted a cross on a (now Virginia) beach, it continued through days subsequent to World War II. Two fundamental things worked in that period, Robertson contends. First, we were one nation under God — the God of the Bible — who really exists. Second, the Bible was the ultimate authority for our lives and nation.

Robertson pointed to his Baptist background (LaHaye is a Baptist, also), and the fact that his father was a US senator from Virginia. Robertson's father told him of Virginia Baptist ancestors who were beaten, jailed, and fined by representatives of the established Anglican Church. Virginia Baptists also suffered whipping and jailing for preaching the gospel, said Robertson.

At the urging of Baptists, Robertson says, James Madison presented Thomas Jefferson's "Statute for Religious Freedom" to Virginia's legislature. Robertson boasted that he and his father well understood James Madison's thinking when he authored the First Amendment to the United States Constitution, which forbids an "establishment of religion." Robertson mentioned the religious tyranny (established religion) that Thomas Jefferson, James Madison, and his Virginia ancestors experienced. None liked it.

Robertson distinguished between established churches and belief in God. The founders considered belief in God and the Bible as vital. But Jefferson, Washington, and Madison never linked belief in God and the scriptures with the establishment of religion. The above founding fathers considered belief in God and established religion as two separate issues.

Robertson expressed shock that the Supreme Court of the United States disallowed reading the Ten Commandments in public schools as it did in 1980. He deplored the fact that 23 years later, a judge of a US district court ordered the removal of a monument containing an inscription of the Ten Commandments from the Alabama Supreme Court building rotunda.

Most American people support prayer in schools, opinion polls show and, Robertson wrote, they also want retention of the phrase, "One nation under God" in the pledge of allegiance. Too, they favor displaying the Ten Commandments in public places. Robertson thinks that there is an agenda on the part of people in the arts, the media, law, psychology, medicine, and education to obliterate biblical morality and God from this country. As a group, they object to any moral absolutes.

According to Robertson, God gave the Ten Commandments to this country to bless it, and Americans must return to their sacred roots. He urged America to stand strong for its foundational principles. James Madison studied theology at Princeton[10] under John Witherspoon, Robertson noted, and joined George Mason in drafting ten amendments to the US Constitution. They meant those amendments (the Bill of Rights) to resemble the Ten Commandments. The First Amendment reads: "Congress shall make no law respecting an establishment of religion or prohibiting the free exercise thereof...." As Robertson pointed out, when the Constitution's authors wrote the famous First Amendment they wanted to restrict congress, not states, individuals, or groups.

In a section titled "Stripping the Nation of Faith," Robertson traced Supreme Court rulings that eroded Christian and biblical influence from society. It's presently being done, he said, by a group of "liberal elites — the academics, the think tanks, the press, the big foundations, and, of course, the judges."[11] They want to replace faith with secular humanism. At the same time, they protect folks with lifestyles and actions considered illegal and immoral by the majority of Americans. The strife over Supreme Court nominees stands as major evidence of the opposing agendas.

Have Tim LaHaye and Pat Robertson correctly assessed what is taking place in American society? In many ways, they have, I suppose. Was this country founded as a Christian nation? LaHaye and Robertson don't agree on that point. LaHaye says, "No," Robertson, "Yes." Both deplore the negative effects on Christian religious expression in this country.

The approaches of both LaHaye and Robertson create their own questionable results. Their argumentation and disputations stir Christians to anger and agitation. However disappointed and indignant we might be about the country's morals, I doubt whether the Lord wants us riled and infuriated.

Was this country founded as a Christian nation? Who can really say what motivated all the signers of the Declaration of Independence and the writers of the Constitution. Some presume to know the founders' intentions. Whether God considers this a Christian nation, no one can assume. Christians need to ask themselves this pressing question: "Did the Lord assign Christians the task of nation building or kingdom building?" There's a vast difference as we'll see in the closing chapters.

The challenge remains: What should be done about evident trends toward irreligion and immorality? Before we treat that we need to look at a few other influential voices in American society.

Mennonites

Though Conrad Grebel, in 1525, founded the Mennonites, they took their name from Menno Simons. In many parts of Europe, early Mennonites suffered persecution. At first called Swiss Brethren, the sect arose from the Anabaptists in Zurich.

The Mennonite sect became notable for several things. They rejected the authority of the state church and seceded from it; they practiced adult baptism only. Founder Grebel was the first adult to be baptized. Today the million-plus Mennonites reside in sixty countries.

Mennonites presumably accept the Bible as their rule of faith but over the years have used a succession of explanatory confessions of faith. The first permanent Mennonite settlement (1863) took place in the Americas in Germantown, Pennsylvania, although many Mennonites came here more than 200 years earlier. In 1688, that initial group of 35 people made the first formal American protest against slavery. For the most part, Mennonites remain a closed community. They educate their own children and form their own schools and colleges.

Early Anabaptists met to draw up a confession of faith known as the Schleitheim Confessions (1527). This united the various groups on seven points. Two of the seven need our attention. Number six, known as "The Sword," became the basis for Anabaptist pacifism and for their rejection of governmental office holding. Number seven forbade taking oaths. Mennonites later united behind a second comprehensive declaration known as the Dordrecht Confession of Faith. Other confessions and statements of faith have ensued.

Mennonites adamantly support the separation of church and state. Starting in 1925, the group held world conferences to organize congregations, but many of the conservative Mennonite groups don't participate. Mennonites began mission work in 1847 and have been active in relief work during war and peace. They do little proselytizing. According to their website, they spread their beliefs through their relief work, their dedication to peace, and commitment to social justice.

During the French and Indian Wars (1689-1763), Indians retaliated by killing many Mennonites. Mennonites refused to use force when Indians attacked them. They responded by giving the Indians food, grain, and hay. Mennonites joined with Quakers in "friendly association" with Indians. They purchased land from the Indians by negotiating with them.

Before 1777, Mennonites received exemption from militia fines and duty. That changed because of the need for more militia participation. Also the government wanted to create revenue in order to finance the war. Mennonites faced a difficult decision; either hire a militia substitute or support the war by non-military means. Later, the government forced Mennonites to pay special war taxes.

Congress enacted the first American military draft during the Civil War (1863). Under the law, a man could pay a $300 commutation fee or hire a substitute. Many Mennonites paid fines or hired substitutes. A few conscientious Mennonites refused to hire someone to do what they would not do. Congress revoked the privilege of hiring substitutes in 1864, but Conscientious Objectors (COs) could:

- accept assignments to hospital duty in order to care for sick and wounded soldiers;
- care for freedmen; and
- pay a fee that would benefit wounded and sick soldiers.

Numerous Mennonite men simply joined the military service or acceded to the draft.

World War I brought new challenges for Mennonites. The principle foe in the war was Germany, homeland of most Mennonites. This forced many German-speaking Mennonites to switch their language to English and caused others to change their allegiance from Germany to the United States.

Second, the US government didn't provide for alternative service. The 1917 Selective Service Act made it possible for COs to serve in non-combatant capacity. Mennonites along with other pacifists objected to this provision. They wanted liberty to give humanitarian and medical aid to the enemy.

The government drafted a few thousand Mennonites. Several hundred migrated to Canada. Many obtained relief through the Farm Furlough Bill. It allowed Mennonites to work on farms in lieu of military service. About ten percent declined military service, suffered court martial, and were jailed. A few Mennonites underwent persecution because of their stances, and small numbers of church buildings were burned. After the war, the Mennonites re-energized their relief work and helped needy people on a worldwide basis.

As war developed in 1930s Europe, "Historic Peace Churches" (Brethren in Christ, Mennonites, and Quakers) convened so that they could present a unified strategy to President Franklin Roosevelt. They foresaw the United States eventually joining the war, and they wanted the government to understand their peace position.

Congress passed the Selective Service and Training Act in 1940. It provided that those who opposed the war because of religious beliefs could be detailed "to work of national importance under civilian direction." Local draft boards decided which persons were truly COs.

Churches joined with the government in negotiating alternate services. They formulated a program known as "Civilian Public Service" (CPS) in early 1941. By their request, the Historic Peace Churches funded and operated the plan. CPS workers became involved in several fields including agriculture, forestry, mental health, public health, and soil conservation. Mennonites expressed their faith and compassion through their participation. More than 8,500 Mennonite men and women served either in CPS or as military non-combatants.

197

Mennonites recognize their conflicting views with society over the issue of pacifism. It came to the fore during the Vietnam War, and they acknowledge it as a continuing question. They appear committed to aiding both sides in war with money, food, and relief work.[12]

Amish

The Amish also arose from Anabaptist roots. They derive their name from Jacob Amman, a Swiss bishop who broke away from the Mennonite movement in 1693. The Amish share many beliefs with the Mennonites, such as basic Bible doctrines, adult baptism, and non-resistance. Most of their differences with Mennonites center around such matters as attire, form of worship, Bible interpretation, language, and technology.

Church Of The Brethren

From Anabaptist roots also, the Church of the Brethren fellowship formed when a group considered the established churches too rich, corrupt, and powerful. In their view, those churches neglected to proclaim the simple New Testament message. The new group sought to form a church similar to the New Testament church. Alexander Mack and some Pietists (those who emphasize holy living) led the movement in the early years of 1700. Many of them migrated to the United States in 1720.

Church of the Brethren members accept basic Christian doctrines, and they practice numerous rites "neglected" by other Christian groups. These consist of: Commitment to peace and reconciliation, an emphasis on simple living, an opposition to taking oaths, the maintenance of a strong and wholesome family life, service to neighbors, and the practice of outward symbols taught in the New Testament including foot-washing and the sisters' veiling.[13]

On the basis of Matthew 5:44-45 and 26:52, Church of the Brethren members believe it unscriptural for Christians to participate in war. They share this belief with Quakers, Amish, and Mennonites.

Some Church of the Brethren members join Quakers and Mennonites to form Christian Peacemaker Teams (CPT). According to

198

an April 16, 2004, Church of the Brethren newsletter, two members of one team were in Iraq, March 2003, when bombs began falling on Baghdad. They still resided there one year later. During the period October 2002, until March 2004, they spent several months in Iraq.

A CPT team left Iraq on the advice of Iraqi colleagues in April 2004. "The extremely aggressive actions of the US and Coalition forces throughout Iraq and especially in Fallujah have created widespread suspicion and fear," a CPT release said. "This suspicion puts all internationals at risk."[14]

"We were there before the war with the hope that we could stop a war," one of the team members said.[15] He contended that the team's efforts along with massive anti-war demonstrations helped "delay the war" (they don't think that terrorism can be combated by any kind of violence). They regarded neither Iraqi nor coalition forces as the enemy.

The team contended that the coalition forces lost the war. According to CPT workers, only corporations whose business increased benefited from the war effort. CPT workers saw little hope in the situation in early 2004. They expected "more hell" in the area, but acknowledged that some "good things" happened. Those included the belief that God was raising up leaders with visions of a more peaceable society. They credited many Iraqis who disliked the occupation but resisted violence.

The long-term effects of war concerned the team. They cited the loss of United States credibility, the effects of war on troops, and consequences of weapons developed from depleted uranium. One member also worried that further violence would foster more Iraqi opposition.

In November 2005, four CPT workers were kidnapped and held hostage by a radical Moslem group in Iraq. An Associated Press release from Baghdad quoted a statement from The CPT organization. CPT blamed coalition forces for the kidnapping. "We are angry because of what has happened to our teammates is the result of actions of the US and UK government due to the illegal attack on Iraq and the continuing occupation and oppression of its people," the communiqué said. A spokeswoman refuted charges that CPT is a fundamentalist organization.

The next paragraph in the AP article illustrates CPT's goals: "We are very strict about this: we do not do any evangelism, we are not missionaries," Jessica Phillips told the Associated Press in Chicago. "Our interest is to bring an end to the violence and destruction of civilian life in Iraq." Phillips also stated that the group aims primarily to document "alleged human rights abuses by US forces."[16]

The above report points to two questions about CPT's mission. First, why wouldn't an ostensibly Christian organization try to teach people about Jesus? Second, why point out only the abuses of the US military. That appears to fix blame on one side.

The Quakers (Religious Society Of Friends) — American Friends Service Committee

Quakers founded the AFSC in 1917. They aimed to find opportunities for young Quakers and other conscientious objectors to perform services of love during wartime. Basic Quaker beliefs form the foundation of it:

- There is that of God in every man; and
- The power of love can take away the occasion for all wars.

Thousands of people from varying faiths and backgrounds work with and in the Committee, despite the Society's relatively small numbers. The Committee's major goal: work for the relief and rehabilitation of war victims. They started in 1917 by aiding refugees in France, feeding and caring for refugee children, rebuilding homes, and founding a maternity hospital. As World War I came to a close, service committee members worked to fight disease and famine in Russia, they established orphanages in Poland, and fed hungry children in Austria and Germany.

The AFSC formed small Quaker centers in many of the above countries and gave them the following tasks:

- After the relief workers went home, supporting the small groups of nationals interested in Quakerism.
- Supervising the turnover of projects to locals.

Work renewed just a few years later when refugees poured out of Germany because of Hitler's policies.

Subsequent to that, AFSC workers functioned in numerous times of war and emergency. Workers unselfishly acted in Asia, Europe, South America, and the Middle East. During the Biafran-Nigerian War, Quaker workers helped minister on both side of the battle.

Quakers take the position that most conflicts are rooted in injustice. Therefore they concentrate on trying to eliminate injustice at home — that is, in the United States. They assist American Indians, Mexican-Americans, migrant workers, prisoners, blacks, and the poor.

> *The AFSC's approach is to help these people find the tools with which to organize themselves for community action and thus obtain better schools, better housing, better working conditions they deserve.*[17]

AFSC representatives attempt to influence public opinion on war and peace issues. They also participate in vigils, demonstrations, and protests, with the aim of ending the military draft, arousing Americans concerning militarism's dangers and informing Americans of the "status of the military-industrial complex in the United States."[18] "Young people are drawn into the AFSC," says their website, "by their desire to make a positive witness against war and injustice."

One must admire the Mennonite-Quaker-Church of the Brethren consistency and their unselfish dedication to their belief. I question their understanding of the Great Commission. Mennonites and Quakers appear to neglect Jesus' orders in order to promote pacifism and their relief work. Had they simply preached the original message of Jesus, there might be more peace, and less relief work necessary. The question remains: Should Christians overtly attempt to influence governments?

Some might wonder why I've not included Mormons and Jehovah's Witnesses in this work. Both of those groups take unique positions respecting governmental relations; Jehovah's Witnesses refuse to take oaths, and will not salute the flag. Early Mormons formed standing armies and militia. I chose not to include them because neither group uses the gospel for the core of its message. Both probably qualify as cults.

---

1. Tim LaHaye, *The Race for the 21st Century* (Nashville: Thomas Nelson Publishers, 1986), p. 97.

2. Quoted by Wesley D. Camp, *Camp's Unfamiliar Quotations from 200 B.C to the Present* (Paramus, New Jersey: Prentice Hall, 1990), p. 254.

3. Herbert V. Prochnow and Herbert V. Prochnow, Jr, *The Toastmaster's Treasure Chest* (Edison, New Jersey: Castle Books, 1988), p. 348.

4. *Op cit*, LaHaye, p. 98.

5. Tim LaHaye, *Faith of Our Founding Fathers* (Brentwood, Tennessee: Wolgemuth & Hyatt, Publishers, Inc., 1987), p. 4.

6. *Ibid*, Edmund Burke's speech, "Conciliation With America," p. 67.

7. *Op cit*, LaHaye, *The Race for the 21st Century*, pp. 103-104.

8. Some Jewish traditions say that Isaiah was of noble birth, but there is no biblical substantiation for it.

9. Pat Robertson, *The Ten Offenses* (Nashville: Integrity Publishers, 2004), p. ix.

10. It was then called College of New Jersey; an anachronism that slipped by Robertson and his editors.

11. *Op cit*, Robertson, p. 23.

12. http://religiousmovements.lib.virginia.edu/nrms/mennonites.html

13. Harold S. Martin http://www.brfwitness.org/Articles/1968v3n2.htm

14. Quoted in the May 2005, issue of the *The Pulse*, newsletter of the United Church of Christ/Church of the Brethren newsletter, Kingsley, Iowa.

15. *Ibid.*

16. *Sioux City Journal*, Wednesday, November 30, 2005, Section C10. Three of the hostages were later released, but one was slain by the insurgent captors.

17. http://www.nobel.se/peace/laureates/1947/friends-committee-history.html

18. *Ibid.*

Part Three

Fixing The Mix

11

Answering Troublesome Questions: *An Overview Of Christians And Governments*

Jesus said, "If you hold to my teaching, you are really my disciples. Then you will know the truth, and the truth will set you free." — John 8:31-32

Years ago, one of the Hollywood Church of Christ deacons rode with me to a conference. He excitedly read from a recently purchased commentary on the book of Revelation. The deacon eagerly shared the author's promised answers to hard Revelation questions. He wanted to show me the author's "profound and scholarly" conclusions.

In the early chapters of the book the commentator pledged to answer those difficult issues. As my friend and brother progressed through the chapters, he read additional promises by the author. The deacon expressed growing consternation as he turned from chapter to chapter, front to back, hoping to find those answers. The author promised a lot. He never delivered. I, too, have made numerous promises. It's time to make good on them.

In this chapter, I will try to anticipate your concerns and answer the questions I raised earlier.

Why Is It Important To Use New Testament Examples And Models?

People commonly assume that knowing abstract truth brings freedom. Intellectual knowledge benefits one's mind, but it doesn't always lead to liberty. Some folks who can parse obscure verbs and do calculus in their heads serve peonage to pride. They pass SATs but can't figure out why they flunk interpersonal relationships.

Truth and freedom unequivocally connect with Jesus' teaching. Detached from it, we're lost, confused, and fettered. No wonder we face so many personal quandaries and crises. We're detached from our soul-supplier. If Jesus is the Son of God, the only one of his kind, then his is the sole authorized version of life-instruction. "If you hold to my teaching," he said, "you are really my disciples. Then you will know the truth, and the truth will set you free" (John 8:31-32).

Jesus gave simple, direct, potent instruction. New Testament churches and individuals that followed the Lord's teaching and stayed sensitive to his Spirit enjoyed compelling results (cf Acts 2:41; 4:32-35; 6:7; 11:19-21; 16:4-5). As a result a robust, resilient church advanced in the first century. Since then it's faltered much of the time. What happened?

The church currently sends confusing messages. By their opinions, traditions, and dogmas, early church fathers, popes, and councils encrusted, splotched, obfuscated, burdened, and warped Jesus' pristine message. Subsequent reformers, pop-preachers, and televangelists continue to layer it with complex tiers. It's now perverted, pasted, and glazed with centuries of variegated, rusty, and flake-infested paint. Until we return to the simplicity of Jesus' original methods, teachings, and principles, we'll be befuddled and the world will be turned-off.

You ask, "What changed?" Plenty. At first, the church followed the apostles' doctrine, that is, Jesus' teaching. Second, the word "church" originally meant the people, not the building. "Church" described the budding, vital people of God, not brick and board buildings. Third, each congregation operated autonomously; elders (local overseers appointed from among mature men in every church) administered each congregation (Acts 14:23; Philippians 1:1; 1 Timothy 3:1-7; Titus 1:5-9; 1 Peter 5:1-4). Fourth, the church knew only one mediator — Jesus. All Christians accessed God through Christ. They shared in prayer and the Lord's table (Acts 2:42).

As hierarchy evolved, doctrines, polity, and teachings developed then crystallized. The church no longer consisted of a priesthood of believers (those saved by the blood of Christ) who could pray directly to God. Professional clergy emerged. Soon the church (through its priests and bishops) became the dispenser of salvation. Only priests administered the Lord's table, and no one could be saved apart from the church. Church traditions became equal to Jesus' teachings. In many cases church leaders preferred the teachings of men because of their convenience and acceptability.

Can we remove centuries of colored encrustations and regain the formula for that unsoiled paint? Is it possible to restore the Spirit's power to the pew — to wrest it from prelates, pulpitarians, and priors? Can it be reinstated by God's people? Definitely. When Jesus' followers devote themselves daily to the apostles' teaching, to the Lord's table, fellowship, and prayer, God's Spirit works mightily in them as he did in the first century.

In order for Christians to forestall the dictates of ecclesiastics and resist being carried away by every breezy doctrine, they need a daily diet of the Word, and they require the personal leading of God's Spirit. With the abundance of Bibles available in just about every language spoken today, there's little excuse for any individual to be disconnected from God and Jesus' blood-bought freedom.

A Christian missionary from England said, "As Christ's witnesses in India, we have to try to show that Jesus Christ, though he lived in a foreign country, and at a distant period in history, is yet in truth the center and Lord of all history, that his cross is one all-sufficient mercy seat where all men's guilt is taken away and men are reconciled to the family of God."

But the Hindu replies: "That is what you say, but you do not believe it. If you did believe it, you would not find it necessary to live in 250 separate denominations with 250 separate names on your church boards. You would not need to say, 'I am of Paul,' 'I am of Apollos,' 'I am of Calvin,' 'I am of Luther.' You would be content to simply name the name of Christ and live in one household called by his name."

At a college reunion, one classmate exclaimed, "Jim, you've changed. You had thick, blond hair, but now you're bald. You used to be tan, but now you're pale. You were trim, now you're obese. You've changed so much."

"But I'm not Jim."

"Good grief, you've changed your name, too."

That's what's happened to the church. It goes by many aliases, and it's changed so much, no one recognizes it. How can any unbeliever or seeker identify what it is? It's not known anymore as just the church of Jesus or the way or as the followers of Christ.

Buildings boast all kinds of names on the door: Methodist, Baptist, Presbyterian, Lutheran, Reformed, Free, Roman Catholic, Orthodox. Why can't we be followers of Jesus without other designations or names? How did we get to the place where denominations compete?

Here's how I see what happened: Many people follow diets to lose weight. Suppose that only one diet of all the diets out there is fundamentally sound. It's the true human regimen. Every person should follow it to enjoy good health. This lone diet follows the fundamentals, the life-principles that God built into our bodies.

There's no charge for it. It's completely free. The Lord wants every person on the planet, and those yet to be born, to know about it and to use it. He forces no one to follow it, however. In the same way he let Adam and Eve decide whether to eat from the infamous tree, he permits each individual the choice of diet.

But some participants over-eagerly promote this true diet. They want everyone to accept it and aren't satisfied with the Lord's approach to tell others about it and let them decide. They aggressively vend it in order to make this true diet trendy. In their desire to have everyone accept it, they get carried away.

Let's say they go to Russia where no one knows of the plan, and they attempt to disseminate it. "It sounds good to us, and we think it's healthful," say the Russians. "There's only one problem. Our folks eat potatoes. Russians will never give up spuds. We'd like to follow your diet, but don't expect us to give up our staple."

So the diet promoters consider it and say, "That's not a bad deal. We add 300 million persons to the roll. We compromise only on spuds. Let's do it." So the Lord's diet takes on a Russian modification. It makes everybody "happy" except the Lord.

Then the promoters go to China to enlist the Chinese. Of course, they love their rice. "With just this one compromise, we can enlist a billion Chinese," the promoters insist. So the Chinese also obtain their separate modification. Now Russian and Chinese formulations add to the list.

When the zealots go to Japan, the Japanese want fat beef. Soon scores of dubious nationalistic and cultural adaptations gain acceptance. Hundreds of variations encumber the Lord's perfect diet. All the participants claim to follow the proper diet. Only a few do. Most wonder why their altered regimens accomplish so little.

Compromises like this led to our many denominations. Lifeless churches named after leaders, teachers, countries, doctrines, and dogmas exist everywhere. As a result, they contaminate Jesus' original "diet," the food of life.

Do we want the Spirit's life in the church? Do we really want to exalt Jesus? In order to find the right regimen — life's true bread — we need the original recipe. We discover it only in the New Testament. We go there not to establish our righteousness but to glorify God and utilize his wisdom. The object is to praise God and to benefit all who willingly submit to him.

While watching a television program a few years ago, advice given a young woman about her fornication shocked me. It was in effect, "You are an adult. If it seems right, do it."

The logic prevails among many folks. A guy goes into a liquor store with a gun. Equipped with the judgment that he's reached a responsible age, and it seems right, he reasons: "I'm old enough to know what I'm doing. I need money. This guy in the liquor store owns more than enough. Therefore, I'm justified in using force to get what I need."

The logic that says, "If it seems okay to you, do it," has brought the world to near chaos. This same reasoning, "if it seems right do it," strongly infiltrates the church. That's why it's important to use New Testament patterns and examples, not as laws but as principles that connect us with the living Christ and glorify the Father. Paul advised the new Christians in Colosse:

> Don't let others spoil your faith and joy with their philosophies, their wrong and shallow answers built on men's thoughts and ideas, instead of on what Christ has said. — Colossians 2:8 (TLB)

211

Do We Just Forget And/Or Neglect Social Causes?

Advocates of the social gospel thought that simply saving a person from hell wasn't sufficient. People require more than insurance that indemnifies them against a flaming future or protection from the devil's agents. They need something that improves their lives now. "Social gospelers" sing "What's now is important" lyrics. It's as if they hear not Jesus, but Ernst Renan, who declared, "Science alone can ameliorate the unhappy situation of man here below."

Social gospel promoters presumed that if people lived in a blemished society, the society would corrupt them, because society molds people. The only corrective: make society perfect.

Ministers rallied behind social issues and railed against those responsible for "social inequities." They took up the causes of slavery, labor's right to organize, religious intolerance, and agricultural dislocation. Matters of race relations, equal rights, and peace currently dominate. Concerning the latter, many feel that the kingdom of God cannot appear without war's abolishment.

Did social gospel advocates succeed? Without question they helped ameliorate many effects of injustice, but they also miserably failed to accomplish Jesus' mission goals. Not only that, they created new problems virtually non-existent before they started. Welfare moms are a pregnant example.

Two major factors always obstruct social gospel efforts. First, hardly anyone agrees on what constitutes a perfect society. Only God knows for sure. Most human definitions fall tragically short. Ask 100 independent thinking persons on the street what comprises an ideal societal structure and you'll receive 99 different opinions. Ask those 100 people a similar set of questions tomorrow, and some will have altered their estimations. If you could ask the same group thirty years from now, you'd have substantial variation from their original opinions. Some will have changed 180 degrees.

When I was young and poor, I saw no reason why all of the wealthy people shouldn't be forced to share with us poor folks. My "poor" perspective in the 1950s was limited to those Americans like my family, who toiled weekly for petite paychecks. It didn't include destitute folks in Africa, Asia, Central and South America, or even Appalachia. A slight correction: When I wanted to pitch cold, greasy, fried eggs, my mother usually reminded me of famished African children. The eggs were usually cold and greasy simply because I didn't get up on time.

As it turned out, wealthy people helped us more than I'll ever know. For a few weeks, an abundantly wealthy man in Bartlesville, Oklahoma, employed me as his personal attendant and chauffer. He allowed me to listen to his personal and business conversations. One day, he visited with the CEO of a Bartlesville-based oil company. The local county hospital needed funds to continue operating. The incident predated Medicare and massive public medical funding.

The two benefactors decided to give the hospital several thousand dollars apiece in order to keep the hospital out of the red. They apparently donated like that for several years. Both felt it was their duty to help. About eight months later, my wife gave birth to our first son in that hospital. We still marvel at the small amount of the bill for that eight-day hospital stay.

I never thanked my boss or the other executive for their assistance. Other charitable people supported the schools and universities I attended. Rich people helped me in ways I rarely appreciated. Nonetheless, I felt that wealthy people should be compelled to contribute so I could live a more comfortable life.

In the meantime, other events shaped my view of sharing. During our college time, my wife and I labored long hours. I worked forty hours per week and went to college full time. We paid my tuition by the month, fed our kids, and economized every way we could imagine. The Lord put us in touch with many generous people who helped us along the way. We've gained things we never thought possible when we began.

I'm older now. The Lord granted us a few possessions, and I've discovered an amended "social perspective." One major difference: I don't as readily hold to the "share" idea, especially if someone forces me to do it.

Life experience also shows me that well-intended, but injudicious assistance to others often results negatively. Helping people who possess the ability to take care of themselves often makes them dependent on outside help. It destroys their initiative and self-esteem. I witnessed this in my own family. My elder brother lived comfortably for many years and generously hosted numerous family gatherings. My wife and I saw some of our relatives take advantage of his hospitality. We probably did ourselves on occasion. He never complained. Nonetheless, some kinfolk continued to take with little gratitude and with the ongoing expectation that he should continue his generosity because "he could afford it."

Abraham Lincoln said, "You cannot help men permanently by doing for them what they could and should do for themselves." Given the fact that too frequent gifts often kill resourcefulness and breed laziness, how do you redistribute wealth and give everyone an equal chance? Even if you conceived a perfect formula, administrators of the program would favor their friends and relatives. Nepotism and corruption plague every society and system.

Investigators are currently focusing on the U.N. "Oil for Food Program." Iraqi dictator, Saddam Hussein, received millions so he could feed starving children in his country. Much of the money found its way to high echelon U.N. leaders. The greatly heralded 1964 US efforts to build the Great Society testify that money and the United States Congress definitely can't construct a perfect place. Never was so much spent with so little result.

Here's the second obstacle: If society is evil (a point I'm not arguing), its citizens can't create anything perfect. Five-year-old illiterates could more easily prepare a calculus course than could the brightest human beings build a perfect society or even define what constitutes one. Yet, for some reason, just about every generation of "intellectuals" attempts to craft a perfect culture.

Reinhold Niebuhr recognized an inherent flaw in the liberal quest for the perfect society. The liberals aimed to correct civilization's defects through education and by changing society. Here's the rub. Sin causes society's evils as much as it results from them. Actually, sin causes the imperfections and more sin results from the imperfections. It's a double-edged sword.

We can't make history completely safe, said Niebuhr. According to him, one works on behalf of justice while understanding that we'll never achieve perfect impartiality and fairness. Yet we can't escape involvement in the quest for it, he concluded, by assuming that it's a pointless endeavor because excellence can't be attained.

I question whether Christians should directly enter the quest for an ideal social order. Here's what I mean. Countless legitimate social causes confront us. Every society, past and present, contains folks in need of dress and foodstuff. Accidents, congenital problems, and illnesses produce widows, orphans, and permanently disabled people. Ethnic and economic groups tend to be closed and exclusive resulting in discrimination and prejudice.

Many American church groups seriously attempt to influence the US government toward more humane policies. Claiming to represent people who can't help themselves, church lobbyists pressure Congress to make "right decisions" for the well-being of people and the planet. They feel it necessary to counter the work of lobbyists that represent such groups as the National Rifle Association, corporate America, and "big oil."

According to the official bulletin of one vocal church group, their lobbyists attempted to pressure congressional representatives in numerous areas of concern.

They wanted Congress to:

- increase the federal minimum wage and assistance to needy families, provide additional low-income housing, give affordable, comprehensive health care for everyone, but they opposed tax supported school vouchers;
- eliminate the debt burden that encumbers many developing countries, halt military aid to a certain foreign government, and give political prisoners legal justice while promoting stronger legislation against hate crimes; and
- study their concerns about greenhouse gas emissions, federally funded embryonic stem-cell research, and the provision of clean drinking water.

Along with many other denominations, this group maintains a permanent lobby team in Washington that echoes the decisions of the church's general synod. How this team makes its contacts and whether the team's personnel might be people of moral turpitude, folks whose background might be shady, we're not told. The lobbyists' ethics and methods don't appear to be issues. Most important to them is influencing Congress concerning the social issues already listed. The gospel isn't mentioned.

Jesus commissioned us to take the good news to every nation. When churches and individual Christians follow Jesus, they work to correct defects within the church, and they urge brothers and sisters in Christ to do the same. New Testament churches fed widows and orphans.[1] They preached to all people and expected converts to accept one another as brothers and sisters without exception.[2] The church in first century Antioch appointed leaders of various races and backgrounds.[3]

We can't forget, however, the parameters of the programs and policies, which the apostles instituted. First, Jesus taught us to remember the poor. Early Christians helped the needy. But neither Jesus nor his apostles ever petitioned or urged governments to set up programs to assist the poor. Second, giving was always voluntary. The church assessed no one or forced anyone to give. Third, the church took care of its own and presumably others in need. It didn't solicit outside help to finance its mission.

The apostles designated only certain folk worthy of church aid. Here social planners usually miss a crucial point that Paul addressed in the book of Ephesians:

> *He who has been stealing must steal no longer, but must*
> *work, doing something useful with his own hands, that*
> *he may have something to share with those in need.*
> — Ephesians 4:28

Those we help, if able, need to make serious efforts toward improving their lot so that they can begin helping others.

The church's primary task must always be proclaiming Jesus' message. Once people believed, the apostles expected them to repent of wrongdoing, tell others about Jesus, and then join in helping others. The modern "gospel of Oprah," that God accepts you the way you are, corrupts Jesus' message.[4] Jesus told us about and showed us God's love, but he expects us to change. Paul pointed to radical alteration in him and his contemporaries:

> *Remind the people to be subject to rulers and authorities, to be obedient, to be ready to do whatever is good, to slander no one, to be peaceable and considerate, and to show true humility toward all men.*
>
> *At one time we too were foolish, disobedient, deceived and enslaved by all kinds of passions and pleasures. We lived in malice and envy, being hated and hating one another.*
>
> *But when the kindness and love of God our Savior appeared, he saved us, not because of righteous things we had done, but because of his mercy. He saved us through the washing of rebirth and renewal by the Holy Spirit, whom he poured out on us generously through Jesus Christ our Savior, so that, having been justified by his grace, we might become heirs having the hope of eternal life.*
>
> *This is a trustworthy saying.* And I want you to stress these things, so that those who have trusted in God may be careful to devote themselves to doing what is good. *These things are excellent and profitable for everyone.*   — Titus 3:1-8 (author's emphasis)

When we accept him, the Lord demands transformed lives. We jettison hate and living only for pleasure. Once we repent, we help other individuals — "share with those in need." If we don't commence this alteration, our conversions are definitely suspect. "Religion that God our Father accepts as pure and faultless is this: to look after orphans and widows in their distress and to keep oneself from being polluted by the world," said James, Jesus' half-brother in the flesh (James 1:27). James addressed Christians there, not governments. We shouldn't expect the world or the state to do what Jesus commanded us to do.

Church elders must hold believers accountable for the new life. A generation ago the church lacked encouragers. Now the church lacks "rebukers." The press loves political correctness, but Christians need to admonish one another when necessary. Paul's advice to the Thessalonians should suffice here: "And we urge you, brothers, warn those who are idle, encourage the timid, help the weak, be patient with everyone" (1 Thessalonians 5:14).

We save people by leading them to the Lord, and we build a better society on a one-by-one basis. The Good Samaritan used his money to help the wounded stranger on the road. Wherever practicable, Christians use their means in the same way. But Jesus didn't go looking for people to help. His key task was proclaiming the message of God's kingdom.

Jesus made crucial points about offering help to others. Remember his conversation with the paralyzed man at the Pool of Bethesda? (John 5:1-15). To the 38-year-old invalid, Jesus said two things that some consider demeaning. First, "Do you want to get well?" Modern social workers spend huge amounts of time, energy, and resources on people who don't want a "cure." If the government wants to operate that way, so be it. But the church can't afford to waste the Lord's time or his resources. Jesus taught the disciples to preach about his kingdom. If people refused to accept the message, however, the Lord instructed his followers to fling the dust off their feet and look for receptive audiences.

Jesus said something else to the man that some find impertinent. He charged the newly healed man: "See, you are well again. Stop sinning or something worse may happen to you." We don't always know the connection between suffering and sin. But sometimes it is evident. In those cases it's necessary to humbly point it out. Paul noted the procedures for warning an erring brother:

> *If anyone does not obey our instruction in this letter, take special note of him. Do not associate with him, in order that he may feel ashamed. Yet do not regard him as an enemy, but warn him as a brother.*
> — 2 Thessalonians 3:14-15

Christian leaders remind brothers and sisters of other duties. I wonder how often the following charge by Paul has been fulfilled in the last 1,900 years:

*Command those who are rich in this present world not
to be arrogant nor to put their hope in wealth, which is
so uncertain, but to put their hope in God, who richly
provides us with everything for our enjoyment.*
— 1 Timothy 6:17

Paul wrote the above about wealthy Christians. Jesus gave us no authority or commission to tell non-Christians what to do.

Modern political correctness forbids making moral judgments. But the Bible makes a distinction between trying to help Christian brothers and sisters cross the finish line as opposed to passing judgments on non-believers. We don't condemn the world. God will take care of them, but:

*Brothers, if someone is caught in a sin, you who are
spiritual should restore him gently. But watch yourself,
or you also may be tempted. Carry each other's bur-
dens, and in this way you will fulfill the law of Christ.*
— Galatians 6:1-2

The gospel positively affects society in demonstrable ways that advocates of political correctness don't want to admit. When people take the good news to heart, they build stable families and more secure relationships. There's less need for outside intervention in the lives of people and families.

Psychologist, Patrick Fagan, related numerous statistics that illustrate this correlation. First, according to a 1995 survey, ten percent of families with mom and dad in their first marriage lived in poverty. In families where couples cohabited, 42 percent lived in poverty. Divorced-separated families were at 49 percent and al-ways-single families (where mothers try to raise children without a spouse), 66 percent.

Even more compelling are risk rates of serious child abuse. Statistics for this evidently aren't kept in the United States, but the United Kingdom records them. According to the study that Fagan quoted, in a traditional married family, the risk rates of serious child abuse were one percent. For a single mother alone with her children, they were fourteen percent; a single father under the same circumstances, twenty percent; cohabiting natural parents, twenty percent; and for a mother cohabiting with her boyfriend, 33 percent.[5] After relating the results of several studies, Fagan summarized his findings:

> *The key ... about American men and women is that most cannot stand each other enough to raise the children they ... brought into existence. And government is absolutely incompetent to correct that. But the data is ... clear. If men and women worship God, God has the power to correct it.*[6]

I relate the above not because I want to see Christians petition their governments to increase or to diminish social aid. A spate of bureaucrats stands ready to administer government programs regardless of their effectiveness. Neither am I criticizing any particular program nor wanting other Christians to disparage government efforts. I simply want to illustrate our two main tasks. First, Christians share Jesus' good news, and second, their money. When people accept the gospel and live according to Jesus' principles, they create more stable families and societies.

Changed hearts become compassionate hearts. Once we experience God's forgiveness, we patiently work to help others discover and appreciate God's love. We don't make societal improvement, personal popularity, or economic success our goal. Jesus gave us the objective of warning people to repent so they can first, avoid condemnation, and second, participate in God's kingdom. The Lord's people look for open doors while they proclaim Jesus' sovereignty. Christians seek receptive hearts, those wanting change, and desiring to glorify God. Society improves as people accept Jesus' message and live as he did.

Christians also learn to live by the principle Jesus taught in Luke 12. Are you concerned about redistributing our society's wealth? Consider how Jesus handled the following matter: One of two brothers came to Jesus wanting him to render a "fair" judgment concerning their dad's estate (I wonder how many cases of the following are handled a year by US judges): "Teacher, tell my brother to divide the inheritance with me." "I deserve the goodliest portion of the family pot." The request commonly splits families and societies.

Why shouldn't we try to work things out between people? Aren't we supposed to be peacemakers? Shouldn't we endeavor on behalf of justice? Jesus' answer should caution those who think that they possess the acumen to resolve every human inequity. He replied, "Man, who appointed me a judge or an arbiter between you?" God doesn't grant us that gift of discernment. The devil deceives us into thinking that we have it.

Jesus avoided money quarrels for good reason. He warned us about the root of those clashes. "Watch out! Be on your guard against all kinds of greed; a man's life does not consist in the abundance of his possessions" (Luke 12:13-15). Some people genuinely need financial assistance. We can't shirk our responsibility to them. But greed and power lubricate many social programs. If the government chooses to be in the heavy petroleum business, that's their business, and it's up to politicians, social workers, and budget people to work out the details. They're answerable to God for their conduct. But Christians shouldn't be grease merchants for greedy rich, for the poor, or for politicians. We're fishermen.

The Kingdom Of God

Some of the reformers neglected the "kingdom of God." At the least they evidently misunderstood what the term means. Many current evangelists suffer the same misapprehension. The kingdom doesn't relate to borders, physical territory, or geography. Its domain is the human mind (heart). God's governance is the issue. If God manages you in Christ, that makes you part of God's kingdom, because as Jesus said, "The kingdom of God is within you" (Luke 17:21).

The Kingdom Message

Before Jesus ascended into heaven (circa 30 A.D.), he traveled with his apostles to a mountain. There the twelve asked him a question relating to a long-time concern: "Lord, are you at this time going to restore the kingdom to Israel?" (Acts 1:6). They failed (so do many contemporaries) to comprehend the plain messages Jesus delivered. Jesus' generation didn't and ours doesn't grasp what Jesus meant by his kingdom.

Here are some straightforward examples of his kingdom teaching:

- "If I drive out demons by the Spirit of God, *then the kingdom of God has come upon you*" (Matthew 12:28, author's emphasis). Jesus' mastery of evil spirits authenticated his ministry. His domination of demons indicated the kingdom's presence or imminence. Jesus made it clear that he meant the kingdom's nearness when he told his disciples this: "I tell you the truth, some who are standing here will not taste death before they see *the kingdom of God come with power*" (Mark 9:1, author's emphasis). In other words, the kingdom would appear during the lifetime of most folks present with Jesus that day. Eleven of those twelve apostles received power on the day of Pentecost, and they exercised the kingdom's power.
- Paul considered the kingdom a present reality when he wrote to the Colossian church: "For he has rescued us from the dominion of darkness and brought us into the kingdom of the Son he loves, in whom we have redemption, the forgiveness of sins" (Colossians 1:13-14). One can't be delivered into something that doesn't exist.
- The apostle John spoke as if the kingdom existed in his time. "I, John, your brother and *companion in the suffering and kingdom* and patient endurance that are ours in Jesus, was on the island of Patmos because of the word of God and the testimony of Jesus. On the Lord's Day I was in the Spirit, and I heard behind me a loud voice like a trumpet ..." (Revelation 1:9-10, author's emphasis).

The above scriptures show that after the day of Pentecost, the apostles spoke of the kingdom in the present tense. It came and is here, even if not in its fullness or completeness. Its growth and expansion continue through each generation as people accept God's rule in their lives through Christ. But the breadth and comprehensiveness of the kingdom won't be complete or revealed until the last day.

The New Covenant To Be Written In The Peoples' Hearts

In the same way that God's kingdom exists in believer's hearts, Jeremiah (circa 600 B.C.) prophesied that the new covenant replacing Moses' Law would be written in hearts and minds.

> *"The time is coming," declares the Lord, "when I will make a new covenant with the house of Israel and with the house of Judah. It will not be like the covenant I made with their forefathers when I took them by the hand to lead them out of Egypt, because they broke my covenant, though I was a husband to them," declares the Lord. "This is the covenant I will make with the house of Israel after that time," declares the Lord. "I will put my law in their minds and write it on their hearts. I will be their God, and they will be my people."*
> — Jeremiah 31:31-33[7]

For man's part, the new covenant would not depend on performing outward ritual. God would put the law in their hearts. It would be "within" them. Obedience wasn't mere conformance to regulation. It meant voluntary submission to the Lord of the universe. Even under the Law of Moses, love for God and one's neighbor were the basis for the whole law. Yet the majority resisted loving the Lord.

A territorial kingdom defined only by physical boundaries always has unwilling subjects. No government in history ever gained 100 percent assent on an issue. Dissenters create disharmony and dishearten the willing subjects. That's why it's hopeless for Christians to attempt geographical kingdom-building or societal-improvement. Hearts must change and be renewed before a territorial kingdom can remain permanent. For this reason the new arena, said Jeremiah the prophet, would be the individual's heart or mind, not physical province.

223

We should understand God's kingdom, not geographically or territorially, but personally and individually. It exists whenever or in whomever God rules. If God controls and manages your life, if his will regulates your morals and behavior, and if you submit yourself to his Son, Jesus, in pure service and loving gratitude, then you participate in the kingdom.

Stephen, one of seven men, full of the Holy Spirit, rendered special service to the church in Jerusalem (Acts 6). He believed Jesus to be the Messiah. The kingdom resided in him. But Stephen's faith incited his countrymen to fury. Members of the Jewish high court rabidly gnashed their teeth; Jerusalem dentists probably stayed busy for months.

Then those prominent religious leaders, who so vociferously desired a territorial kingdom free of Roman presence, covered their ears, screamed at Stephen, rushed at him like seventy NFL line-backers, ripped off their coats, and stoned him, mortally wounding him. He died surrounded by men boasting knowledge of God but untouched by God's love. Their anger exposed their allegiance. Rage and wrath symbolize Satan's kingdom. They're never God's kingdom badges.

To his death, Stephen kept his allegiance to the God of peace. The Lord's kingdom grew strong within him. He died seeing his king at God's right hand. Stephen's final words illustrated that he qualified for membership in God's kingdom, "Lord, do not hold this sin against them" (Acts 7:60).

A geographical territory wherein 100 percent of the people submit to God isn't necessary for the beginning of his kingdom, though that should make pleasant surroundings. God's kingdom started once Jesus fully and willingly subjected himself to the Father. Setting up the kingdom took one king and one subject. It enlarges every time someone like Stephen submits to Christ. It grows in progressive generations and will increase until history's conclusion.

The kingdom expands as individuals repent of their sins and submit fully to Jesus. We become members of God's kingdom as we share in Jesus and willingly surrender ourselves to God. It's neat knowing that no outside power can separate us from his love

(Romans 8:31-39). And that because of God's love, we become more than conquerors.

The rigors of the departure from Egypt and the hardships of travel put Israel's faith on trial (Deuteronomy 8:1-5). In the same way, the king of the universe today leads his subjects through difficult and challenging circumstances including living under autocratic rulers and among antagonistic neighbors.

Sports enthusiasts understand that winning requires rigorous exercise. Godliness, too, requires training (1 Timothy 4:7-8). Jesus referred to the testing as the denial of self and the willingness to bear our own crosses and follow him (Matthew 16:24). Those ready to suffer with Jesus obtain a share in his victory. We shall be "fellow heirs with Christ, *provided we suffer with him* in order that we may also be glorified with him" (Romans 8:17, author's emphasis).

Many see no benefit from testing and discipline. They want to enjoy a kingdom void of struggle and strain. A few decades ago, several of my friends became excited about an engaging, popular television minister in the Los Angeles area. Skillful, knowledgeable, and entertaining, he quoted scripture as he paced before the cameras with Bible in hand. Jewish friends, Christian friends, and even unbelievers urged that I watch that minister's program.

His most frequent theme: *being a Christian brings one speedy and lasting success.* In other words, Christians always thrive. Once you profess Jesus, your days of suffering end. Distress signifies that you don't live correctly. God intends for everyone to prosper and to enjoy plenty right now. To paraphrase the preacher and some of his colleagues: "Turn to the Lord and you will have your own house with a garage big enough to house your boat, your sports car, and your spouse's SUV. God will pay your bills. All your suffering will become past tense."

Does the Bible promise a peace that passes understanding? (Philippians 4:7). Definitely, but it is peace of mind that prevails in the midst of trial, not avoidance of every stressful situation. Hardship and difficulties, said James, give opportunities for a blessing from the Lord (James 1:12). Peter echoed the thought: "If you are insulted because of the name of Christ, you are blessed" (1 Peter 4:14).

225

The lesson derived from watching virtually every Old Testament figure is the benefit of enduring suffering. The book of Hebrew's faith "Hall of Fame" delineates dozens of Old Testament heroes and heroines (Hebrews 11). Each of them endured a severe faith test. The "hall" acquaints us with the successes of those in the past.

Before our children entered college they had to take either the SAT or ACT tests. As every college student knows, certain books and some internet sites give sample questions. By using those sources, students gain an idea of what's on the real examinations. At test time the student should meet with few surprises. In the same way, reading the Word prepares us for life. The Old Testament is like an SAT introduction manual.

The people we meet in the Bible and the adversity they endured show us, first, what types of ordeals we may expect, and second, how God expects us to react to tribulation. The response he wants in every case: *trust him*. The Bible offers more than information about life's testing. God assures victory if we "lay aside every weight, and sin which clings so closely, and ... run with perseverance the race that is set before us, looking to Jesus" (Hebrews 12:1-2 RSV). People in whom God's kingdom resides gladly do that.

Why Didn't The New Testament Writers Condemn Slavery?

The book of Philemon illustrates how the early church dealt with the slavery problem. It appears that Onesimus, an evidently worthless[8] slave owned by wealthy Philemon, stole something and deserted. Whether in Rome or Ephesus, scholars aren't sure, Onesimus and Paul met. Paul led the slave to Jesus. Paul also helped the slave's owner, Philemon, know the Lord.

The book of Philemon is a brief letter, which Paul sent by Onesimus' hand. The seasoned apostle requested Philemon to forgive his runaway slave. He also entreated him to accept Onesimus as a "dear brother." Paul didn't order Philemon to do it. He appealed to Philemon "on the basis of love" (Philemon 9). Christians undergo that change. We love all people and treat them as we wish to be treated because Jesus forgave us.

226

Here's the fact that shocks some. Neither Paul nor Peter became involved in the slave issue, except to urge slave owners to treat their slaves as brothers. Godly slaves rendered faithful service to their masters. Christian masters remembered that their slaves were brothers and sisters in Christ. When both parties do as the Lord taught, slavery ends because no Christian mistreats a brother or sister.

Had the early church directly involved itself in the slavery issue, it would have resulted in the loss of the Great Commission's incisiveness. When we stay on target with our message, God's Word goes throughout the world. The Word and Spirit change people. People whose hearts are not softened by God's love and the Holy Spirit will not convert.

If we expect the world to listen, we demonstrate that the Spirit of Jesus works in our lives. For many years, I taught a Bible study for business and professional people in Los Angeles. Two women, the publisher and the editor of a popular area newspaper, invited me to teach a weekly class in their newspaper boardroom. Both lacked background in the scriptures, but each seemed eager to learn.

In the same way that Cornelius, the seeker, in Acts 10 did, my friends invited many of their friends. Most who attended were successful business and professional people in the area. They included bankers, realtors, car dealers, travel agents, and a plumber with a flourishing business. They came from varied backgrounds including Jews, Catholics, Christian Scientists, agnostics, and others from mainline churches.

At a memorable session, an agnostic made antagonistic comments. I attempted to show the way of the Lord by logic. I could tell that I made only scant progress. After the session, I asked the newspaper publisher, a good friend, what she thought of the evidences that I gave for believing in God. She said, "To be honest with you, Bob, I wasn't listening to what you were saying as much as I was watching your body language and how you were reacting to him." I'm thankful that the Lord kept me from expressing my usual arrogant impatience that day.

If you're interested in how the story progressed, the agnostic continued to attend the study. He was of Jewish background; his son is an orthodox rabbi. But as he carried on with the study, I often heard him say concerning Jesus' teaching, "This is good stuff." What about my publisher friend? She and her husband sent us a note this past Christmas describing the *miracle* in their lives. They're now faithfully attending church.

But How Can We Stand By And Allow So Much Wrong To Take Place?

When I was young, I carped about my younger brother's faults. I complained about my elder brother, too, only not quite as much. Our parents used to say what I suppose most people say to their children when one complains about another, "Bob, you take care of yourself, and we'll take care of him." For the most part they did, although I didn't always recognize it at the time. The Lord works through other people if we don't interfere with his program.

On the other hand, we can and should do certain things. As the apostle John wrote,

> *This is how we know what love is: Jesus Christ laid down his life for us. And we ought to lay down our lives for our brothers. If anyone has material possessions and sees his brother in need but has no pity on him, how can the love of God be in him? Dear children, let us not love with words or tongue but with actions and in truth.*   — 1 John 3:16-18

I need to feed and help my neighbor if he can't help himself. I best help my neighbors by letting them know the liberating power of the good news. Those two things I can do something about. Much of what I see on the evening news I can't change. Unselfish assistance to a needy neighbor always trumps fretting about a far-away disaster. One thing I can do. Correct the flaws in my own life.

I can't fix all the world's wrong. Only God knows how to do that. Usually when I try to rectify the wrongs of others, I disrupt his program.

1. See Acts 6, 7 for the model. A board of deacons was created to fairly adminis-
trate (without discrimination) the program. Paul brought monies from Gentile
churches to help support this effort. See Acts 11:27-29; 12:25; 2 Corinthians
8-9.

2. According to Galatians 3:28, in Christ, "there is neither Jew nor Greek, slave
nor free, male nor female...."

3. According to Acts 13:1-3, Simeon was black, and Lucius was from North
Africa. These two were among the prophets and teachers in that exceptional,
exemplary church.

4. This idea is prevalent not only in Hollywood, but in numerous churches. It
doesn't coincide with Jesus' message or his church's. See Matthew 4:17, where
Jesus called people to repent, and Mark 7:20-23, "out of men's hearts, come
evil thoughts, sexual immorality, theft, murder, adultery, greed, malice deceit,
lewdness, envy, slander, arrogance and folly. All these evils come from inside
and make a man 'unclean.' "

5. Patrick Fagan, "Family and Religion," *Faith and Public Policy*, ed. James R.
Wilburn (Lanham, Maryland: Lexington Books, 2002), pp. 94-95.

6. *Ibid*, p. 102.

7. It is not the Abrahamic covenant, which was to be replaced but the Mosaic.
That's the one made with Israel when God took them "by the hand to lead
them out of the land of Egypt."

8. The meaning of the name "Onesimus" is "worthless."

12

Good Messengers
Don't Mess With The Message:
The Church's Mission

Preach the Word; be prepared in season and out of season; correct, rebuke and encourage — with great patience and careful instruction. For the time will come when men will not put up with sound doctrine.
— 2 Timothy 4:2-3a

Some years ago, while browsing in a bookstore, I came across Robert Fulghum's book, *Words I Wish I Wrote*. In that small volume, he included an unknown wag's witty wish: "When I die, I want to go peacefully and quietly in my sleep like my grandfather did — not screaming and shouting like the passengers in his car at the time."[1] That's how today's popular religious teachers and philosophers impress me. They kick and scream like victims of forces beyond their control as they perceive this nation careening toward calamity.

Instead of basing their hope in God, they worry. Their angst originates from a misapprehension. To them the only way to preserve Christianity is to "restore" eighteenth-century principles and the ideal society they think existed then. They don't see that past theological paint-mixing, color-blending, smearing, and flinging obscure the mission and the options the Lord provides for societal improvement.

There is irony in what these religious leaders attempt. Read contemporary writings of any era. You'll find authors wistfully writing of the "good old days." Two things militate against the view that our day's misery and immorality exceed that of other ages. For one, it's a route to self-glorification. If conditions never were this

231

bad before, it must take extraordinary people like those leaders to correct them. These are always "the worst of times."

There's a second error in talking about how much better things were in the good old days. The Bible cautions against it. Here was Solomon's advice: "Do not say, 'Why were the old days better than these?' For it is not wise to ask such questions" (Ecclesiastes 7:10).

Here's an example of the smudged-eye efforts many modern ministers make. In his book, *Nation Without a Conscience*, Tim LaHaye made numerous recommendations on how to save America.[2] Issues that concern LaHaye and his peers include the liberal press, evolution, abortion, homosexual behavior and AIDS, crime and violence, New Age faiths, materialism, pornography, welfarism, and secularism.

As solutions, LaHaye listed many "What ifs?"[3] I like to play golf with a friend who just turned ninety. Two years ago, my friend scored a hole-in-one on a local golf course. He's a superb chipper. If he's within 125 yards of the pin, he usually clubs the ball close to, if not in, the hole. I'm rarely close to anything except trees, water, sand, and other fairways. He often says to me, "Bob, if you could keep your ball on the fairway, you'd be a good golfer." "If I had brains and ambition," I reply, "I'd be rich." "What ifs" typically drown in impracticality. Moreover, Jesus didn't send us to do the "what ifs" LaHaye suggested.

What is a Christian's mission? What does Jesus want us to do about the sinful conditions around us? Does he expect us to attempt changing them? Or does he want us to do something else?

The Lord wants transformation. It's vital that we restore something to its original, biblical example. To do that, we clear our smeared eyes and look again at Jesus' action plan. What mission did Jesus assign his disciples? Was it nation-building and/or restoration?

Not long before he ascended, Jesus gave his followers vital marching orders:

All authority in heaven and on earth has been given to me. Therefore go and make disciples of all nations,

> *baptizing them in the name of the Father and of the Son and of the Holy Spirit, and teaching them to obey everything I have commanded you. And surely I am with you always, to the very end of the age.*
>
> — Matthew 28:18-20

Jesus assigned us to go to every nation, lead people to him, baptize them, and teach them to go to every nation, lead people to him, baptize them, and teach them.

Preach The Good News

How did we lose sight of that mission? Picture a group of the Lord's soldiers. He orders them not to fight and kill, but to tell dying people about his rescue operation. In the process of doing this, they're to keep in mind that they help others and show genuine affection because that's the Lord's way. The main mission is, tell folks about Christ.

Once people accept Jesus' lordship and forgiveness, and are baptized into him, they should be instructed on how to advance Jesus' cause. New "recruits" become fresh soldiers who continue to do what Jesus taught his original followers: "Go and make disciples of all nations, baptizing them in the name of the Father and of the Son and of the Holy Spirit, and teaching them to obey everything I have commanded." Disciples keep doing this until every person in the world hears the message.

In case the message isn't evident to some readers, a quick review of the New Testament's good news follows. The sermons recorded in Acts make it clear that the message has about six major points. They are:

1. God sent Jesus into the world.
2. We crucified him.
3. God raised him on the third day.
4. Jesus is now seated at the right hand of God.
5. There is salvation in no other name but Jesus.
6. Jesus is coming back to judge all creation (separate the sheep from the goats) and to take his faithful followers to heaven with him.[4]

The above points contain the substance of apostolic teaching. They serve as the basis for ethical teaching (cf Philippians 2; 1 Peter 2-3). The New Testament epistles shout this message.

As New Testament scholar, Stephen Neill, noted:

> *The New Testament is concerned with proclamation. It is a Kerygma, the loud cry of a herald authorized by a king to proclaim his will and purpose to his subjects. It is Euangelion, good news sent to those who are in distress with the promise of deliverance.*[5]

Twenty-first-century Christians share the same obligation that Jesus gave first-century believers:

- make disciples of all nations;
- baptize them in the name of the Father and the Son and of the Holy Spirit; and
- teach them to obey everything Jesus commanded.

We use the methods Jesus used in his ministry and the apostles modeled. When people accept this message and live by it, it changes them for the better and makes them more endearing. The world around them receives a positive influence. But the main task remains, glorify God by telling people about Jesus.

Jesus readied himself to suffer humiliation and to forgo retaliation in order to fulfill God's mission. He vigorously worked for God. His example clearly shows us what he expects from his followers. Peter emphasized Jesus' paradigm:

> *For it is commendable if a man bears up under the pain of unjust suffering because he is conscious of God. But how is it to your credit if you receive a beating for doing wrong and endure it? But if you suffer for doing good and you endure it, this is commendable before God. To this you were called, because Christ suffered for you, leaving you an example, that you should follow in his steps. "He committed no sin, and no deceit*

was found in his mouth." When they hurled their in-
sults at him, he did not retaliate; when he suffered, he
made no threats. Instead, he entrusted himself to him
who judges justly. He himself bore our sins in his body
on the tree, so that we might die to sins and live for
righteousness; by his wounds you have been healed.
For you were like sheep going astray, but now you have
returned to the Shepherd and Overseer of your souls.
— 1 Peter 2:19-25

In the face of suffering, Jesus never hesitated to declare God's coming kingdom. He calls us to do the same. Christians don't retaliate or threaten. Telling Jesus' message is our primary task. We leave judgment to God. How do we contemporary Christians fulfill our calling?

We Live To Please God

Ephesus was a large, Hollywood-like city in what is now the country of Turkey. Paul spent several months establishing the church there and in the surrounding area. He later wrote those converts about their goals and behavior. In the same way that contemporary Christians neglect and overlook important matters, the new Christians in Ephesus evidently forgot the new life to which God called them.

For you were once darkness, but now you are light in
the Lord. Live as *children of light (for the fruit of the*
light consists in all goodness, righteousness and truth)
and find out what pleases the Lord.
— Ephesians 5:8-10 (author's emphasis)

If you asked 100 people in your favorite mall "What does it take to please God?" you would probably get 120 answers, the majority having to do with self-fulfillment. Most of us try mightily to please ourselves. Grocery store breakfast food aisles illustrate how we try to satisfy every taste and whim. Want high-tech evidence of our pleasure kick? Walk through an electronic store.

These many options aren't creating positive results. Children whose parents allow them to please themselves become tyrannical and spoiled. Adults focused on pleasing themselves are despotic, wrinkled children.

God's people consciously try to please him. They endeavor to gratify God in their marriage, at work, among friends, in sports, hobbies, recreational activities, and their budgets.

Why try to learn what pleases God? Isn't it a given that he wants us to join a church, attend services, teach our children right from wrong, and get them to attend church? What's there to find out? Don't we know what pleases him?

"The fruit of the light," said Paul, "consists in all goodness, righteousness, and truth." Most of us try to be good. But some things about righteousness and truth we just assume. Here's what I mean.

An important part of pleasing God is knowing who and where God's enemies are. Chief difficulties that Coalition troops in Afghanistan and Iraq faced from the beginning included knowing the enemy and the enemy's location. When armies attack where the enemy isn't, they fail.

Many Christian preachers, broadcasters, writers, and churches don't seem to know the enemy's identity or his location. They spend all of their energy and a lot of other people's money shooting at decoys and erroneous targets. They sight their big guns on issues like:

- prayer in public schools;
- abortion;
- exorbitant taxes;
- governments going to war;
- civil rights;
- cleaning up the entertainment industry; and
- public display of religious symbols such as crosses or copies of the Ten Commandments.

They target these issues because someone persuaded them with powerful sounding arguments. The above concerns aren't the

236

enemy's main forces. They're merely decoys or to use another analogy, symptoms of the major problem. In the meantime, the enemy keeps massing forces.

All of the above seem like worthy causes. Big name preachers who espouse them expect to save lives and to create a better quality of life. They hope to fix what's wrong with American society assuming that attempting these corrections pleases God.

But they base these efforts on a mistaken idea of what pleases God and a miscalculation of the enemy's position. Waging war in this fashion only hardens the enemy, and I don't consider it pleasing to God.

Let's back up the truck to New Testament times. What conditions existed then, and how did Christians deal with them? For one, the Romans ruled most of the world. With what kind of government did the Romans dictate? It was pagan; a near dictatorship. It taxed heavily. Adoration and worship of pagan gods proliferated. Slavery was common. The Caesars usually went to war when they chose.

How did Jesus and the apostles deal with those miserable societal conditions? Almost nothing directly. They never protested. Never picketed. You won't find one whisper of public complaint by God's people in the New Testament. "Render to Caesar the things that are Caesar's and to God the things that are God's," said Jesus. In other words, "Pay your taxes and be done with it. Submit to governmental authorities."

Remember that the Roman governmental authorities were 99.9 percent pagan, but Jesus and the apostles taught respect for governments. Christians refused to obey the government only when emperors commanded Christians to honor them as gods or Roman officials forbade the worship of God.

Was Jesus concerned that improper political and governmental actions would bring suffering to ordinary people? Yes, he wept over Jerusalem as he foresaw its impending disaster (Matthew 23:37-39). Jerusalem's salvation though, could come about only through the repentance of its people and not by any change in governmental policy. Jesus and his apostles preached and warned. The people didn't listen. Therefore, suffering came upon them *by means*

237

of the Roman government. General Titus destroyed Jerusalem and many other Israelite cities.

Neither does the New Testament tell us to expect schools to teach our children morality, prayer, or instruction about God. That job belongs to Christian parents. "Bring your children up in the training and instruction of the Lord," Paul said to Christian fathers (Ephesians 6:3).

In the same way that we daily feed and clothe our children before they leave for school, Christian parents spiritually nourish their children every day. God gave parents the responsibility of guiding and instructing their children in Christian morality. The Lord's followers don't foist it off on schools. Consider those parents who protest the loss of prayer and Bible reading in public schools. Do you wonder how many of those moms and dads actually study God's Word and pray with their children at home?

All of our children went to public schools, graduating from Hollywood High in Los Angeles. We knew that in some of their classes they'd face exposure to teaching counter to our beliefs. My wife and I often discussed with them beforehand how to prepare for what they would hear. We didn't want them taken by surprise. Further, we nearly always prayed with them at breakfast.

We think they are great children. Were our children perfect examples of Christian behavior? Hardly. I don't think any of our children suffered loss of faith as a result of what they heard or didn't hear at school. Their parents shaped their lives more than any other factor.

It's our job to teach our children the scriptures, to pray with them, and to give them moral guidance. If they happen to receive some of this at school, we consider it a blessing, but we can't and shouldn't depend on it happening.

Teaching our children in the way I described was one of the correct things we did. We're also thankful that we eliminated all television in the household until our youngest was a high school sophomore.

I wish that we had done more to prepare them. For one, I regret that we didn't have the children select a Bible passage each day, encourage them to research that particular section of scripture, and then have a family discussion so that all could give their ideas, opinions, and thoughts on what the passage meant and how it applied to them.

I erred in other ways. One of my greatest mistakes was the notion that I could help shape public school policy. For many years, I was a member of the LeConte Junior High Advisory Council (in Hollywood) and later the Hollywood High School Advisory Council. I hoped that the involvement would give me insight into what took place at our children's schools and help me exert some influence.

Christians must decide for themselves how to please God; each person's calling differs. Perhaps if I relate my mistakes, though, it will help you avoid making the same types. I refer to my service on the advisory councils. Some friends convinced me that I could have a positive influence. I lack educational training. In working for my degrees, I emphasized textual and theological studies and had only one dud class in Christian education. My education skills are deficient.

I discovered, too, that I made enemies simply because I took sides on certain educational matters. That meant that I put stumbling blocks in the way of certain people by virtue of stands that I took on issues not related to belief in Jesus. It probably cut me off having conversations about the Lord with those folks because they perceived me as an enemy. Were some of them potential seekers? I'll never know unless the Lord confronts me about them in the judgment.

In addition, many of my allies on certain issues held moral beliefs much different than my own. Here's an example. For a few years, I was the chair of the Hollywood High School council's student motivation and conduct committee. I headed a group of twelve to fifteen people, some of them representing various governmental and quasi-governmental agencies in the Hollywood area. Our goal was to encourage and motivate students to attend class and to get serious about their education. The committee held seminars, sponsored health fairs, and conducted surveys.

One pleasant, bright couple (both single and in their twenties) often volunteered to help assemble and summarize data from polls

239

and surveys that we took. The two were efficient, fair, friendly, and helpful in every way. I enjoyed working with them.

One Sunday, the *Los Angeles Times* travel section featured the Grand Canyon. For many summers, my wife and I spent about a week at the canyon's North Rim, so I read the article with interest. The piece described a couple that offered nude raft tours of the canyon. You guessed it — my friends conducted those cool, au naturel cruises.

That wasn't the worst of my experiences. The people on my committee represented the diversity of Hollywood. Members came from numerous cultural, ethnic, and moral directions. We conducted a student health fair. Subcommittees handled various aspects of the event — advertising, student participation, displays, and so forth. What I discovered on the day of the fair shocked me and upset the principal, a man of high moral principles. My committee had arranged an event at which the Chinese Communist government sponsored a booth, as well as a booth that openly displayed and offered free condoms.

When Paul cautioned about being "unequally yoked with unbelievers," he didn't have only marriage in mind. It's extremely difficult to form associations with unbelievers because it nearly always leads to compromises and embarrassing partnerships for Christians. Any Christian who retains active membership in a political party quickly and painfully learns this. I am not saying that political party membership is necessarily wrong — each Christian has to make that judgment. It may be beneficial to attend public functions and discreetly join organizations. But we keep in mind the goals of sharing the message of Jesus and pleasing God.

I joined a service club and belonged to it for many years. My membership in the organization led to numerous Bible studies. Several people came to Jesus as a result — one of our sons-in-law included. Nonetheless, that involvement led to frequent hard choices — especially when storytellers at meetings told raunchy tales, demonstrated bigotry, or used expletives.

Considering that I was in a definite minority and that the service club wasn't a church organization, I chose not to take issue with every offense of my conscience. Rather, I tried to deal with people on an individual basis hoping I could lead them to Jesus. As you know, people in the world often disdain preachers, especially self-righteous ones.

Christians In A Secular Society

In a 2004 issue of *Christianity Today*, Charles Colson, with Anne Morse, wrote a piece titled "Reclaiming Occupied Territory: The Great Commission and the cultural commission are not in competition." Colson said that he exhorted a group of ministers to "engage today's cultural battles, particularly to support the Federal Marriage Amendment."[6]

Some of those ministers expressed confusion by his remarks. One of them asked: "But won't engaging the culture this way interfere with fulfilling the Great Commission? Isn't this our job — to win people to Christ?" Colson seemed amazed by the question. "Of course we're called to fulfill the Great Commission," was his response. "But we're also called to fulfill the *cultural* commission." Colson contends that Christians must sustain and renew God's creation by defending and upholding God's creations — "family and society" and by "critiquing false worldviews." He described the ministers' response to his logic as a "great 'Aha' moment."

Colson based his argument on the Genesis creation story wherein on the sixth day God ordered human beings to act as "agents in his ongoing work." Colson worried that if Christians didn't become involved in this way that there might not be anything to save.

The New Testament doesn't teach us to try to change society. We tell people about Jesus. We fight the Christian warfare with the sword of the Spirit (God's Word), not with money, influence, and power. If we feel strongly about certain issues, and we want to vote for them, we prayerfully and judiciously choose.

It's appropriate for Christians to use their opportunities to vote, but telling other people how to vote or advocating the position of one political party over another in a church setting has no biblical precedent. It leads only to division. I also question whether the Lord wants us to lobby governments and organizations concerning moral issues. Too many churches are so involved in political and social issues they neglect to preach the good news.

241

The New Testament pointedly teaches us to work on correcting evils within the church, but not those outside the church. Consider what Paul wrote to God's church in Corinth.

> *I have written you in my letter not to associate with sexually immoral people — not at all meaning the people of this world who are immoral, or the greedy and swindlers, or idolaters. In that case you would have to leave this world ... But now I am writing you that you must not associate with anyone who calls himself a brother but is sexually immoral or greedy, an idolater or a slanderer, a drunkard or a swindler. With such a man do not even eat. What business is it of mine to judge those outside the church? Are you not to judge those inside?* — 1 Corinthians 5:9, 11-12

Many church leaders disregard this New Testament procedure. They condemn folks outside the church:

- for their immorality;
- for their positions on prayer in public schools;
- for their beliefs on abortion, taxes, civil rights, gay rights; and
- concerning governments waging war.

When churches use this approach, they're trying to change the attitudes of unbelievers without changing their hearts. Material must be pliable or moldable before you can modify its shape. As iron can't be altered without heat, unrepentant people aren't moldable. We lead them to Jesus first; he softens their hearts.

"I will give you a new heart and put a new spirit in you; I will remove from you your heart of stone and give you a heart of flesh" (Ezekiel 36:26). God's love transforms people. Force and coercion ossify them. You can more readily shape dried bricks than unconverted hearts. According to 1 Corinthians 5, judging outsiders is the Lord's task. The church cultivates, nurtures, and cares for believers. Those outside the church are God's responsibility.

242

Most church leaders get the Lord's instructions backward. They want to ensure greater numbers and bigger collections so they do little about immorality in the church, but they constantly judge outsiders on their "lax morality." They condemn the world's transgressions, but allow all sorts of sin in the church. Many seem fearful of offending well-to-do Christians who might stop giving. The New Testament teaches us to leave judgment of the world to God. Christians are responsible only for reminding fellow believers of their need to be pure, loving, and generous.[7]

Churches inconsistently deal even with sinners in their fellowships. Here's what I mean. Referring again to 1 Corinthians 5, note the types of brothers or sisters that Paul insists we disfellowship. He meant any person who is "sexually immoral or greedy, an idolater or a slanderer, a drunkard or a swindler."

Are you aware of any churches that consistently follow Paul instruction? I've known some people who have been put out of the assembly because of immorality. It happened to one of my friends after she married a divorced man. It was a second marriage for her, too. I found it odd that the church she attended approved of the man as long as they were dating, but once they married, church elders acted to exclude them from the assembly. Did the couple deserve the exclusion? The Lord only knows. I don't. That's up to him to judge.

I'm familiar with actions of other churches in shunning people. Most instances I've known were for alleged immorality. It's a painful, but necessary process at times.

Here's the part that troubles me. Paul said we should also eliminate the greedy, the slanderers, and the swindlers from our midst. I've never known of that to happen. Have you? I have had preachers slander me and perhaps I've slandered others. I also suffer bad cases of greed on occasion, but I've never heard of a church taking action against parsimonious pew-sitters.

Church leaders including preachers, deacons, and elders — those ensconced in the heavily cushioned chairs on Sunday morning — often exhibit itchy, covetous palms. Some of those preachers who eagerly pressure our government on issues of school prayer, abortion, and other issues, may be the greediest of all. Our job is maintaining purity in the church. It's time that we work on this neglected assignment — deal with the greedy, gossips, swindlers, and liars among us.

Do we live in an evil era? Unquestionably, but so did people in all past ages, "This is a wicked generation," Jesus said of his earthly contemporaries (Luke 11:29). Some thirty years later, conditions hadn't changed. Paul assessed his fellow earth inhabitants as a "crooked and depraved generation" (Philippians 2:15). "I tremble for my country when I reflect that God is just," said Thomas Jefferson. He knew the evil even in good men. There has never been a perfect or just generation.[8]

I find no New Testament example of a Christian preacher or prophet attempting to change government or society. Christians called individuals to repent. We rarely do that anymore. Instead, many Christian leaders concentrate on changing governments and their policies.

A few years ago when I started on this project, I discussed it with a woman minister who regularly criticizes the government. I voiced my view to her that Christians shouldn't be telling governments how to do their work. "We should leave that to the politicians," I said. "But they're doing a lousy job," she replied. I wish I'd had the presence of mind to say that we ministers do a lousier job with the Great Commission. Too few tell the good news anymore.

We neglect another part of Jesus' tutoring. It was a crucial part of Jesus' instructions to the apostles. Paul utilized it in his ministry. We inform people about the good news, but if they refuse to accept it, we move on. Repeating for emphasis what Jesus said, "If anyone will not welcome you or listen to your words, shake the dust off your feet when you leave that home or town."[9]

Suppose a large apartment building is afire. Occupants and their building are at risk. You want to notify as many people as you can. You call, go door-to-door, and try to enlist others to help you warn the residents, but you will also conclude that everyone deserves to hear the message once far more than any deserves to hear it twice. If certain folks, for whatever reason, refuse to listen, you quickly go to the next apartment. Everyone deserves to be warned.

We waste effort on uninterested people. In the meantime others needlessly die in their sins because no one takes the message to them. Some of us are trying to save a doomed building while we neglect to warn most of the residents that they face impending disaster. If people won't listen, we move on to others who will.

We declare the good news, nurture those who accept Jesus, and we help the poor. We keep the right priorities, though. The apostles' emphasis in Acts 6 illustrates what I mean. Public preaching and teaching were the vanguard. The church rapidly grew in numbers. Within a few days it was comprised of several thousand members (Acts 2:41; 4:4).

We noted earlier that the New Testament word "church" always denotes the people, not the building. "Church" connotes "an assembly." In its early years the church built no houses of worship. Followers of the way met in homes, in rented rooms, and in the Jewish temple courtyard. Almost daily they gathered. Many of the converts were Jews from outside Jerusalem. Many were widows. Church leaders recognized the need to care for those with no income. First-century citizens in Israel had no welfare programs, no pensions, and no Social Security, yet church people rarely went needy. God's people took care of their own poor.

Many wealthy disciples voluntarily sold property and gave the proceeds to the apostles. Barnabas liquidated a piece of real estate and gave the proceeds to the apostles so they could buy food and necessities for hungry widows and their families. The church assessed no one. Its needy program was voluntary (Acts 4:32-37). In the meantime, the apostles continued preaching and teaching about Jesus (Acts 5:42).

An unforeseen problem developed. The out-of-town converts (the Grecian Jews) complained that the local widows received preferential treatment. When the out-of-towners grumbled, the apostles requested them (the Grecian Jews) to select men of good standing and filled with the Spirit to administer the food program.

The apostles gave instructive reasons and methods. "So the Twelve gathered all the disciples together and said, 'It would not be right for us to neglect the ministry of the word of God in order to wait on tables' " (Acts 6:2). Job one, the apostles insisted was "attention to prayer and the ministry of the Word" (Acts 6:4).

The twelve did three things vital to church growth. First, they made their verdict with everyone present. The apostles didn't make decisions behind closed doors. They held no secret meetings. The apostles met in open sessions. After hearing all sides present their cases, the leaders openly rendered their judgments.[10]

Second, the apostles recognized the importance of feeding the poor, but never lost sight of the church's primary task, ministry of the Word. The apostles knew they must keep preaching the Word and training others to do so.

Too many churches burden their ministers with board meetings to discuss the color of new carpets, meetings to discuss the church's position on political issues, visitation of shut-ins, and numerous other matters that elders, deacons, and various gifted members should cover. Ministers have little time to evangelize and to train others to do it. It's no wonder that many major Protestant denominations currently lose members and abandon church buildings.

Third, the church didn't attempt to shuffle responsibility for the poor to the government or to non-believers. The church's poor are the church's duty. Most modern churches invest heavily in buildings (that is, shrines to preachers) that suck the major resources of Christians. Victor Hugo's nineteenth-century comment still applies: "Jesus said, Love; the church says, Pay."[11] New Testament churches owned no buildings. God's people evangelized for Jesus, met in homes or rented buildings, and cared for believers.

I spoke by phone with an elderly widow who lives in a large midwestern city. Because of certain physical conditions she's unable to drive anymore. A local mainstream church uses a van to pick up people who can't get to worship services otherwise. The church also feeds them before bringing them home. The church invites homeless people to eat at the same time. The behavior of certain people at a recent church meal shocked her: "They grab food even though they appear well fed."

Something else troubled my friend. She said that no one says prayers of thanks at these church meals. She heard that it had something to do with the ACLU. Why would the ACLU object to saying grace at a church meal? Can you imagine the apostles not thanking God because either Jewish or Roman authorities objected? Here's a chance to publicly show gratitude to God, and church leaders wince because of some attorneys.

Why does no one offer thanks? The church probably accepts public funding to pay for the meals, and therefore regards it as illegal to thank God. That's what happens when churches ask non-Christians to help them do their work.

One final thought. In certain circles, you hear murmuring about all the illegal immigrants in this country. Some of my American Indian friends enjoy pointing out that my ancestors were immigrants. My great, great grandmother, a Seneca Indian, was here to meet many immigrants. But to those who complained about the presence of other people in Hollywood, we used to say that the Lord told us to preach the gospel to the whole creation. We didn't obey him, so he's sending the world here to make it easier for us.

I pray that we can rediscover the color of the original paint and begin to use Jesus' artistry so all the world, near and far, can be led to Jesus. The apartment building is already ablaze.

---

1. Robert Fulghum, *Words I Wish I Wrote* (New York: HarperCollins, 1997), p. 157.

2. Tim LaHaye, *Nation Without a Conscience* (Wheaton, Illinois, Tyndale House Publishers, Inc., 1994), p. 252-253.

3. *Ibid*, pp. 269-270.

4. The New Testament scholar C. H. Dodd helped identify these.

5. Stephen Neill, *The Interpretation of the New Testament: 1861-1961* (London: Oxford University Press, 1964), p. 347.

6. *Christianity Today*, August 2004, p. 64, "The Back Page" by Charles Colson with Anne Morse.

7. But Paul even cautions about making judgments concerning the behavior of other Christians. Only the mature should be engaged in attempting to do that. See Galatians 6:1-3.

8. "Notes on the State of Virginia," Quoted in Camp's *Unfamiliar Quotations*, p. 64.

9. Matthew 10:14; for Paul's observance of the method, and see Acts 13:49-52 and 18:5-6.

10. The Acts 15 conference to consider matters of the Law and circumcision for Gentile Christians is an example.

11. Victor Hugo, *La Légende des siècles*, 1859.

13

The Spirit's Fluid Grace:
Finding Harmony And Achieving Unity

*For I resolved to know nothing while I was with you
except Jesus Christ and him crucified.*
— 1 Corinthians 2:2

I love to watch rowing teams. Arms work fluidly, oars dip rhythmically, trim sculls scud toward their goal. Harmonious action and unified motion send neat sensual invitations.

Our young friend, Nick, is an outstanding high school runner and hurdler. Watching Nick compete exhilarates folks. His muscles, frame, brain, and lungs work in perfect synergy. Nick recently won the high hurdles event at the Drake University Relays in Des Moines, Iowa. That meant that he beat the state's best high school hurdlers for the third year in a row.

We depend on our bodies responding in a unified way. It's trouble when they don't. At the wellness center where I attempt to play racquetball, a man in his forties comes to walk around the track. It probably takes Glen[1] twenty minutes to make the circle that I can run in ninety seconds; Nick probably in 25 seconds. Because of a congenital condition, Glen's muscles operate with jerky, unpredictable motion. He strains to make his limbs cooperate. It's sheer exertion just to enter a door.

Glen inspires me. His voice quavers, but his smile never fades. His body resists his brain's commands, but his attitude never flags. He's always positive.

The modern-day body of Christ operates in worse fits and starts than Glen's. In most cases, its attitude doesn't compensate for its lack of concord. Churches become wan from disunity and often surly. Because of their discordance, many churches deserve an F grade.

249

Did you ever sing "The Song Of The Volga Boatman"? It's a folk song based on the experience of Russian laborers. They struggled on a path along the riverbank gripping ropes that tugged loaded boats and barges up the Volga River. As they grappled they sang a rhythmic song: "Yo-o-heave-ho. All together once again ... Haul the barge my brothers; Bend your shoulders to the line! As along the shore we run, sing our chorus in the sun." All pulled on the "heave." If a guy heaved on the "heave" they probably replaced him.

Thoughtful accord is crucial to every endeavor. "How good and pleasant it is when brothers live together in unity!" wrote King David in Psalm 133:1. You can sense Paul's emotion as he begged the Corinthians:

> *I appeal to you, brothers, in the name of our Lord Jesus*
> *Christ, that all of you agree with one another so that*
> *there may be no divisions among you and that you may*
> *be perfectly united in mind and thought.*
> — 1 Corinthians 1:10

The word translated divisions "schismatic" means rend or tear. In contrast, "perfectly united" refers to the setting of a fractured bone, outfitting a ship to sail, mending nets, or adjusting parts of an instrument so it can work properly. The Greeks might use it today to describe a well-tuned engine.

Few things frustrate us as much as trying to drive a vehicle that misfires. My wife and I use an old tractor to power our snow blower. That antiquated machine gets ornery in cold weather. When I first start it in winter, it coughs, sputters, and backfires on three cylinders. Until all four cylinders cooperate, I can't move it, let alone blow snow with it. Our cat could probably out-pull it. Meanwhile, I sit shivering.

You can mend a net, tune an engine, and repair most broken bones, but finding the secret to church harmony continues tougher than finding perfect pitch at a convention for the tone-deaf. How do you get church members to say the same thing? How do you get them to avoid division? How do you get them to unite themselves in mind and purpose?

250

Meeting together under one roof doesn't guarantee unity. Many church groups share a building, a common creed, and one leader, but they quibble and spat with one another worse than three kids trying to share one handheld video game player.

People differ so much. Years ago, I drove from Dallas to Abilene, Texas, where I planned to attend some lectures at Abilene Christian University. Some old friends lived in Weatherford, Texas, at the time. I wanted to stop and visit them on my way. As I drove through Weatherford, I came to a stoplight and waited for the light to change.

Two women sat in the car ahead of me. I judged them to be about my age. Their gestures indicated that they were talking. Long after the light changed to green, they still chatted. I gave them a polite amount of time to finish their conversation — far longer than customary in Los Angeles — then "patiently" honked the horn.

The strangest thing happened. They didn't speed off in haste, and they didn't get angry. They didn't even gesture to me to button up or to partake in some other physical activity. Both of them rubbernecked looking back at me. I couldn't understand why those women kept staring at me. It became finally evident that they were trying to see if they recognized me.

In small Texas towns like Weatherford, it's apparently customary to honk at your friends as a greeting, not in impatience. For some reason, those gabbing women never understood my gesture, either. People differ, don't they?

Corinth citizens constituted a potpourri of cultures — Middle Easterners, Greeks, Romans, slaves, and sailors. It lacked only Texans. Paul told the church members what Jesus earlier said to the disciples, "Get it together. My brothers, some from Chloe's household have informed me that there are quarrels among you" (1 Corinthians 1:11). The Lord abhors arguing and bickering, yet many churches pack padded pews with folks who can't get along. Two elders (both nearly ninety) oversaw the first church where I preached. Those two shouted and pouted for years over a trivial and unanswerable Bible question.

No two people agree on everything. My wife and I often carry on a loving conversation about some decision I'm facing. She will patiently say, "Bob, I would do it this way." And I impatiently retort, "But *you* aren't doing it!" It is hard for people who share common goals to get along. How can we ever unify a diverse church?

Christ Must Be The Focus

A young man came to the Hollywood church in the early '70s. Though intelligent and sincere, he had trouble adjusting to our group. At his home church where his father preached, they did everything according to an inflexible pattern. At one time the group was sizable, but it kept getting smaller. Why was it losing members? Simple. People kept "departing from the faith."

Those who left didn't actually lose faith in Jesus as God's Son. They broke from rigidity. They deserted because they didn't agree with the boy's father's strict interpretation of the scriptures. The church had been reduced mostly to members of the preacher's own family. If the preacher's wife ever disagreed with him, he could be sunk.

Some have tried to organize the church along lines of perfect conformity to the Word. It's always according to the way that they see it, however. No other views are tolerated. Fifty years ago, I was certain about thousands of things. Some of them I'm not sure about now. Many of them I don't even care about. But some essentials, I'm more convinced of all the time. Here are a few:

- Jesus, the only Son of God, lived in human form without sinning.
- Jesus died by crucifixion to pay the penalty for our failures.
- Three days later, many people saw Jesus alive.
- Jesus proved his resurrection to numerous people in various ways.
- We can share his resurrection victory by faith in him, repentance, and being baptized for the remission of our sins.
- God's Spirit lives in all those who obey in this way.
- Jesus will return to judge all people according to his righteousness.
- In the meantime, the world recognizes Jesus' followers because of the love they show for one another.

These things constitute the heart of the good news, the core of the message the apostles proclaimed. If you checked the board minutes of your church and listened to the conversations of the members, would you hear and see this focus on Christ? Unity in Christ must always trump personal preferences.

Think of the way that people get upset over church dinner menus, building configuration, carpet colors, worship times, the size of the savings account, the clothes of the minister or his spouse, and a million other things not related to the good news.

When We Lose The Cross Focus, The Church Misfires

"For the message of the cross is foolishness to those who are perishing, but to us who are being saved it is the power of God" (1 Corinthians 1:18).

In the 1980s I went to visit an elderly friend who lived alone in Los Angeles' Wilshire area. After my knocks on his apartment door got no response, I contacted the apartment manager. Together we went inside and found our friend on the floor cold and lifeless.

The paramedics came. The police arrived. I waited with them for the coroner. As I stood watching, I couldn't help but feel the contrast between the motionless form on the floor near me and the man that I once considered a dear friend — a very powerful and influential person in his day.

Before his retirement, he served as the number four person in one of the biggest southern California-based corporations. He'd been highly influential in Los Angeles community activities. Now he was inert, his impact a memory. The same thing happens to many powerful churches. Loss of purpose and disunity renders them comatose if not lifeless.

Vital churches unify and strongly emphasize the good news of Jesus' death for our sins, his burial, and resurrection. Guided by the Word, they desire the Spirit's presence and steerage. Healthy churches don't brag about anything except Christ. Paul said, "I resolved to know nothing while I was with you except Jesus Christ, and him crucified" (1 Corinthians 2:2).

We commonly try to "sell" people on the church instead of proclaiming Jesus' resurrection and urging people to repent of their

253

sins. It's our praise team, preacher, Sunday school, attractive program, or the size of the church that we talk about. When we do that, folks attend because of the church's popularity, not because they've repented and developed a personal relationship with Jesus.

It's important to help people become a part of the congregation once they're led to Jesus. However, we err when we try to bring people into the church without helping them become disciples of Jesus.

Our attempts at church building reflect the loss of mission that Jesus gave the apostles — to make disciples of all the nations. After the first few centuries, the church became institutional and planted, instead of mobile and missionary in nature as Jesus intended. Reformers worked on reshaping the institution and neglected to restore missionary zeal. Only rarely do disciples recognize that.

I recently attended my fiftieth high school reunion. Describing the emotions the experience ignited in me would fill boring volumes. At the registration table, a few 1954 annuals lay open so we ancients could see what we looked like five decades ago. Many with whom I'd once been close I didn't even recognize. I couldn't even identify some of the girls I'd once dated.

All school annuals share one similarity. They show head photos. To my knowledge, no annual depicts knees, elbows, and feet — with one possible exception — one from a podiatrists' school. We use face photos because that's how we identify people. The church needs to illustrate, advertise, exalt, and make its head prominent. We preach Christ and him crucified. When we try to sell people on "our church" it's like showing elbows, knees, and bottoms.

The focus remains on Christ when we allow others liberty of their own consciences. Worshiping with believers who emphasize the cross and exalt the Father should make every Christian happy. It's not necessary to have conformance on every issue.

People's experiences in Christ don't always match. We live on an acreage near the most remote place in Iowa. Several old friends from California and relatives from various states have visited us. Few find the way on their own. Often folks call from about forty miles away and say, "How do we get to your place?" I ask them,

"Where are you?" I can't direct people unless I know their location. Suppose I gave the same directions to folks driving east from California that I gave to those traveling west from Indiana?

It's also senseless trying to press all believers into the same mold. In order to properly respond to Christ, some folks will need work in one area and some in another. We allow people to exercise liberty in areas where scripture doesn't give firm instruction. We emphasize the good news and encourage believers to study the scriptures, but we can't insist that each person sees them in the same precise way. Paul instructed the meat eaters not to pass judgment on the vegetarians and vice versa.

The apostle John informed Jesus that he and his fellow apostles discovered a man who exorcised demons in Jesus' name. They ordered the man to stop because he wasn't one of them. The twelve assumed their exclusive right to Jesus' name. The Master didn't agree. In fact, he scolded them for their elitism. He intimated that they should be thankful the man did works in Jesus' name and for his glory (Mark 9:38-41). When I hear reports of others' successes in the Lord, I often envy rather than express gratitude. I pray that I can more humbly glorify God when others succeed in the Lord.

Vital churches always demonstrate another characteristic.

We Love God And Lovingly Serve all People, Even Our Enemies, As Jesus Taught And Acted

Here's a test: Next time you visit any public place, look around you. Whose feet would you least like to wash? Whom would you not want to serve for a day? If we want to be honchos and receive five-star treatment wherever we go, we shouldn't hang around the church. Sinners who know they need God's grace comprise the church. They confess their own sins, and continue to pray for one another. No person is more important than another.

> But because of his great love for us, God, who is rich
> in mercy, made us alive with Christ even when we were
> dead in transgressions — it is by grace you have been
> saved. And God raised us up with Christ and seated
> us with him in the heavenly realms in Christ Jesus, in

255

*order that in the coming ages he might show the in-
comparable riches of his grace, expressed in his kind-
ness to us in Christ Jesus.*

*For it is by grace you have been saved, through
faith — and this not from yourselves, it is the gift of
God — not by works, so that no one can boast. For we
are God's workmanship, created in Christ Jesus to do
good works, which God prepared in advance for us to
do.* — Ephesians 2:4-10

Our continuing focus must be honoring Christ for his loving sacrifice. When churches and individuals do that, they accomplish
mighty things for God.

Using New Testament Models

Do you remain unconvinced of the need to use New Testament
models? Do you ask, "What's the point of returning to congregational autonomy?" Why use apostolic examples for church-state
relations? Why do we need to give up beloved, long-established
religious traditions? No one agrees on New Testament examples
anyhow, why try? Why go back 2,000 years? Aren't civilization
and ethics advancing?

It is crucial to use the New Testament because no other way
pleases the Lord and presents an effective witness in the world.
This may seem shocking, brash, and opinionated, but sometimes
brutal candor is vital. My wife often has to deal with me that way
to get my attention. It is the same with my doctors, and my friends.

We toured the *Queen Mary* ocean liner soon after its restoration and relocation in Long Beach, California. The guide told us
that during the renovation, workmen removed the huge smokestacks
to make the inside of the ship's hull accessible for the work. After
cranes lifted the stacks off of the ship and placed them on the dock,
the much-traveled smokestacks collapsed. Over the years, the inte-
riors of the stacks rusted and eroded. What remained were several
layers of paint, but no metal.

What remains of the Lord's church in some instances is more
facade than substance. We've encrusted, smeared, and caked the

256

Lord's church with so much human opinion and so many man-made traditions, it's hard to tell that the body of Christ is in there any more.

Are You Sure We Must Use New Testament Models And Examples?

Before he went to the Garden of Gethsemane, Jesus prayed for his disciples and for future believers. He asked:

> ... that all of them may be one, Father, just as you are in me and I am in you. May they also be in us so that the world may believe that you have sent me. I have given them the glory that you gave me, that they may be one as we are one: I in them and you in me. May they be brought to complete unity to let the world know that you sent me and have loved them even as you have loved me.   — John 17:21-23

Church unity is scarcer than rats at a cat show. Some denominations have joined together in recent years. But a few mergers hardly constitute the oneness Jesus desired. A Hispanic preacher friend once said, "If you tie two cats together by the tail, you have union, but not unity." In some instances amalgamations represent survival efforts more than commonality. Some modern church mergers resemble scads of tail-tied cats.

The church began losing its unity when leaders and church-men departed from the apostles' teaching. Human opinions and traditions began counterbalancing Jesus' plain instructions. Many denominations now virtually countermand his authority. As a result, much of Jesus' church lies divided, hacked, and chopped like cheap pâté. His prayer for complete unity is largely unanswered.

Recently, I sat in a meeting of ministers representing the northwest Iowa cluster of a certain denomination. That group publicly advocates positions not in accord with the New Testament, such as the promotion of ordaining homosexual ministers.

Should the church protest activities of so-called gays and lesbians in American society and its workplaces? Absolutely not.

257

Should the church allow its members to practice homosexual behavior? Not according to the New Testament. Some Corinthians lived that lifestyle prior to their conversion to Jesus, but they gave it up in order to follow Christ (1 Corinthians 6:9-10).

Ministers of the denomination whose meeting I attended expressed frustration in their efforts to get members involved. Most of their congregations are dying. Older members expire; conversions are rare. The group reviewed several programs designed to engage people. But aging, tired, overworked folks don't want to volunteer. The leaders face another problem. Many members disagree with the church's public positions on numerous issues. I know that to be true because I'm close to several of their people.

The ministers and a denominational representative conversed about the need for societal justice and world peace. One subject I didn't hear discussed. As they deplored the non-involvement of their members, they ignored Jesus' commission to all his disciples — "tell the good news to every person."

At that meeting of ministers, not one person spoke of personal evangelism. The subject came up only during a report that related to mission work in a Latin-American nation. When I asked how they evangelized in that country, a church representative who'd just returned from a visit answered vaguely. That denomination apparently has lost touch with the core of Jesus' good news. They're interested only in the effects. It's like talking with overweight people who want their knees and backs to feel better, but don't want anyone tell them to exercise more and eat less.

Few mainline Protestant churches evangelize. Most preoccupy themselves maintaining musty buildings, talking about societal improvement, and burying their dead. The good news that Jesus commissioned his church to proclaim whispers like an occasional gasp from a nearly moribund body.

In its original form, the Word of Christ changed people and brought God's indwelling Spirit. As a result the church grew mightily. It increased despite the fact that it owned no buildings and made no efforts to change society except to proclaim Jesus' resurrection. It required its people to fully repent; it suffered intense persecution and exercised no political influence. Families were happy, individuals were filled with purpose, God's people dearly loved others, and they praised him.[2]

Subsequent generations of teachers and leaders think it necessary to alter the message, popularize it, and make it more palatable. It's as though a brilliant general formulates a perfect plan for pacifying a nation that's intent on complete world annihilation. The general's strategy will guarantee minimum loss of life, and happy results for all involved. He informs his colonels and majors of his design, and they in turn tell their subordinates. Each time the plan is passed on, however, underlings add ideas and/or modify it to their preferences.

After all that filtering, amending, and adding, the original becomes so altered it's pathetically ineffective. In fact, many troops sally forth attempting to use the variations only to suffer embarrassing defeat. In the meantime, the renegade enemy increases its strength and lethal weaponry.

If you think I'm stretching the point about additions, consider all the laws that churches and denominations enact for their members. The Catholic church presently carries about 4,000 different laws — down a few thousand after Vatican II — a priest once told me. Compare that number with the Old Testament's mere 600-plus laws.

Nearly every denomination formulates laws (written and unwritten) by the bunch. Local church treasurers transfer money collected in the pews to clerical hierarchy. At the headquarters, clerics busily make new decisions and precepts that the local churches often disagree with — some that aren't even biblical.

Churches need laws dictated from comfortable cloisters like they need outhouses for their air-conditioned sanctuaries. Today's churches suffer ecclesiastical top-heaviness. They're fatuous with flabby preachers, pastors, and attorneys. Churches will win only when the troops jettison this bureaucratic burden, rally behind the General Jesus, and follow his original plan.

Jesus' Word gives the unbeatable strategy. I pray that we can unite to put it into motion. When modern churches insist on rallying behind certain traditions it's like subordinates wanting to vary the perfect original. That's why it's vital to peel the encrustations

259

and undo paint-mixing of the last 1,900 years. Restoring congregational autonomy, we can begin making disciples who will make more disciples for God's glory not to attain denominational laurels.

A 2005 issue of *Christianity Today* featured an intriguing interview with a prominent minister and professor of an eastern US theological seminary. The minister-professor just published a book in which he criticized the consciences of evangelical Christians. The magazine interviewer asked the book's author about his statement deploring congregational autonomy. All congregations need to be accountable to a denomination, insisted the author. "It is flatly unbiblical and heretical for an individual congregation to say, 'We'll just be by ourselves and not be accountable to anybody,'" said the author.[3]

I'm wondering how he supports the allegation that congregational autonomy is unbiblical. The Bible indicates otherwise. On their first missionary journey, Paul and Barnabas made converts in the cities of Antioch, Iconium, Lystra, and Derbe (south central Turkey). On their return trip, the missionaries revisited those cities, and the official church historian Luke tells us that Paul and Barnabas "appointed elders for them in each church and, with prayer and fasting, committed them to the Lord, in whom they had put their trust" (Acts 14:23).

The missionary duo didn't turn over those churches to denominational leaders or even to the apostles in Jerusalem. They turned them (the elders and churches) over to the Lord. It's denominations that are unbiblical and heretical. In Acts 20, Paul challenged the Ephesian elders to oversee the flock of God in their city (Acts 20:17-31).

Modern churches get in trouble because they're led astray by single "pastors" who aren't unanswerable to anyone. The apostolic pattern holds ministers accountable to elders within the congregation. Denominational leaders and hierarchies created most of the obfuscating paint-mixing the church now suffers.

Using our analogy of the general's perfect plan helps illustrate this error carried out by his subordinates. As the individual underlings revise and reform — put their personal spins on the original

— they place their names over the doors of local headquarters. A captain's name appears or a lieutenant's. In some cases, the names aren't posted, but they just as well could be. The subordinates want their particular divisions identified by the modifications that they have made in their local outposts.

General Jesus' name isn't over the doors of most church buildings. Some reformer's name is, or the particular modification or reform that makes the local church identifiable. We won't have unity until we give up allegiance to the subordinates, the various Reformers, and return to the general's specific instruction (the New Testament).

Modern believers claim to follow the Reformed tradition or the Lutheran tradition. Jewish tradition drew harsh criticism from Jesus (cf Matthew 15:1-20). There's no reason to think that Christian traditions make him any happier. Customs established by subordinates keep us from unifying in Jesus' name.

Creeds also divide us. Constantine commanded the formulation of the first creeds, not Jesus. God's Word is sufficient to guide us. All other definitions and laws are extraneous.

Most of your town's church buildings probably boast the names of reformers. Other marquees feature types of church polity and doctrine. That's what we do when we identify ourselves as Presbyterian, Episcopalian, Baptist, Pentecostal, Reformed, Free, Methodist, or Lutheran. Paul considered such factionalism scandalous. He excoriated the Corinthians practicing it.

> One of you says, "I follow Paul"; another, "I follow Apollos"; another, "I follow Cephas"; still another, "I follow Christ." Is Christ divided? Was Paul crucified for you? Were you baptized into the name of Paul?
> — 1 Corinthians 1:12-13

Paul forbade people to use his name or anyone else's to identify themselves as followers of Christ. Yet we regularly do it! It's because we follow the recommendations of subordinates, not our general. As long as denominations compete with one another, Satan wins.

Efficiency stands strongly as a second reason to use the original. Jesus gave his church an awesome assignment — teach the good news to every nation. Years ago in Hollywood, I visited a newly arrived family. It wasn't a "traditional" family. It was comprised of a woman in her late sixties, her forty-year-old daughter, and the daughter's two children. The grandmother attended services with her grandchildren. She asked if I would visit the home and speak with her daughter. I arranged to do that one day and allocated about an hour for the visit.

When I arrived at the arranged time, the grandmother greeted me at the door. The daughter was in her bedroom applying makeup. Forty-five minutes later she was still "fixing" her face and my hour was quickly passing. So was my patience. When the daughter finally came through the door, it didn't appear that her lengthy facework helped much. The daughter spent so much time on her appearance that she left little opportunity for substantive talk, a conversation she badly needed.

Churches spend inordinate time on makeup, too. They fuss over window dressing — the right seasonal colors to lavish on pulpits and sanctuaries. Ministers sport distinctive, dignified robes. Ecclesiastical accoutrements such as reverse collars are so commonplace no one questions their usage.

Meanwhile, the general's advice goes unheeded by his minions: "While all the people were listening, Jesus said to his disciples, 'Beware of the teachers of the law. They like to walk around in flowing robes and love to be greeted in the marketplaces'" (Luke 20:45-46). Window dressing consumes a lot of the members' time and energy. In the meantime, they neglect the substance — Jesus' good news.

Lately I've been receiving unsolicited information packets from a certain denomination's regional office. Those multi-page parcels demonstrate evidence of bulky bureaucracy. One recent packet contained nine pages of "vital" information on how to hold a fundraising pancake breakfast at "your church." It included sample flyers and pages on how to motivate involvement of members. I wondered how many hours of an "expert's" time it took to produce those nine pages. I was also curious about whether the few hundred dollars that a church might make from the breakfast would cover that denominational worker's salary.

A more recent packet (33 pages worth, many printed on both sides) provided a calendar of events for church leaders as well as other information. Here are some examples of the way many denominational leaders spend their time. Of the scores of meetings for the quarter, there was a Church Life Cycle Transformation Summit (I don't know what that is) on Sunday, a Cluster Meeting on Monday and a regional staff meeting on Tuesday and two Spirit Fests on Saturday.

The next Sunday there was an IRMS Twentieth Anniversary Recovenanting Service (I don't know what that is, either) on Monday, a Regional Nominating Task Group meeting and more cluster meetings followed by a Saturday All Licensed Ministers Meeting. A minister was being installed the next Sunday followed by a Monday Investment and Property Unit meeting. Other meetings in subsequent days included a Stewardship and Mission Interpretation Unit (I think I know what that is), Interim Minister's Support Group, a #18 Post High Camp, Interim Minister's Retreat, Regional Licensing Unit of Commission on Ministry, Grand Camps, Canoe Camps, Women's Events, Couple Canoe Camps, and on and on.

Recall the Interim Minister's Retreat? The theme of that meeting was "Congregational Transformation as an Appropriate Interim Ministry Agenda." A media services meeting featured the following topics:

- Worship in the Digital Age;
- Whole Community Catachesis (sic);
- Developing Spirituality in the Life of the Church: A Holistic Approach; and
- Godly Play.

I'm sure these people have good intentions. I think you'll agree, however, that we've burdened the good news ship with so much tradition, organization, and custom, it is listing badly.

How Can We Possibly Unify When There Are So Many Interpretations Of The Bible?

I offer no easy solution, but it's simpler than most folks want to admit. Modern Christians often hear only the Sunday text and little else. A large percentage doesn't even hear the text before they fall asleep, engage in pew-people-watching, or football reverie.

First, we'll take giant steps toward unity when Christians read the Bible for themselves and not depend on "experts" to digest it for them. Today we benefit from numerous modern language versions so we're not forced to interpret King James's English before we can figure out what Jesus and his apostles meant.

I recently led my Tuesday night study group through the Old Testament book of Judges. Some of the students formerly attended churches for years, and even taught Sunday school, but many could not identify or locate most Bible books.

Judges' content shocked some of them although I warned them of its "R" rating. Earlier I mentioned Ehud, who drove a dagger into the belly of an unpopular, overweight king. Judges 5 contains the story of a general who fled for his life into the tent of a woman whose people he presumed were allies. After inviting him in, she gave him some milky grog that sedated him. When he fell asleep, she drove a tent peg through his temple.

Abimelech murdered 69 of his brothers, but later died when a woman cracked his skull with a huge millstone. Samson slaughtered Philistines by the hundreds and then died when he forced the collapse of a temple housing 3,000 partying Philistines.

Civil war developed in Israel after one tribe refused to correct known killer-rapists in its borders. The "rapee" was a concubine. The victim's husband incited punishment of the guilty tribe by carving up his concubine's corpse and sending the parts to representatives of the other tribes.

What's the point of learning from such a gory, violence-filled book? Tales from Judges demonstrate what happens when people depart from his teaching. Our Judges-review illustrates the Old Testament as a "How not to do it" book. When the Lord led Israel to the promised land, he warned them not to depart from his Word. But retention of God's Word wasn't just the leaders' responsibility.

The Lord ordered each father to teach his children the Word every day. He wanted God-focused daily family discussions (Deuteronomy 6:7-9; Psalm 78:5-7). Israelite parents failed to do that. Instead they succumbed to the loose sexual practices of the nations they were supposed to have driven from the area.

When Christian fathers allow their children to become electronically steeped, media saturated, and computer literate, but remain ignorant of Jesus' teaching, they err in the same way. Males in the upper-midwest customarily attend Sunday school until they arrive at age ten or twelve. In many cases after that, only women, small children, and the elderly attend Bible school. Worship services take a distant second during hunting season and special days like Super Bowl Sunday. Our task is demonstrating the Word's worth and how Jesus' message is for tough, mature people, not just the weak. In fact it teaches us how to be gallant and strong in Christ.

The Lord instructed Israelite fathers to talk about God every day with their kids. Families' members grow in respect for one another, and the church's message broadcasts boldly when Christian fathers follow this example. Christian fathers put away the sports and pleasure gods and exalt the only true God. The New Testament gives us the positive — how to do it — example.

Paul instructed fathers to rear their children in the "training and instruction of the Lord" (Ephesians 6:4). English translations don't fully convey Paul's intended meaning in this verse. The Lord planned that instruction to children about him come through their fathers. According the Lord's design, fathers play the major role in the child's learning about God. Fathers have to stop abdicating responsibility to mothers, Sunday school teachers, Christian schools, and chance. God holds us accountable.

A second path to unity is to read all the way through the various Bible books instead of studying by subject — at least for the first several times that we read the scriptures. Many ministers in my own fellowship, Churches of Christ, can quote scores of scriptures, but I wonder what percentage has read the Bible from cover to cover.

My early church experience illustrates what happens when one uses the Bible only as a source of haphazard reading. I familiarized

265

myself with numerous passages on the subjects of baptism, the nature of Christ, the Godhead, music in worship, the church, and the faith-works controversy. I felt that I could quote or find the necessary scriptures to convince a person of the correctness of my position on these subjects. I mostly based my approach to salvation on logic and human reason. Along with theological and biblical training, I studied Greek and Hebrew and read substantial parts of the Bible in the original languages.

I relate this to brag a little, I suppose, but mainly to make my point about my technical preparation to preach the Word. Much of my training and background, however, lay in proving the correctness of teachings that others in my fellowship and I believed — no one is more "expert" than a first-year Greek student.

In 1963, my wife and I lived in Redding (northern), California. The Hollywood Church of Christ called us to work with and for them. Taking a train from Redding to Los Angeles, I planned to meet with the elders and to find a residence before we moved south to Hollywood. Late at night, I relaxed in the train's dome car observing the stars and watching the section lights turn from green to red as we passed them. Several Lutherans were on board that train traveling from Minneapolis via Seattle to San Francisco for a church conference.

I didn't intend to eavesdrop. After all, what could I learn from Lutherans? But, I took notice of conversations unlike anything I'd heard in my life. I listened like a gossip at a sex-addict session. Those Lutherans spoke of their spiritual experiences. They talked of their personal relationship with the Lord, something I'd never enjoyed up to that time.

In our fellowship, we usually studied to find the correct doctrine. Then we followed it hoping that we'd have done all the right things before Jesus returns to judge us. Until that train trip, I had little conception of God's grace. For me, Jesus ranked just a little ahead of Paul in religious stature. Knowing doctrine was important. God judges you on the rightness of your beliefs.

I reflected on that "providential" train with those Lutherans, and continued reading the Bible all the way through several times. It became evident to me that I was guilty of the same thing for which Jesus condemned his contemporaries — using God's Word as a mere rulebook. I'd made the very mistake that moved Jesus to say: "You diligently study the scriptures because you think that by them you possess eternal life. These are the scriptures that testify about me, yet you refuse to come to me to have life" (John 5:39-40).

If the scriptures we're reading don't make us trust God, increase our faith in Christ, and help us love God and appreciate others, we're probably misusing them. It's especially helpful to read the New Testament books at one sitting as opposed to using proof texts. One gains an entirely different perspective from reading the Bible a book at a time. Inspired authors wrote the books to be read in that way. Possessing and knowing scripture doesn't save us. That sprouts pride. Knowing Jesus humbles and saves us.

When people become familiar with scripture, they're also less likely to be carried away by every wind of doctrine. Luke commended the Christians in Berea because when Paul preached there, they verified everything he said (Acts 17:10-12).

The Bereans made noteworthy effort. It's unlikely that any of them owned a copy of the Old Testament or even a copy of one Old Testament book. Paul quoted Old Testament scriptures to them to prove Jesus was the Messiah. The Bereans verified what Paul said by going to the synagogue where the scrolls were kept as we would go to a library to consult a reference book. They would unroll a holy scroll until they found Paul's quotation or assertion so they could validate it.

Doing that was far more difficult than it would seem because the Old Testament had no chapter and verse divisions at the time. Those helps weren't added until centuries later. I've read the Bible more than sixty times and have taken various groups of students through it, but I occasionally struggle to locate certain passages; my memory gets worse with age. At this moment, my timeworn Young's *Analytical Concordance* sits open beside me because I had trouble remembering where to find one of Jesus' sayings. Mr. Young made it convenient for me to locate the chapter and verse.

The Bereans lacked these helps. Still, they wanted to check everything Paul said. They didn't assume that he was a "sound" preacher and that they could trust his judgment after that. They continued their verification process. God bless them.

Strong, unified churches emerge when God's people exalt the cross, dedicate themselves to daily Bible reading, scripturally verify what their leaders advocate, submit all things to prayer, and allow God's Spirit to harmoniously lead them. I pray that the church will understand its mission and effectively carry it out to God's glory.

---

1. Not his real name.

2. The book of Acts regularly reports these details, for example, 2:14-47; 3:11-26; 4; 5; 7:59—8:40; 11:19-30; 13:13-52; 16:22-34. There were exceptions, of course, otherwise we wouldn't have the New Testament epistles.

3. *Christianity Today*, "The Evangelical Scandal," interview of Ron Sider by Stan Guthrie, April 2005, p. 73.

14

Summation:
Christians And Governments

We are most like beasts when we kill.
We are most like men when we judge.
We are most like God when we forgive.
— William A. Ward

Can Christians Serve In The Military?

New Testament support for objections to Christian military service is scarcer than roast boar at bar mitzvahs. In contrast, sympathy and favorable attitudes toward Roman officers and soldiers appear more often than dance requests to a prom queen. It is hard to dispute with Tubingen scholar, Otto Bauernfeind's assessment:

> *The question whether a Christian should undertake or refuse military service is not put in the NT (New Testament), nor can it be directly answered from the NT.*[1]

In the same way Paul urged vegetarians not to pass judgment on meat eaters and vice versa (cf Romans 14), it's a matter of one's own conscience. Instead of condemning others for their decisions, I think it best to let the Lord judge.

Should Christians Serve In Government Positions?

It is unlikely that the early evangelists would have passed up an opportunity to bring anyone to Jesus. Slaves and affluent, both women and men comprised first-century converts. A few were in government service. The historian, Luke, recorded Paul's conversations with governmental representatives Agrippa, Felix, and Festus. The apostle did his best to bring them to the Lord, too (Acts 24-26).

Nothing in the exchanges between Paul and those Roman agents indicates disapproval of their positions. He called for them to repent of their sins and to think about the judgment to come — but service to the Roman government seemed not a concern.

Though the New Testament gives no specific commands about governmental service, it yields one example of a Christian serving in a government position. In Paul's closing remarks to the Romans, he mentioned "Erastus, who is the city's (Corinth) director of public works" (Romans 16:23b). Because Paul only occasionally offered details of a person's background, it appears that the mention of Erastus' employment indicated that Paul thought it a positive thing.

Did Erastus' governmental position compromise his discipleship? As novice politicians soon learn, it's very difficult to be fair and just with every constituent in all circumstances. "An honest politician is one who, when he is bought, will stay bought," Simon Cameron jested. Cameron might have spoken of contemporary politicos, but that wasn't the case. He died in 1899.

Given the trifling amount of information we possess concerning the duties of Corinth's public works director (treasurer) in 50 A.D., we must be circumspect. It's impossible to draw conclusions concerning Erastus' possible temptations and difficulties.

Elected representatives are pressured by various groups to act in accordance with their wishes. Can a Christian fairly represent all of the special interest groups that expect him/her to do favors for them? Only people faced with the task know for sure. This much is evident, however. Nearly all jobs present temptations and potential compromises. No perfect employer exists, and no flawless corporation, church, government, or individual exists, either.

In the late '50s and early '60s, I worked for a major oil company. My bosses at times did things of which I disapproved. For several months I worked in a bulk plant where the company stored large quantities of petroleum derivatives like gasoline, oil, solvents, paint thinners, and weed killers.

The company had a contract with the highway department to provide weed killers for application along state roadways. On one occasion, there was a surplus of hundreds of gallons of a green-colored weed killer. It was returned to the bulk plant. Though the state paid for it, it had no further use for the balance of the chemical. The plant manager needed to decide how to dispose of it. He chose to add it to the huge regular gasoline storage tank. In doing so, he conveniently made up for some gasoline storage losses.

I imagined what the green, foul-smelling liquid would do to the insides of automotive engines. When we asked the boss about it, he considered the amount of weed killer contamination to the total volume "slight and harmless." I yielded to his judgment, but 45 years later I still wonder about it. I needed to feed and house my family then and jobs were scarce. I looked forward to working for the Lord, when I wouldn't be a party to decisions of such a nature.

Later as a minister, I learned that some of the ethical choices I faced equally challenged and frustrated me. No church attains perfection. Paul criticized even Peter for his prejudice toward Gentiles in Antioch. The Lord calls us to sharpen and hold one another accountable. Thank God for friends in Christ who have done that for me. I pray that I've helped others in the same way.

Some good friends served in elected positions and did so with apparent integrity. Whether all of their decisions pleased God is for him to say. I face plenty of my own temptations every day and plead his mercy in Christ.

Should Christians Criticize Their Governments?
Luther's use of scripture to support his rebuke of civil authorities seems to some scripturally sound and logical. Isn't Jesus the perfect example for all Christian behavior? Modern merchandisers adroitly sell pins and bracelets with WWJD (What Would Jesus Do) stamped on them. If that means forgiving people as Jesus did, acting from pure motives, and practicing patience, it's a worthy aspiration.

Jesus acted in ways that he never authorized us, however. He drove money changers from the temple (John 2:13-16). He possessed that authority. He's the divine, supreme Judge. He warned us against adjudicating another's guilt (Matthew 7:1-2). The Lord expects us to leave verdicts to him.

271

Jesus also reprimanded Pilate. The Father gave him that mandate. You and I lack both the discernment to know when censure is appropriate and the license to convey it. As we recognized earlier, Jude saw that condemnation remains God's domain. The Lord never granted it to us.

> *But even the archangel Michael, when he was disputing with the devil about the body of Moses, did not dare to bring a slanderous accusation against him, but said, "The Lord rebuke you!"* — Jude 9

During Jesus' earth-tenure, Rome did many things Jesus could have protested. However, we lack a record of Jesus saying things like the following:

- Caesar stifles the democratic process. We're booking a ship to Rome next week to protest our lack of local representation in Israel.
- Join me and the disciples in our protest of Tiberius' war against the Germans.
- God wants all people to be free. Beginning Monday we're going to boycott all farmers and pottery-makers that use slave labor.
- In Israel, we are overtaxed, forgotten, and mistreated. Join me in rallying against this travesty.
- Rome orders us not to pray publicly. Join our letter-writing rally and send your contribution to help finance our campaign against the government's ungodliness.

Paul's pointed questions to the Corinthians amply illustrate what he thought of Christians passing judgment on the world: "What business is it of mine to judge those outside the church? Are you not to judge those inside? God will judge those outside" (1 Corinthians 5:12-13). The New Testament contains no precedent for protest, criticism, or boycotting non-Christians or governments. From start to finish of his ministry, Jesus warned all people to repent of their own sins (Luke 13:1-3). God will pass judgment on other's flaws.

272

The book of Revelation describes Christians facing horrific treatment. Jesus' letters to the seven churches of Asia (Revelation 2-3) describe the poverty, affliction, slander, and martyrdom they endured. Those communications contain no suggestion or hint that the churches involved protest the maltreatment or hire lawyers to preserve their freedom. Instead, Jesus cautioned them that conditions would worsen and urged those beleaguered Christians to prepare themselves to face them.

The Lord wants his people to confront persecution's fire with faith, not complaint. He never riled his followers to dissatisfaction with society or government. Doctor Jesus prescribed patience.

The seven Revelation letters impart something else. They contain:

- admonitions for church members to act morally pure;
- severe reprimands about unfaithfulness to the Word;
- warnings about lapsing in belief; and
- repentance demanded from those losing faith.

Is it my conclusion that Christians should never offer criticism? The US government allows us to voice dissent through elected representatives and by voting. I consider that legitimate. But there's no precedent for churches encouraging letter-writing, rallies, telephone, or email campaigns to protest governmental decisions or corporate policies, however good the motivation or seemingly righteous the cause. It's too easy to become distracted from the kingdom mission. Our task continues to be telling the good news, not perfecting society.

The Lord wants us to be model citizens of whatever country or state in which we reside. The current nonstop grumbling of both right-wing and left-wing Christians suffocates the effectiveness of Jesus' message and generates hostile audiences for those who share the good news.

The world associates Christianity with censure and complaint, not love. That's why Peter cautioned: "Live such good lives among the pagans that, though they accuse you of doing wrong, they may see your good deeds and glorify God on the day he visits us" (1 Peter 2:12).The apostle followed that statement with his command:

> *Submit yourselves for the Lord's sake to every author-*
> *ity instituted among men: whether to the king, as the*
> *supreme authority, or to governors, who are sent by*
> *him to punish those who do wrong and to commend*
> *those who do right. For it is God's will that by doing*
> *good you should silence the ignorant talk of foolish men.*
> *Live as free men, but do not use your freedom as a cover-*
> *up for evil; live as servants of God. Show proper re-*
> *spect to everyone: Love the brotherhood of believers,*
> *fear God, honor the king.*   — 1 Peter 2:13-17

Paul advised, "Give everyone what you owe him: If you owe taxes, pay taxes; if revenue, then revenue; if respect, then respect; if honor, then honor" (Romans 13:7). That leaves miniscule space for criticism. When Paul wrote, "If you owe taxes, pay taxes," he used rapid-fire two syllable and one syllable words in the original. His language is balanced, but blunt and forceful. Paul didn't bother with eloquence. He meant business. We pay taxes, and we treat governmental leaders with respect, not just the ones with whom we politically agree.

The nineteenth-century scholars, Sanday and Headlam, noted in their classic commentary on Romans:

> *To designate this or that form of government as "Chris-*
> *tian" and support it on these grounds, would have been*
> *quite alien to the whole spirit of those days (first cen-*
> *tury). The Church must influence the world by its hold*
> *on the hearts and consciences of individuals, and in that*
> *way, and not by political power, will the Kingdom come.*[2]

Tim LaHaye, Pat Robertson, and many other preachers appear to say to the Lord: "Protect me, my family, and possessions by preserving the 'American Way' so I can serve you." In other words, "Unless the government, its agencies, and schools maintain a Christian atmosphere, we and our children can't faithfully serve the Lord." This is at odds with Jesus' following challenge:

Once when large crowds of people were going along with Jesus, he turned and said to them, "Whoever comes to me cannot be my disciple unless he loves me more than he loves his father and mother, his wife and his children, his brothers and his sisters and himself as well. Whoever does not carry his own cross and come after me cannot be my disciple ... none of you can be my disciple unless he gives up everything he has.

— Luke 14:25-27, 33 (TEV)

Jesus prepared the disciples by telling them of the persecutions they'd face if they remained his friends and continued their testimony about him. Jesus predicted a troublous future. They'd be handed over to "local councils and flogged in the synagogues." Also, they'd appear before "governors and kings as witnesses to them" (Mark 13:9). In other words, "When they arrest you for preaching in my name and they haul you into court, that's a good opportunity to witness to the dignitaries."

Jesus never taught us to influence society so life would be comfortable for us and conducive to faith. At present, about half of the church spends its time whining that the government doesn't maintain a society supportive of its convenience, comfort zone, and ease.

What about the other half of the church? Despite Paul's caution not to let the "world around you squeeze you into its own mold" (Romans 12:2),[3] the second half of the church is not only squashed, it's been compressed into a gelatinous mass, capped with fruity fuzz, and stuck in a politically correct freezer.

Paul gallantly declared God's rule before the elite Areopagus in Athens. Peter and John courageously pronounced Jesus' resurrection in the Jerusalem courthouse. Stephen intrepidly preached as angrily thrown rocks and stones pelted his head. But we meekly tag along the media's way, truth, and light fretting about social acceptance, cringing before academia, and worrying about creature comforts. Will our short-term security, be converted to eternal shame when Jesus "comes in his Father's glory with the holy angels"? (Mark 8:38).

275

Is There Such A Thing As A "Just War"?

What conditions justify a government's conduct of a war? Solomon's pick favoring one prostitute mother over another was easy compared to the "just war" issue.

Some rely on Augustine of Hippo's definitions of a "just war." As we've noted, Augustine didn't formulate the full theory. He originated the concept that the "motive for war must be love." Has any nation ever fought a war under the pretense of loving its enemy — the nation it set out to conquer? Augustine's view might echo well in the hallowed halls of the Vatican, but will thud at West Point. What about the "love test"?

It's less realistic than expecting the groom not to think of the honeymoon bed during the wedding. It's pious but not practical, devout sounding, but not realistic. As is true of the Edsel plans, it should have died on the drawing board. The concept is suspect because no group can be that purely motivated, whether military or mendicants.

It's also not possible to make judgments about an adversary's worthiness. We don't know the intentions of people. Friends and relatives often give me credit for righteousness I don't deserve. They make assumptions because I'm supposed to be a minister. Discussing the justness of a war compares to medieval contemplations of how many angels sit on a pinhead.

Is It Right For Governments To Wage War?

Is it wrong for governments to engage in war? I find nothing in the scriptures that restricts governments from declaring and conducting war. Evidence suggests that Christians should not protest their governments' military actions, however.

The role of individuals contrasts with that of governments. In the Old Testament, the Lord established Israel as a theocracy (ruled by God). Through Moses, the Law, and the prophets, God gave Israel strict instructions. He reckoned his spokesmen immediately accountable for informing Israel, and he held Israel answerable for keeping his will.

No government since exists as a true theocracy. Zwingli attempted one in Zurich, Calvin in Geneva, and others made abortive attempts. But Israel was the only God-ordained theocracy. Therefore, it's impossible to use the Old Testament as a model for dealing with governments or for measuring governmental responsibility to the Lord.

According to the New Testament, governments are established to keep the peace and regulate society. However, the Lord gave no minister, prophet, or religious person responsibility for holding governments answerable. God does that.

Do we find an exception to this principle in John the Baptist's fateful criticism of Herod the tetrarch's scandalous marriage? (Matthew 14:1-12). John was possibly the boldest, most honest and direct preacher who ever lived. He criticized the king's morality, and he challenged all to live better lives. He targeted just about everyone he met. All heard his command to "Repent!" But John lived and died under the Jewish system.

Jesus affirmed John's greatness, but the least in the kingdom, said Jesus, is greater than John (Matthew 11:11). Because the kingdom came into existence after John died, we can't use his excoriation of the king as our precedent. John lived in a different country under an entirely separate system.

Although the New Testament records John's life, he lived at the end of the Old Testament era. God's kingdom wasn't yet established through Jesus' death, burial, resurrection, and the arrival of the Holy Spirit. John achieved distinction. He was a good guy, but he wasn't a Christian. He lived under Mosaic Law.

Whether it's right for governments to wage war isn't our call. The state accounts to God. The Lord gave us the responsibilities of witnessing for Jesus and acting as good citizens. The New Testament advises us to pray for our heads of state. When leaders make incorrect decisions they answer to the Lord.

The first-century Roman government bore no resemblance to a democracy in a republic. Pagan and ruled by dictators, it promoted idolatrous religious beliefs. Yet Jesus taught his disciples to honor the Roman government. Would he also silence Christians who protest war?

When Jesus said, "Render to Caesar," I think he meant that his followers should let Caesar decide whether the Romans went to war. His followers were too busy themselves making disciples of all the nations. The New Testament gives no advice or instruction to governments or leaders of governments unless those leaders are disciples of Jesus.

What Should Christians Do When Their Governments Do Things That Are Clearly Un-Christian?

On their way to the Jerusalem temple one day where they planned to preach and teach, Peter and John met a crippled beggar. Typical preachers, their pockets were empty. Peter brought something better; the ability to heal in Jesus' name. He ordered the man to walk.

Not long ago I made a hospital call on a sixty-year-old woman who awaited knee replacement surgery. Following her recovery, she wanted to dance again. She hoped for other things, of course, but she definitely wanted to waltz. I doubt whether that first-century beggar ever boogied. But he could once Peter and John healed him. The beggar did what every long-term lame person and many elderly long to do. He kicked up his heels, leaped, ran, and praised God. Peter and John credited the Lord Jesus Christ of Nazareth.

The incident seized attention in the busy temple courtyard. Many people witnessed the healing and saw the formerly bedridden man exuberantly running and then grasping the apostles. Those people praised God, too. Peter preached about Jesus' death, burial, and resurrection to the excited audience, but disclaimed human power. He attributed the incident to this: "It is Jesus' name and the faith that comes through him that has given this complete healing to him, as you can all see" (Acts 3:16).

That didn't close Peter's homily. As Jesus often did with his sermons, Peter ended with a call to repentance. By then the authorities arrived and wanted to know what happened. The healing didn't bother them. Here's what agitated the leaders; the apostles kept proclaiming Jesus' resurrection. The authorities jailed Peter and John over night. The next day the high Jewish court met to question the two. By what power did the apostles heal? That's what disturbed them.

278

If you mean the healing of the crippled man yesterday, and want to know the power behind it, the Holy Spirit prompted Peter to say,

> *Then know this, you and all the people of Israel: It is by the name of Jesus Christ of Nazareth, whom you crucified but whom God raised from the dead, that this man stands before you healed. He is " 'the stone you builders rejected, which has become the capstone.' Salvation is found in no one else, for there is no other name under heaven given to men by which we must be saved."*
> — Acts 4:10-12

Peter preached the good news again, and he repeated the gospel's main elements. The facts created a quandary for the authorities. In the apostles, they saw unabashed courage and unbending conviction. Jesus' men weren't first-century Ph.D.s or seminary grads. They hadn't even attended junior college or a recognized preacher's training school.

Their dads taught them how to fish, repair boats, mend nets, and maybe tell fish tales, but not talk to crowds. Yet, there the apostles stood, poised and confident, as if trained by an Athenian elocutionist. Unambiguous evidence stared at them. Right beside the apostles was the guy they'd healed. The message about Jesus kept spreading faster than swine flu. The exasperated Jewish leaders had no vaccine or treatment.

Like ineffectual parents they threatened gravely. Don't speak anymore or "teach at all in the name of Jesus" (Acts 4:18). The highest court in the land commanded the apostles to desist their proclamation. Suppose the United States Supreme Court delivered a similar charge today: "Under penalty of death no more preaching in the name of Jesus!" How would Christians react? Would they call a massive protest? Hire the best lawyers? Would James Dobson make impassioned radio pleas, and Pat Robertson and D. James Kennedy appear before television cameras to exert "Christian" pressure?

The ensuing verses provide our paradigm. At a meeting with the brothers and sisters, the apostles prayed to God acknowledging

279

his sovereignty. They quoted the description found in Psalm 2 of how the world's rulers often oppose God. Then the apostles reviewed the way authorities, both Jewish and Gentile conspired against God's anointed one, Jesus. In their prayer, they also recognized that events developed along lines according to God's long-established plans. Then those disciples asked an amazing request.

They didn't petition the Lord to change the authorities' hearts or to alter the high court's decision. They didn't beg for leadership skills and the money to form a popular protest. The church solicited two things from God. First, they wanted boldness to continue their witness in the face of the threats. Second, they asked God to do something else few Christians request today — "Stretch out your hand to heal and perform miraculous signs and wonders through the name of your holy servant Jesus."

God answered their prayer in ground-rattling, back-tingling fashion. "After they prayed, the place where they were meeting was shaken. And they were all filled with the Holy Spirit and spoke the word of God boldly" (Acts 4:30-31). Current Christians depend too much on lawyers, letter-writing campaigns, political clout, and legal maneuvers. Jesus' real followers fearlessly declare his good news and pray powerfully. They do not demand a cozy, comfortable, safe environment.[4]

Most Christians know Jesus' parable of the sower. Matthew, Mark, and Luke all include it (Matthew 13:1-23; Mark 4:1-20; Luke 8:4-15). Ministers preach on its themes and also base children's sermons on the sower's planting methods. Slight differences appear in the gospel accounts (the kinds of differences you'd expect from three honest witnesses), but interpretations don't vary concerning the seeds sown on rocky and thorny ground. Those seeds lasted only until trouble came.

Why the seed impermanence? Association with the Word made life difficult for those folks so they gave up. Jesus' way proved too demanding, too grueling, and too life-threatening so they quit. Wealth's deceit and the worries of life choked the Word sown among thorns.

Christians need to stop complaining about societal impediments and begin asking God to grant us boldness to complete the real undertaking he assigned us. He demands fruitfulness from us in sharing the good news.

Why Does The New Testament Use Such Warlike Language And What Kind Of War Do Christians Fight?

Battle shields and swords seem strange symbols for Christians. Here's a sample of the militaristic expressions used by Paul and other New Testament authors: "Finally, be strong in the Lord and in his mighty power. Put on the full armor of God so that you can take your stand against the devil's schemes" (Ephesians 6:10-11). How can Christians associate themselves with war symbols?

Combat seems alien to the love of Christ. Inconsistent with his teaching. If Jesus taught love, forgiveness, compassion, gentleness, and meekness, how can his followers use war metaphors? Someone recently asked me about that contradiction.

Here's what some military leaders have said about warfare:

- General George S. Patton: "In planning any operation it is vital to remember and constantly repeat to oneself two things. In war nothing is impossible provided you use audacity; and do not take counsel of your fears."
- Admiral Bull Halsey: "Hit hard, hit fast, hit often." Does that sound like turning the other cheek? The world uses strike, cut, and run; Christians don't.
- Dwight D. Eisenhower: "When you appeal to force, there's one thing you must never do — lose."

If the above accurately describe war, how can Christians properly use warlike metaphors? In the first place, Jesus taught about interpersonal relationships, not international relations. Jesus directed no teaching toward governments or their leaders. Paul implored Christians to pray for political-governmental leaders so that we can "live peaceful and quiet lives in all godliness and holiness" (1 Timothy 2:2). But no New Testament writer or apostle directed a teaching toward lawmakers or political leaders. The New Testament targets individuals and churches.

281

Misunderstanding Jesus' teaching leads many Christians to march in the streets — to gripe, boycott, and battle in the name of Christ. Picketing, protesting, and war don't befit what Jesus taught. That being true, is war a fitting Christian symbol? I think so, but only after we clearly understand three things. We need to know first, "Who is the enemy?" Second, "What or where is the battlefield?" Third, "What is the weaponry?"

In Christian warfare, who is the enemy? Most people wage war on numerous fronts. In a single day, I might be upset with my wife, one of our children, or a grandchild (family conflicts rarely occur these days, and I thank God for that), a neighbor, the IRS, or a big corporation.

We skirmish with all kinds of people. The following illustrates the preponderance and pain of battles among exes: "I still miss my ex, but my aim is improving." Some people constantly war with varieties of folks and scores of institutions. If we watch the news often, we get angry enough to do battle with people all over the world. But others aren't the enemy.

People blame others. But it's never the blamer's fault. Fault-finding didn't originate recently. It started with the first couple. I blame Adam for starting this blame-fixing when he excused himself by saying: "It was that woman you gave me." We mistakenly fault other people for our problems, and err when we battle with them.

"The art of war," said U. S. Grant, "is simple enough. Find out where the enemy is. Strike him as hard as you can and keep moving." We compound our trouble because we don't know the enemy's identity let alone his location or how to fight him.

The New Testament identifies the real foe. Satan is the enemy, not our spouses, friends, neighbors, or coworkers (Ephesians 6:11). As long as we war with other people, Satan wins. We'll lose no matter how right or wise, astute or smart we think we are.

Where is the battlefield? It's in our wills. It's the battle of faith, belief, trust in God, and loving as Jesus loved. We want to do things our way. Paul knew that struggle.

I do not understand what I do. For what I want to do I do not do, but what I hate I do ... I know that nothing good lives in me, that is, in my sinful nature. For I have the desire to do what is good, but I cannot carry it out. For what I do is not the good I want to do; no, the evil I do not want to do — this I keep on doing. Now if I do what I do not want to do, it is no longer I who do it, but it is sin living in me that does it. So I find this law at work: When I want to do good, evil is right there with me. — Romans 7:15-21

The apostle recognized the perpetual tussle of his will against the Lord's. I battle in the same way. Each day I start with new resolutions and "good" intentions. But even during my morning prayers, my stubborn will mines my mind. I more easily let go of money than I do my scheming, bitterness, pride, and lust.

Will-battles constantly arise. Checkout stand magazines allure us though we've vowed mental purity. With a single word, decades-old resentment against a sister or father reignites. Our mouths refuse to remain closed at the opportunity to deride a coworker. Inane television shows consume time. Pride pops up more often than lust.

We also scorn the poor. In one of the most misunderstood passages in the Bible, Jesus talked about our eyes being the "lamp of the body. If your eyes are good, your whole body will be full of light" (Matthew 6:22-23). Many preachers use this text to address moral purity. "Bad" or "evil" eyes lust after women — look for the best chests and the sexiest "hindquarters." We need "good" or pure eyes, preach the ministers. They argue lustily for this "evil eye" interpretation.

It took me years to understand what Jesus meant by "evil eyes." It baffled me that Jesus raised this topic in the midst of a section on the use of money. He taught about not storing up "treasures on earth," and afterward warned about master cash. How does an "evil eye" relate to monetary gain?

One day, while studying the book of Deuteronomy, I found the mystery's solution. Here's what the Lord told Israel about helping the destitute:

*If there is a poor man among your brothers in any of
the towns of the land that the Lord your God is giving
you, do not be hardhearted or tightfisted toward your
poor brother.* — Deuteronomy 15:7

The human side of us tends toward selfishness, doesn't it? Our personal wants scream for attention muffling the pleas of the deprived.

Few societies lack poor people. In telling Israel in advance what choices they'd face, the Lord warned them not to squeeze their money too tightly. Verse 9 counseled them against having "ill will toward your needy brother." The King James Version translates closer to its literal Hebrew wording, "thine eye be evil." The expression probably reflects our body language when someone requests help. We squint disapprovingly. That puts evil and darkness in our minds because first, we don't love a brother, and second, we don't love God enough to trust him to care of us when we generously give.

The battleground for these decisions is our will. Scores of times every day we face choices about loving God and his creations. The weapons we choose determine whether we shall win or lose this battle over our souls. Unless we're led by the Spirit and armed with generosity, honesty, righteousness, peacemaking, prayer, sporting the bulletproof vest of faith in Christ, and protecting our brains with a sure-salvation helmet, we'll be will-war casualties.

What Is The Church's Work?

According to the New Testament, God assigned the church three basic missions. First, the church makes our Creator's wisdom known to rulers and authorities in the heavenly realms to his glory (Ephesians 3:10-12). Second, we preach Christ and him crucified to every person occupying the globe. That means bringing people to Jesus and encouraging them to stay close to him and to one another without prejudice, impurity, or greed.

Jesus gave the assignment to every follower:

*Go and make disciples of all nations, baptizing them in
the name of the Father and of the Son and of the Holy*

284

Spirit, and teaching them to obey everything I have com-
manded you.   — Matthew 28:19-20a

If the Lord graded your church, its leaders, members, and you on the completion of the first and second assignments, what letter grade would he give?

Will the Lord evaluate us that way? Jesus' parable of the vine and the branches warns that he will. "He cuts off every branch in me that bears no fruit" (John 15:2).

Jesus further cautioned us to follow his teaching:

> *If anyone does not remain in me, he is like a branch*
> *that is thrown away and withers; such branches are*
> *picked up, thrown into the fire and burned.*
>   — John 15:6

Does your church base its decisions on God's Word or on politically correct resolutions made by some hierarchy behind closed doors?

Here's the third calling Jesus gave us: unselfishly help the poor. According to Jesus' Matthew 25 parable, all nations will be gathered, but people will be separated individually as shepherds divide their animals. As the critters pass by, they're directed either to a sheep pen or goat sty. Here's what marks one group from the other. Did they feed and slake the thirst of destitute folks? Did they welcome strangers, minister to the sick, and visit prisons?

This parable teaches that the Lord intends to ask you and me those questions on the last day. I doubt he'll be happy with the answer, "Well, I was an activist in urging more generous government programs." Or, "I think we should help our own first." We'll account for whether we kept our pockets full while others starved, and how we used our time.

My wife and I currently live in northwest Iowa. The average age of the population here stands well above the national average. Thousands of graying people live alone. For those not capable of self-care, nursing homes abound. Federal and state governments keep creating programs for elderly assistance. Most persons in need of medical help receive it. Yet one problem persists — that of loneliness. Among the elderly, it's epidemic in every state and among all socio-economic groups. Walk the halls of convalescent homes; forlorn eyes implore you to stop and chat.

Is manpower available to assist with the loneliness problem? No and yes. Most rural and small town churches face budget crunches. Many churches share ministers with nearby congregations. One local minister preaches at three different churches every Sunday. A lone minister, regardless of energy, planning, and gifts can't possibly visit all of the sick and shut-ins, and shouldn't.

Most northwest Iowans expertly and regularly play cards. Every day, area residents play thousands, maybe millions of card games in homes, community centers, and cafes. Physically able elderly folks drive miles to engage in that pastime. Meanwhile, people of their own generation or a little older sit or lie alone in nursing homes longing for someone to visit them. Within a few years, today's card players will sit solitary in nursing homes. But only a minority of the current players regularly visits shut-ins.

The fact that people tend to live longer now increases the incidence of lonesome folks. Jesus gave us a remedy for elderly loneliness. It's evident from reading 1 Timothy 5 that the first-century church faced similar difficulties. But, it expected all people young and old to minister. The church cared for its widows; Paul reminded Timothy of the requirements for such assistance:

> *No widow may be put on the list of widows unless she is over sixty, has been faithful to her husband, and is well known for her good deeds, such as bringing up children, showing hospitality, washing the feet of the saints, helping those in trouble and devoting herself to all kinds of good deeds.* — 1 Timothy 5:9-10

This passage informs us first that all Christians engage in helping others. Second, church leaders are obliged to remind their people of the responsibility to do that. I pray that we can mobilize the Christian card players, tea party gossips, coffee shop experts, casino junkies, domino addicts, and chronic golfers. They could measurably shrink the loneliness black hole.

Our goal, however, is not attaining a perfect society or kingdom in this age. The New Testament teaches a different perspective. Karl Barth, for one, recognized the fact that the church resembles a group of pilgrims.

The writer of Hebrews gave us a clear example of this:

> *And so Jesus also suffered outside the city gate to make the people holy through his own blood. Let us, then, go to him outside the camp, bearing the disgrace he bore. For here we do not have an enduring city, but we are looking for the city that is to come.*
> — Hebrews 13:12-14; cf 1 Corinthians 10

When Moses led the Israelites out of Egypt, the Lord didn't want them to settle until they reached the promised land. The enduring society won't be found this side of heaven. We'll reside permanently with the Lord only in the afterlife. There the Lord promises rooms for all who make reservations. No one will grow old there or ever be lonely.

Patient Witnessing

Revelation's symbols baffle most folks. Some spend so much time speculating about "666" and the mark of the beast they never discover the book's primary message — perseverance.

The mysterious book introduces us to a great body of water. It is a

> *... sea of glass mingled with fire, and those who had conquered the beast and its image and the number of its name, standing beside the sea of glass with harps of God in their hands. And they sing the song of Moses, the servant of God, and the song of the Lamb.*
> — Revelation 15:2-3 (RSV)

You probably recognize the picture. The Israelites sang Moses' victory song once they traversed the Sea of Reeds. God had parted the waters for their safe passage and conquered their enemies for them. Moses' Song didn't rocket to the top only to be forgotten. Heaven's tenants will sing it again but with an additional refrain — the song of the Lamb. Both stanzas of the melody will be heard on the glassy sea's victory shore.

Fire mingles with that smooth-as-glass sea. That symbolism indicates at least three things. First, to the ancient Israelites, seas represented threat and disaster (Psalm 93:3-4). That signification originated with the Exodus. The Israelites preferred terra firma. Centuries after Moses, Solomon (circa 950 B.C.) built a maritime fleet to bring gold and other treasures from abroad. Yet he depended on sailors from Tyre to skillfully sail his ships (1 Kings 9:26-27). Tyre's King Hiram evidently designed those vessels (1 Kings 10:11).

Generations later, King Jehoshaphat tried to duplicate Solomon's fleet experience but his native navy met disaster. His ships never got out of port (1 Kings 22:48; 2 Chronicles 20:37). Water in larger bodies than in buckets or, at most, wells and aqueducts usually represented the enemy to the Israelites.

Revelation's glassy sea perhaps indicated solidarity and placidity but its fire probably signified testing (1 Peter 4:12).[5] The first-century recipients of Revelation knew about Caesar's pyrotechnics. In Peter's closing years, Nero impaled many Christians, doused them with oil, and used them to light his well-known paved highways. In the first century's nineties, Emperor Domitian banished Revelation's author John to Patmos, a lonely island. John and his Christian contemporaries found themselves in the cruel flaming crucible, which Peter predicted.

Some cities of the Roman Empire required people to take loyalty checks before they could be involved in business endeavors. Allegiance tests often included burning incense to a figure of Caesar. Christians obeyed their governments but could never bow to or burn incense to idols.

The "beast" of Rome insisted that all worship it. Revelation predicted the "beast's" defeat, but assassination or civil disobedience wouldn't bring it about. While Christ would defeat the beast, the disciples' faith and loving commitment to Jesus the Lamb would save them. The verses of the song demonstrate that: "Who will not fear you, O Lord, and bring glory to your name? For you alone are holy" (Revelation 15:4).

Many Christians remained faithful even in the face of martyrdom. In the same way that God's agent Moses earlier led Israel through the Red Sea, the Lord rewards Christians' faith by safely leading them through the fiery, glassy sea. The Lord's people from all times in history will join together. To the king of the ages, the entire congregation will sing the "song of Moses and the Lamb."

No part of the New Testament urges physical or political action against ungodly governments. The apostles faced a hostile government that ordered them not to preach about Jesus anymore. Despite threats and jail time, the apostles took their commands from higher authority. An angel of the Lord released them from confinement one night and instructed them to "Go, stand in the temple courts ... and tell the people the full message of this new life" (Acts 5:20).

The authorities rearrested them, reiterated their warnings, and flogged them. Undeterred, the apostles now with aching, lacerated backs left the offices of the nation's highest court rejoicing because the Lord counted them worthy to suffer disgrace for his name. So in "the temple courts and from house to house, they never stopped teaching and proclaiming the good news that Jesus is the Christ" (Acts 5:42).

Even though Peter suffered because of the rulers' jealous rage, he later wrote to Christians (God's elect):

> *Submit yourselves for the Lord's sake to every authority instituted among men: whether to the king, as the supreme authority, or to governors, who are sent by him to punish those who do wrong and to commend those who do right. For it is God's will that by doing good you should silence the ignorant talk of foolish men. Live as free men, but do not use your freedom as a cover-up for evil; live as servants of God. Show proper respect to everyone: Love the brotherhood of believers, fear God, honor the king.*   — 1 Peter 2:13-17

Regardless of injustices they might suffer, Christians bear witness to Jesus and use his humble, forgiving, example as a behavior-model.

Instead of complaining when judges bar plaques containing the Ten Commandments from courthouses, real Christians witness to judges, attorneys, and prisoners about Jesus' love. In place of crabby complaints about the illegality of public school prayers, we pray with our children before we send them to class. Rather than taking adversarial positions against those who disagree with us on abortion, we ask God to open our opponents' hearts as he softened the heart of the Tarsus-born murderer Saul. We temper our anger toward those who wage war or refuse to by remembering that Jesus advised us that wars and rumors of wars will always be present (Matthew 24:4-6).

Many prominent Christians seem to ignore or disregard our primary assignment — to preach the good news to all people. How has that happened? Once the church started building houses of worship and its hierarchy evolved, it developed a fortress mentality. Jesus meant his church to be an ever-enlarging, loving army that continues to enlist new troops as it conquers by faith. Using a different metaphor, a pilgrim church never settles until it reaches its goal, the fullness of God's kingdom on the last day.

Jesus' church advances to every part of the world reaching people of all backgrounds, races, ethnicity, and language. It lovingly urges people to submit to Christ, the universe manager. Modern churches mangle the message and twist the mission. We rarely go into the world equipped with courage, a knapsack, and a faith that the Lord always keeps us company. The church now tries to be a network of bulwarks, a complex, creature-comfortable citadel — a bastion that gives people protection from the world's assaults.

Jesus called us to a high-risk venture. We're to spread into the most remote islands and villages on the planet as a dynamic spiritual force. Calling all to repent, we help folks achieve victory over guilt and death through faith in Jesus' death and resurrection power.

The church settled instead, and became known for its sanctuaries and cathedrals. It erects attractive marquees, depends on eloquent, high-paid oratory, and sends slick embellished invitations. It prefers padded pews, air conditioning, aesthetics, and unique architecture.

What's the intent of all these procedures? Apparently so that people will attend, give money, and help the churches to provide even bigger and fancier accommodations. Only rarely do churches fulfill Jesus' commission. Jesus assured the disciples that'd he'd be with them to the end of the age (Matthew 28:20). Now we want our ends comfortable to a great age.

Jesus said of his church that Hades' gates wouldn't "prevail against it." Whenever a person accepts Christ and changes his/her life in conformance to him, death loses another of its victims. Faith in Christ is the smart bomb that voids death's one-way ticket. We call no ceasefires, sabbaticals, or time-outs until every living, breathing person hears Jesus' good news and knows that he blasted death's door open by his resurrection.

Many conservative American Christians seem to think they need all the rights and freedoms afforded by the US government in order for the church to survive until Jesus returns. They fix their hopes in the courts and Congress.

It's as if they've anxiously retreated inside those bastions to worry about their fate. They talk good news only when they hear about the appointment of a conservative judge to the federal bench. Otherwise they fret and angst prevails. Only Congress and a conservative judiciary, they teach, can give adequate protection against the world's evils and protect the folks inside. You rarely hear them speak positively.

The liberal side of the church fumes, too — about war and injustice. It seems as if both wings forget or don't read Paul's encouragement to the Roman church:

> *Therefore, since we have been justified through faith, we have peace with God through our Lord Jesus Christ, through whom we have gained access by faith into this grace in which we now stand. And we rejoice in the hope of the glory of God. Not only so, but we also rejoice in our sufferings, because we know that suffering produces perseverance; perseverance, character; and character, hope. And hope does not disappoint us, because God has poured out his love into our hearts by the Holy Spirit, whom he has given us.* — Romans 5:1-5

291

Suppose those brave medics that travel to battlefields in order to treat and rescue wounded soldiers, suddenly stop going out. Soon they build a huge hospital. In the meantime, the field of battle moves so that the expensive hospital sits largely isolated from areas of greatest need. Then those in charge decide that diseased, maimed, or unsightly people should never enter their hospital. That's how many so-called right-wing Christians regard the church.

Robert St. Clair related a sobering vignette about Martin Niemöller, who revealed his heart and conscience. According to Niemöller, God used a dream to make him aware of his witnessing responsibility.

Because Niemöller defied Hitler, he served an eight-year prison term. Toward the last of his sentence, a very real vision startled him. Prior to that time he hadn't felt obliged to talk with his Nazi guards about their need for Christ.

In Niemöller's dream, Hitler pled his case before God saying that he'd never heard the gospel. The Lord then asked Dr. Niemöller: "Were you with him a whole hour without telling him of the gospel?"

In fact, Niemöller remembered, he'd once spent an hour with Hitler and said nothing to him about Christ. Immediately Niemöller "saw that it was his duty to witness to all men, even his guards. The good doctor was so true to his duty that the guards were changed more often lest the Gospel find its mark."[6]

The left side of the church constructs expensive hospitals, too. They err by trying to treat patients using diseased and troubled doctors, nurses, and technicians. They want everyone to walk the halls indiscriminately.

I pray that the church can return to Jesus' medivac model. On the last day, Satan and his forces will capitulate to God. In the meantime, Jesus advised us not to worry about governmental or other types of opposition. He'll take care of our enemies. The Lord always completes his work. Whether he uses us or raises someone else to do it, that's the question.

1. Gerhard Kittel, ed., G. W. Bromiley, tr., *Theological Dictionary of the New Testament: Volume VI* (Grand Rapids, Michigan: Wm. B. Eerdmans Publishing Company, 1969), p. 515, n. 95.

2. William Sanday and Arthur C. Headlam, *The International Critical Commentary, A Critical and Exegetical Commentary on the Epistle to the Romans*, S. R. Driver et al editors, Fifth Edition (Edinburgh: T. & T. Clark, 1914), p. 372.

3. The New Testament in Modern English translated by J. B. Phillip.

4. Some assume that we shouldn't pray for gifts like the ones that God granted the apostles. I don't think it's right to assume anything. One reason we don't have is that we don't ask (Matthew 7:7-12).

5. Translated "fiery ordeal" in the RSV.

6. Robert James St. Clair, *The Adventure of Being You* (New Jersey: Fleming H. Revell Company, 1966), pp. 120-121.

15

Reigniting Those Member Embers:
Letting The Light Shine

People hardly ever make use of the freedom they have,
for example, freedom of thought; instead they demand
freedom of speech as a compensation.
— Sören Kierkegaard

Possibly you worship with a group that shows no interest in the things we've discussed in this book. What should you do? In order to avoid division, I suggest the following fourteen-point plan.

1. Pray that God will help you grow in him and grant you good judgment and insight. He promises to always answer our prayers for wisdom.

2. Meditate on the scriptures daily. Read all the way through the Bible at least once a year. Try reading different translations. When language becomes too familiar, we tend to pay less attention, thinking that we already know what is there.

3. Become a Berean. Humbly request your church leaders to biblically substantiate their decisions. I know that this works because people have often insisted that I be accountable. Recently at our home study, I made an unsubstantiated statement. The group "held my feet to the fire" until I had clarified and actually retracted part of what I had said. Praise God for their courage, biblical knowledge, and sincerity.

295

4. Ask God to give you boldness in sharing the message about Jesus and to open the hearts of the people to whom you witness. God does amazing things when we openly confess his name. I still marvel at an occasion that I experienced on a flight from Los Angeles to Minneapolis. I was seated by a Harvard coed who seemed engrossed in her book. At mealtime, I found an opportunity to speak with her and discovered that she was an atheist. Her objections to God appeared not strongly based on intellectual arguments. They seemed more of a reaction against parents and peers. God opened her heart so much that when we changed flights in Minneapolis we stopped to have coffee together. She read many long sections from my Bible there in the airport. God's Word deeply impressed her. I pray that the Lord continually works in her heart to lead her fully to him.

5. Don't be discouraged by first failures. Not everyone listened to Jesus. He doesn't hold us responsible for the conversion of people, only that we witness to them. It helps to make an objective review of your unsuccessful conversations with people. Did you approach them with humility? Was it your motivation to exalt God? Did you ask God for wisdom and guidance before you spoke?

    People kept asking me years ago, "Bob, why are you so intense?" "The Lord has sent me on a mission," I explained. The Lord keeps telling me to be faithful to his message, but I realized after a long time that people saw my intensity as anger. In some cases their observations were correct. I'm trying to change that so I can convey genuine love to every person I meet.

6. Review how Jesus changed your life and tell your story to people. That's the approach Paul used (Acts 9, 22, 26).

7. Encourage your church leaders to return to biblical foundations and to maintain them. We don't do this as a means

to personal power, prominence, or prestige. If we're motivated by these things we're doing it for the wrong reason. God deserves all credit in the church.

8. Train your children to experience life in Christ. Talk to them about him when you drive, at mealtime, and bedtime.

9. Use your television and your computer with discretion. You and your family will be happier and feel better. Don't watch the news until you have had quality quiet time with God.

10. Pray weekly with like-minded friends and share your witnessing experiences with them so that you can find mutual encouragement (James 5:16).

11. Pray for your religious leaders that God will mightily use them (2 Corinthians 1:11; Colossians 4:3).

12. Stay positive and hopeful. Many Christians fall into the complaining trap. Murmuring and grumbling displeases God. Note what happened to the Israelite complainers (1 Corinthians 10:1-13). The acts of the sinful nature include discord, dissension, and jealousy (Galatians 5:19-21). Spend time every day praising God, thanking others for their efforts, and encouraging them.

13. Pray for soldiers to receive Jesus. Pray for peace. Pray for politicians to make wise, godly decisions.

    Befriend Muslims, Hindus, Buddhists, and people of other faiths. Lovingly tell them about Jesus. Many of them are more open to the Lord than we would ever imagine.

    In the 1980s, one of the Hollywood church deacons was hospitalized for a heart condition. While in the hospital, he befriended a Moslem nurse. He asked if she would meet with me. She agreed and we met for coffee.

During the conversation I learned that she struggled with certain circumstances in her life and planned to leave the Los Angeles area.

I took a Bible to give her and asked if she would accept it and read it. She answered skeptically, "Why should I read a book?" Praying hard for the right thing to say, I inquired if there were someone that she loved very much. Her dark eyes began to moisten. "If that someone you love wrote you a letter, would you read it?" I asked.

"I sure would," she said softly with tears now flowing. She reached for the Bible. I wish I could say that she came to know Jesus. I never saw her again, but I pray that I'll see her in heaven. I pray that I will see you there, too.

14. Give praise to God every day.
To God be all glory!

His intent was that now, through the church, the manifold wisdom of God should be made known to the rulers and authorities in the heavenly realms, according to his eternal purpose which he accomplished in Christ Jesus our Lord. — Ephesians 3:10-11

Bibliography

Ahlstrom, Sydney, E. *Theology in America: The Major Protestant Voices from Puritanism to Neo-Orthodoxy.* Indianapolis-New York: The Bobbs-Merrill Company, Inc., 1967.

Angell, C. Roy. *Iron Shoes.* Nashville: Broadman Press, 1953.

Auden, W. H. and Kronenberger, Louis. *Viking Book of Aphorisms.* New York: Viking Press, 1966.

Bainton, Roland H. *Here I Stand: A Life of Martin Luther.* New York: A Mentor Book published by The New American Library, 1950.

Baker, Daniel B. *Power Quotes.* Detroit: Visible Ink Press, 1992.

Barth, Karl. *Evangelical Theology: An Introduction.* New York: Holt, Rinehart and Winston, 1963.

Bayne, Peter, M. A. *The Christian Life — Social and Individual.* Boston: Gould and Lincoln, 1864.

Bruce, F. F., Editor. *The New International Commentary on the New Testament.* "Commentary on the Book of Acts." Grand Rapids, Michigan: Wm. B. Eerdmans Publishing Company, 1964.

Camp, Wesley D. *Unfamiliar Quotations from 200 B.C. to the Present.* Paramus, New Jersey: Prentice Hall, 1990.

Carroll, James. *Constantine's Sword: The Church and the Jews — A History.* Boston-New York: A Mariner Book, Houghton Mifflin Company, 2001.

Clarke, Adam. *Clarke's Commentary.* New York: Abingdon Press, 1966.

Davidson, Lance. *The Ultimate Reference Book.* New York: Avon Books, 1994.

Davidson, Marshall B., Editor. *The Horizon History of Christianity.* New York: American Heritage Publishing Company, Inc., 1964.

Foster, Richard J. *Money, Sex and Power: The Challenge of the Disciplined Life.* San Francisco: Harper & Row, Publishers, 1985.

Fulghum, Roberts. *Words I Wish I Wrote.* New York: Harper Collins Publishers, 1997.

Gaer, Joseph and Wolf, Rabbi Alfred. *Our Jewish Heritage.* Hollywood, California: Wilshire Book Company, 1967.

Gaer, Joseph and Wolf, Rabbi Alfred. *How the Great Religions Began.* New York: The New American Library, 1954.

Graham, Billy. *Approaching Hoofbeats.* Waco, Texas: Word Books, 1983.

Grant, F. C., Editor. *Ancient Roman Religion.* New York: Liberal Arts Press, 1957.

Guggenberger, A., S. J. *A General History of the Christian Era, Volume I — The Papacy and the Empire.* St. Louis, Missouri: Becktold Company, 1900.

Harnack, Adolf. *What is Christianity?* New York-Evanston: Harper & Row, Publishers, 1957.

Hausdorff, David M. *A Book of Jewish Curiosities.* New York: Crown Publishers, Inc., 1955.

Henry, Carl, F. H. *Christian Personal Ethics.* Grand Rapids: Michigan: Wm. B. Eerdmans Publishing Company, 1957.

Henry, Carl, F. H. *Contemporary Evangelical Thought.* Great Neck, New York: Channel Press, 1957.

Hordern, William. *A Layman's Guide to Protestant Theology.* New York: The Macmillan Company, 1955.

Hughes, Richard T. *Reviving the Ancient Faith: The Story of Churches of Christ in America.* Grand Rapids, Michigan: Wm. B. Eerdmans Publishing Company, 1996.

Hugo, Victor. *La Légende des siècles,* published in Europe, 1859.

James, William. *The Varieties of Religious Experience: A Study in Human Nature.* Garden City, New York: Doubleday & Company, 1902.

Kittel, Gerhard and Friedrich, Gerhard. *Theological Dictionary of the New Testament.* Grand Rapids, Michigan: Wm. B. Eerdmans Publishing Company, 1971.

Kung, Hans. *On Being a Christian,* tr. by Edwin Quinn. Garden City, New York: Doubleday & Company, Inc., 1976.

LaHaye, Tim. *Faith of Our Founding Fathers.* Brentwood, Tennessee: Wolgemuth & Hyatt, 1987.

LaHaye, Tim. Nation Without a Conscience. Wheaton, Illinois: Tynedale House Publishers, Inc., 1994.

LaHaye, Tim. *The Race for the 21st Century.* Nashville: Thomas Nelson Publishers, 1986.

Lamb, Harold. *The Crusades: The whole story of the Crusades* (originally published in two volumes as *Iron Men* and *The Flame of Islam*). New York: Bantam Books, April, 1962.

McManners, John. *The Oxford Illustrated History of Christianity.* Oxford, England: Oxford University Press, 1990.

Meyer, Donald. *The Protestant Search for Political Realism 1919-1941,* Second Edition. Middletown, Connecticut: Wesleyan University Press, 1960, 1988.

Millgram, Abraham E. *Jewish Worship.* Philadelphia: The Jewish Publication Society of America, 1971.

Neill, Stephen. *The Interpretation of the New Testament 1861-1961, The Firth Lectures, 1962.* London: Oxford University Press, 1964.

Niebuhr, Reinhold. *The Nature and Destiny of Man: A Christian Interpretation, Vol. 1, Human Nature,* Volume II, *Human Destiny.* New York: Charles Scribner's Sons, 1941, 1943, 1949.

Peerman, Dean G. and Marty, Martin E. *A Handbook of Christian Theologians.* Cleveland-New York: Meridian Books, The World Publishing Company, 1967.

Prochnow, Herbert V. and Prochnow, Herbert V. Jr. *The Toastmaster's Treasure Chest.* Edison, New Jersey: Castle Books, 1988.

Richards, Lawrence O. *Expository Dictionary of Bible Words.* Grand Rapids, Michigan: Regency Reference Library, Zondervan Publishing Corporation, 1985.

Rilliet, Jean. Translated by Harold Knight. *Zwingli: Third Man of the Reformation.* Philadelphia: The Westminster Press, 1959.

Robertson, Pat. *The Ten Offenses*. Nashville: Integrity Publishers, 2004.

Sanday, William and Headlam, Arthur C. *The International Critical Commentary: A Critical and Exegetical Commentary on the Epistle to the Romans*. Fifth Edition. S. R. Driver, et al, Editors. Edinburgh: T & T Clarke, 1914.

Scott, Ernest Findlay. *The Literature of the New Testament*. New York: Columbia University Press, 1936.

Schaeffer, Francis A. *A Christian Manifesto*. Westchester, Illinois: Crossway Books, 1981.

Smith, Huston. *The Religions of Man*. New York: Harper & Row, 1965.

St. Clair, Robert James. *The Adventure of Being You*. New Jersey: Fleming H. Revell Company, 1967.

Trueblood, Elton. *Foundations for Reconstruction*, Revised Edition. New York: Harper & Row Publishing, 1946, 1961.

Wiesel, Elie. *The Night Trilogy*. New York: Hill & Wang, 1987.

Wilburn, James R. *Faith and Public Policy*. Lanham, Maryland: Lexington Books, 2002.

Periodicals

Christianity Today
National Geographic
New Wineskins
Sioux City Journal
The Pulse, newsletter of the United Church of Christ/Church of the Brethren, Kingsley, Iowa